EPIC
RUNS
of
NORTH
AMERICA

Explore North America's most thrilling running routes and trails

CONTENTS

Easy   Harder   Epic

INTRODUCTION

Today running is more than mere exercise and marathons are no longer just for sinewy fitness junkies. Sure, people still run to stay in shape, but these days just as many do it to meditate. Some run for the high or just to clear their head, while others enter races as a way to make a dozen friends all at once. Many stick to pavements, though many more are running off-road and into the wilderness. Regardless of how or where they do it, most runners agree that it is the great grounding constant in their life.

Most runners will also agree that moving through a landscape and breaking a sweat has an oddly profound effect on one's sense of place. Whether you're repeating a well-worn loop close to home or exploring an exotic new place, running affords a deeper understanding of a town or city and its citizens. Unlike a walking tour, it has a way of forcing more self-reflection, while also covering more ground in a short amount of time.

Running has a surprisingly symbiotic relationship with travel. Experienced globetrotters insist it cures jetlag, while running seems to be the one exercise we actually do when traveling, whether for a short business trip or during a long-distance adventure. Nothing is easier than stuffing a pair of running shoes into our luggage, and those running shoes can now take us into the Grand Canyon, Canada's elemental Vancouver Island, or deepest New York City. As more and more people seek out running travel adventures, organized races are popping up in the most extreme corners of North America.

The other welcome development in running – the growing diversity and inclusivity of running communities across North America – is reflected in the compiling of the 50 stories in the book. Jinghuan Liu Tervalon contributed an account of running in Los Angeles' Chinatown Firecracker race and connecting with that city's Asian community. Alison Mariella Désir, author of *Running While Black: Finding Freedom in a Sport That Wasn't Built For Us*, considers the camaraderie of a group of runners taking on the challenge of a running retreat in Alaska.

In this book are 200 of the greatest runs in the US, Canada, the Caribbean, and Central America. The 50 featured runs are first-hand accounts, written by people who are not only passionate about running – some even do it for a living – but

also about the idea that to have run somewhere is to know it. These are stories that will convince you there are times when a run is the way to see a place.

You'll discover why the Boston Marathon, founded in 1897, has become a symbol of pride for America's oldest major city, and how our cover star, the Kalalau Trail in Hawai'i, was an unlikely first trail run for one writer. You'll understand why running up Pikes Peak sears its way into your psyche, and how a relaxed run around Miami's Art Deco district reveals the city's beauty.

HOW TO USE THIS BOOK

Each of the six chapters in this book includes a special collection of runs from that particular region, from easy-access park runs and city loops to iconic marathons and epic ultras. A color-coded key on the contents page will help you identify which are easy, which require serious fitness and fortitude, and which fall somewhere in between (based almost entirely on distance and elevation gain). Accompanying each main story is some practical information to help you follow in the author's footsteps. The authors have also included three extra routes or races that have a similar character to their featured run but may be closer to home or more accessible.

It's important to point out that there are a handful of insanely difficult runs in this book that only a few of us will ever be able to do. In many cases, the people who have written about them are professional runners, paid to train on a daily basis. But the armchair adventure value of these tales cannot be overstated. You will no doubt become parched just reading about Death Valley's Badwater 135 and become dizzy reading about the notoriously disorienting Barkley Marathons. These are stories that will inspire you to kick things up a notch, to train for something bold and, perhaps, someday sign up for a race you never thought possible.

Whichever runs you decide to add to your bucket list, take the time to source and study detailed maps and to gear up properly for any routes that might take you off the beaten path. Be kind to your fellow runners and even kinder to the wild landscapes you travel through. Be prepared for a few quizzical looks from locals and, most importantly, never forget to pack your running shoes.

Clockwise from left: starting the Boston Marathon; enjoying the fellowship of runners in Alaska; the staggering landscape of the Kalalau Trail on Kaua'i

Opening spreads from left: running in Central Park, New York City; Bixby Bridge on the Big Sur Marathon; Yosemite's trails; Vancouver's seawall

CANADA & ALASKA

A TOUR OF VANCOUVER'S WORLD-CLASS SEAWALL

Hugging 990 acres (400 hectares) of rainforest and parkland, the stunning Stanley Park Seawall wows visitors and inspires even the most jaded local runners.

For local runners, Vancouver's Stanley Park Seawall is their treadmill – part of a routine that belies its beauty, an after-work or weekend ritual that is somehow both routine and rare at the same time. However, there's a reason it's often mobbed with tourists, and all a local needs to do to be reminded how spectacular it is, is to look at the face of one of the hundreds of people who visit each day, as they stroll, cycle, sit, and sightsee.

I certainly never need reminding of how spectacular this stretch of coastline is. These days, I guess you could say I'm both a local and a tourist. I lived in Vancouver for years, but now live 7500 miles (12,000km) away in Amsterdam. I only get to run the Seawall when I'm visiting. But to be clear, running the Seawall is the first thing I do whenever I do return to my hometown – and each time it feels like an embrace from an old friend, rekindling memories I thought I'd lost forever. I have wondered if it would mean this much to me if I did still live here and ran it every day. The answer is yes – it's that good.

During one recent visit, I couldn't wait to lace up my running shoes and make my way downtown. I was starting at Waterfront Station near Coal Harbour. Stanley Park is an island of trees linked to the West End of downtown by a narrow isthmus. But its famous 5.5-mile-long (9km) strand, with its paved lanes separating pedestrians from cyclists, has been extended a little over a mile further east, along Coal Harbour, which makes it possible to do a longer run from downtown than previously. Some say the Stanley Park Seawall is the longest uninterrupted waterfront footpath in the world.

It is certainly the ultimate way to experience Vancouver, as it winds past stands of towering evergreens, skirts along sandy beaches, and even affords sublime views of downtown. It also offers great views of the North Shore Mountains and islands floating in the Strait of Georgia, leading out to the frigid North Pacific.

It was early and I felt like I had the city to myself. I jogged westward along West Cordova St before cutting north along a pedestrian mall and down some steps to West Waterfront Rd and the Winter Olympics' cauldron. A few more steps downward

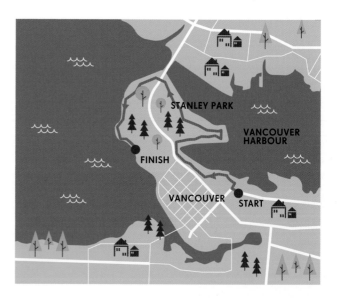

© LeonWong / Shutterstock

landed me squarely on the Seawall's pavement. Floatplanes bobbed peacefully on the docks – later in the day they would all have engines blaring while ferrying people to and from remote islands in the sound.

By the time I hit Coal Harbour Quay further west, I was fully in my stride. Since my last run here the trees over the footpath had grown, as had the height of the glass condominium towers and the size of the shiny white yachts. I smiled when I spotted a couple of my favorite brightly colored houseboats, their more modest façades gleaming red and yellow in the early light, a reminder of a more modest time in the city.

At the end of Coal Harbour I turned eastward and could see yet another enduring landmark: the Vancouver Rowing Club. Its stilted wooden clubhouse, connected to the Seawall by a wooden bridge, has been a permanent fixture since 1911. As I ran toward the city skyline I could see Canada Place, an enormous building that cuts giant sail-shaped silhouettes across the morning sky. It's a building I've marveled at since first seeing it at Expo 86 as a boy. This section of the Seawall weaves in such a way that one moment you are looking at the city, the next you are deep in the park's forest, then, again, looking at the city. This is one of my favorite sections, as I enjoy that juxtaposition of nature and the modern world, which is particularly stark given Vancouver's recent growth.

As I rounded the park's eastern tip and approached Brockton Point Lighthouse, I was staring straight up at the forested upper flanks of the North Shore Mountains. On rare clear winter days, you can see snow-topped summits from here.

I continued westward toward the distant but unmistakable towers of Lions Gate Bridge. The iconic span began to pop in and out of view as I meandered through the trees on the shoreline. But then it appeared in all its glory, and never disappeared again – its inorganic form sprouting from the

TWO-WHEEL TRAFFIC

Vancouverites' love of outdoor activities can actually cause a unique traffic jam on the Stanley Park Seawall. After a lengthy cycling ban – which started in the 1970s – a separate bike-only lane was finally added in 1984 (roller-blading was later permitted in this lane, too), though it has a strict 10mph (16km) speed limit and you are only allowed to travel counter-clockwise. Runners and other pedestrians, meanwhile, can travel in either direction along the Seawall.

Clockwise from top: mild maritime weather makes the seawall a year-round run; Lions Gate Bridge and the North Shore mountains from Prospect Point; downtown Van. Previous page: old-growth forest meets the sea

forest directly above me and arching out across First Narrows. As I ran, a hulking freighter silently made its way between the towers and into the inner harbor. But even a giant ship like this is dwarfed by the bridge's mass.

As I continued around Prospect Point, panoramic views of English Bay opened up before me. A dozen more tankers, scattered like toy ships, dotted its calm surface. Further out, I could just make out the faint outline of Vancouver Island (it's worth returning at sunset for this view alone).

Closer to shore, a couple of kayakers cruised in the shallows. And by the time I reached Siwash Rock, a small but famous outcrop jutting out from the water just off the Seawall, I could see the forests of lofty Point Grey that surround my alma mater, The University of British Columbia, in the distance.

Finally, I passed Third Beach, the perfect respite on a rare scorching summer day. It's a place where, as a child, I spent many hot afternoons, swimming and splashing to keep cool. From here, I could see the high-rise residential buildings of Vancouver's West End coming into view. I increased my pace as I skirted Second Beach, then crossed my imaginary finish line in the sand.

Afterwards, I sat on one of the beach's logs to catch my breath and soak in a little more of the bay view. Still not quite finished, I decided to stroll another mile (1.6km) along the Seawall to English Bay Beach to partake in yet another Seawall ritual. In fact, it's something that has become as much a part of this run as putting on my shoes: a cappuccino and the world's greatest cinnamon bun at Delany's Coffee House. **MP**

Start // Waterfront Station
Finish // Second Beach
Distance // 7 miles (11km)
Getting there // Public transport is extensive, with TransLink (buses, SkyTrain, and SeaBus).
When to go // Mild winters make this runnable year-round. July and August are sure bets for sunshine.
Where to stay // The charming ivy-covered Sylvia Hotel (sylviahotel.com) sits on English Bay Beach, a few strides from the Seawall.
What to wear // Shorts and shirt in the summer. Tights, thermals, and a light rain jacket in winter.
Things to know // Extend this run another mile (1.6km) or so by heading inland along Lost Lagoon from Second Beach to the park section of the Seawall at Coal Harbour.
More info // vancouver.ca/parks-recreation-culture/stanley-park.aspx

*Clockwise from top: Galveston's
Seawall and the Gulf of Mexico*

MORE LIKE THIS
RUNS ALONG COASTAL
AND RIVER DEFENSES

GALVESTON SEAWALL, TEXAS

Completed in 1902, the Galveston Seawall
was a response to the greatest natural
disaster in US history. The 'Galveston
hurricane' of 1900 led to flooding that killed
approximately 8000 residents. A structure
conceived as a memorial has gone on to
become a popular center for recreation
thanks to the Seawall Urban Park, a 10-mile
(16km) stretch that follows Seawall Blvd on
the city's eastern shore, with spectacular
views across the Gulf of Mexico. Start
your run at the western end, Diamond
Beach. The busiest sections are downtown,
between mile 3 (4.8km) and mile 7 (11km),
although this will give you the chance
to stop by Galveston's historic Pleasure
Pier, at 25th St. Go early, or during the
winter off-season, and the pier provides
an additional half mile (out and back) to
your route. Beyond mile 7 (11km) the route
quietens, traveling past tidal marshes to
its eastern extremity, at Fort San Jacinto
Historic Point.
Start // Diamond Beach at the Breakers
Finish // Fort San Jacinto Historic Point
Distance // 10 miles (16km)

PLYMOUTH SEAWALL, MASSACHUSETTS

Start at Nelson Memorial Pk, then take
the exit for Water St. Run southeast along
the seawall, with views across Goose Point
Channel, Plymouth Harbor, and out into
the open Atlantic. Water St delivers you
to Plymouth Rock, the 1620 landing site
for, and now memorial to, the *Mayflower*;
across the street you'll find the Pilgrim
Hall Museum, well worth a separate
visit. Continue your run with a loop of the
beautifully manicured Brewster Gardens,
named for the Pilgrim Father William
Brewster. Exit the gardens at Market St
and cross Burial Hill Cemetery (we advise
walking). Pick up the pace once more
on Allerton St, ending at the National
Monument to the Forefathers. Plymouth was
originally home to the Indigenous Patuxet
people, part of the wider Wampanoag tribal
confederation. For an alternative run, head
to the Plimoth Patuxet Museums, a complex
dedicated to Patuxet history. Starting at
Plymouth Rock, this 2.7-mile (4.3km) route is
direct along Sandwich St.
Start // Nelson Memorial Pk;
Plymouth Rock
Finish // National Monument to the
Forefathers; Plimoth Patuxet Museums
Distance // 3 miles (4.8km); 2.7 miles
(4.3km)

THE MISSISSIPPI RIVER TRAIL/LEVEE
PATH, NEW ORLEANS

Levees have been a feature of Mississippi
life for centuries; the first defenses were
built in the early 18th century by French
traders seeking to protect New Orleans.
The Mississippi River Trail, also known
as the Levee Path, offers 22 paved miles
(35km) along one of the river's best-
maintained levees. Elsewhere in the US,
similar trails have brought environmental
and political considerations into conflict,
resulting in ugly, utilitarian construction.
Not so here, where the trail is beautifully
built. While forays around Baton Rouge are
popular, one of the best routes is in central
New Orleans, starting at the corner of
Wiltz Ln and Patterson Dr. A 15-minute drive
from downtown (or take RTA bus 101), this
5.3-mile (8.5km) section of trail steers clear
of traffic and intersections, ending at the
Algiers Ferry Terminal. Popular with cyclists
and fishers, it's ideally placed for follow-on
activities, such as the Audubon Nature
Institute in Woldenberg Park, accessible via
the ferry.
Start // Wiltz Ln and Patterson Dr
Finish // Algiers Ferry Terminal
Distance // 5.3 miles (8.5km)

DRINK IN SOUTH SHORE SIGHTS ON THE RUM RUNNERS TRAIL

With its alcohol-inspired name, the Rum Runners Trail will pique any runner's curiosity and reward all with its epic historical seaside setting.

'm feeling like the winner of that children's game, king of the castle. Or maybe a rural Rocky when, in the movie of the same name, he raised his arms in triumph on his morning run up the steps of the Philadelphia Museum of Art. Standing atop Castle Rock – an ancient granite hump in the Earth's crust, exposed by retreating glaciers centuries ago – is one of the joys of running sections of the Rum Runners Trail on Nova Scotia's South Shore. Crumbling at the edges, but smooth and rounded at the top, Castle Rock towers over the surrounding forest like the ruins of some great fortress. The views over the coastal lowlands lead the eye to the horizon, where the ferry from the town of

Chester chugs out to Big and Little Tancook islands.

The section of the trail with the short path up to Castle Rock is called the Chester Connection, which begins beside Rte 3 in East River and runs 22 miles (35km) into town. It's my favorite section, not just for the big jewel in the crown, but for the natural surroundings, following mixed forest beside duck-filled Barry's Brook before skirting the shores of little Labrador Lake.

Forest, water features, coastline, small towns – these are the defining characteristics of the Rum Runners Trail from its origins at the outer reaches of urban Halifax to its terminus in the Unesco World Heritage fishing town of Lunenburg. Rum Runners is

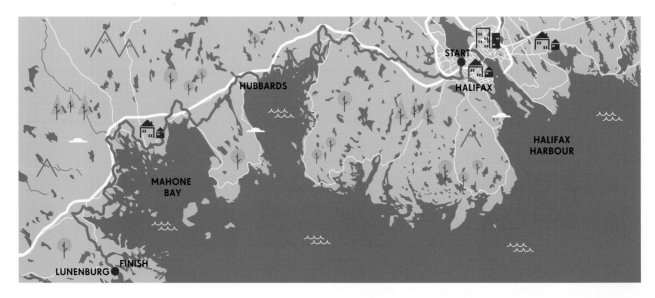

divided into six shorter trail sections, varying in length from 6 to 22 miles (10km to 35km). Open to cyclists and motorized all-terrain vehicles (add cross-country skiing in winter), most sections are nonetheless perfectly suited to running. Much of the trail is built on a former railway bed, so the hard-packed crusher dust surface is flat and predictable. The turns and grades are gentle.

Although some runners start in the heart of Halifax with the Chain of Lakes Trail – which brings the total to seven, including this section – Rum Runners officially begins with the next section, the Beechville Lakeside Timberlea Trail. This is where the trail turns rural and at times wild. On the next section, the St Margaret's Bay Trail, the Atlantic comes into view and the route hugs the coastline. Heading inland again, the Aspotogan Trail cuts across the peninsula of the same name. The Chester Connection is next, followed by the Dynamite Trail – the Rum Runners shortest section – that leads into the town of Mahone Bay. The aptly named Bay to Bay Trail begins in Mahone Bay and ends in Lunenburg.

Trotting down the trail from Castle Rock, I pick up the Chester Connection. The trail rounds Goat Lake before intersecting with Goat Lake Rd for a run of about 5 miles (8km). About a mile (1.6km) beyond is the Graves Island Provincial Park campground, overlooking hundreds of small islands where smuggled rum was hidden back in the day. In the 18th century, three prominent Nova Scotia towns grew up on this bay – Chester, Mahone Bay and Lunenburg. The Rum Runners Trail passes through all three.

For nearly two centuries, Chester has attracted summer tourists seeking cooler weather and a big, protected bay for sailing. Many American families have been coming for generations. Mahone Bay is known for its picturesque waterfront dominated by three shoulder-to-shoulder churches and for its many artisan studios and shops. Lunenburg is Canada's best-known fishing port, partly because of its Unesco-listed status, but mostly as the home of the country's beloved tall ship, the *Bluenose*. Her likeness adorns the

NOVA SCOTIA'S RUM RUNNING

The 1910 Nova Scotia Temperance Act preceded prohibition in the US by a decade. Poorly paid or out-of-work fishermen on Nova Scotia's Atlantic coastline turned to smuggling the 'demon rum'. For over 20 years, ports like Lunenburg bustled with the illegal booze trade. Cargoes of contraband were smuggled in, then out again, always one step ahead of authorities in their 'rum-chaser' boats. Rum running continued even after America repealed prohibition, in 1933, finally ending with the start of WWII.

Clockwise from top: Nova Scotia's trails pass by woods and lakes; Lunenburg's boardwalk; the summit of Castle Rock is your goal for the day. Previous spread: Lunenburg's heritage waterfront

© Natalie Roy / Shutterstock; Joe Regan/ Getty Images

Canadian dime. All three towns are well worth a stop for excellent restaurants, historic accommodations, independent shops, marine museums, and small-town hospitality.

There's a tradition of running along this coast, and not just of the rum-smuggling variety. On the last Saturday of September for the past half century, teams enter the Rum Runners Relay, a 63-mile (102km) road race that roughly parallels the trail itself. About 70 teams enter every year, each member running one of 10 stages from Halifax to Lunenburg. Organized by the Gonzo Adventure Club, the relay has become so popular in recent years, organizers hold an annual lottery to determine which teams get to enter. The three fastest teams get their names inscribed on the victory rum keg. Winners of all other prizes are determined in random draws.

Just a few days after the Rum Runners Relay, on the first Sunday in October, Chester hosts the annual Cut N Run. It's a much gentler dual-length event, with 3- and 6-mile (5km and 10km) circuits. Half of the longer version is run on the Rum Runners Trail. Organizers encourage runners of all ages and abilities to enjoy a non-competitive run or, for beginners, to just give running a try.

Continuing on to Chester just 2.5 miles (4km) further, I'm ready for a hearty, healthy lunch. As usual, the Kiwi Café is buzzing. The Kiwi Lobster Roll sells itself. Chunks of locally caught lobster dressed with dill mayo are served on a buttery, toasted brioche bun with a side salad. I enjoy the lobster roll all the more because I know it was caught in the bay I've been enjoying all morning. As a seaport, Chester has always been a fishing town and a sailing destination. Now, it's also an epic running destination as well. **DR**

Start/Finish // The official (and best) start point is the head of the BLT Trail. Finish in the town of Lunenburg.

Distance // 74 miles (119km).

Getting there // Drive or take Halifax Transit bus #21 toward Timberlea. The nearest airport is Halifax Stanfield.

When to go // April to November.

What to wear // April, May, October, and November runs require warm clothing.

What to pack // Water, light snacks, phone.

Where to stay // Accommodations include Coastal Inn Halifax, Mecklenburgh Inn, Fairmont House B&B, Oak Island Resort, Graves Island Campground.

Where to eat // Many restaurants are available, including Train Station Bike and Bean, Trellis Café, Island View, Rebecca's Restaurant, Salt Shaker Deli.

Things to know // As Rum Runners is a chain of six smaller trails and roughly parallels local roads, it offers many entry and exit points, and you can run the trail in sections.

More info // destinationtrailsnovascotia.com/trails/rum-runners-trail; novascotia.com/see-do/trails/rum-runners-trail/6381

Clockwise from top: the Fundy National Park coast; follow the Harvest Moon signs; Prince Edward Island's Confederation Trail

MORE LIKE THIS
RURAL RUNS IN CANADA'S MARITIME PROVINCES

HARVEST MOON TRAILWAY, NOVA SCOTIA

Winding through tiny towns, past vineyards and orchards, and beside a system of 350-year-old dykes, the Harvest Moon Trailway takes runners through Nova Scotia's agricultural heartland, the Annapolis Valley. Framed by two long, low mountain ridges, the trail begins in the town of Annapolis Royal near the site of the first post-Columbus European settlement north of Florida. At the other end, Grand Pré, a Unesco World Heritage Site, tells the story of the French Acadians who dyked this land off from the sea for farming. Interpretive panels and kiosks along the way provide glimpses into local history and community lore. Much of the trail is flat, built on a former railway bed with bridges that cross streams and span marshlands. Trailside farm markets and u-picks, restaurants and brewpubs break up some of the long straight-aways.
Start // Annapolis Royal
Finish // Grand Pré
Distance // 68 miles (110km)
More info // destinationtrailsnovascotia.com/trails/harvest-moon-trailway

THE ISLAND WALK, PRINCE EDWARD ISLAND

When Bryson Guptill returned from walking Spain's Camino de Santiago to his home on Prince Edward Island – Canada's smallest province – he realized that the island was the perfect size for a walk of a similar length. In 2021, he launched the 'Island Walk', a figure-eight route around PEI. Built for walkers, the trail is broken into 32 sections, but cyclists and runners immediately began using it as well. Guptill says some sections are particularly well suited to running. Of the 13-mile (21km) leg from Northam to Miscouche between waypoints 13 and 14 on the western end of the island, 10 miles (16km) of iconic PEI red-dirt roads runs through farmland and forest. Otherwise, half of the entire Island Walk is on the previously established Confederation Trail, ideal for running. Because PEI is a relatively small island, most of the trail is never far from the ocean, sometimes even hopping onto beaches in locations such as PEI National Park.
Start/Finish // Charlottetown, the PEI capital
Distance // 437 miles (703km)
More info // theislandwalk.ca

THE FUNDY CIRCUIT, NEW BRUNSWICK

Roughly circumnavigating Fundy National Park in New Brunswick, the Fundy Circuit is a challenging 29-mile (47km) loop over rugged terrain. With an elevation gain of 6240ft (1902m) on a series of technically difficult trails, this is a run for those with cross-country experience. Several times over the past decade, a local outfitter called Outdoor Elements has organized the Fundy Circuit Ultra Trail Marathon, a grueling footrace around the entire circuit. Aid stations and race kits supported those who ran the entire circuit, as well as those who preferred options such as the four-person relay and shorter distances. The park considers the Fundy Circuit a world-class course for its mature forest, lakes, rivers, waterfalls and sweeping views of the Bay of Fundy, where the world's highest tides rise and fall.
Start/Finish // Fundy National Park Visitor Centre
Distance // 29 miles (47km)
More info // alltrails.com/explore/recording/fundy-circuit-fundy-national-park--2

VINEYARD-HOPPING ON THE HALF CORKED MARATHON

This wine-themed BC run has nothing to do with achieving personal bests —
unless it's how many Pinots you can sample before noon, says Tamara Elliott.

'If you come in first, you've actually lost.' So goes the joke at the start line of the Half Corked Marathon, which is more about showcasing creative costumes and the sun-soaked Okanagan vineyards than any racing. Every May, more than a dozen wineries in British Columbia's Oliver Osoyoos Wine Country serve as co-hosts for the event, in which participants run a course through the leafy vines and stunning scenery of the Golden Mile and Black Sage Benches. Hydration looks a little different here than at typical water-and-Gatorade stations; participants make a pit stop at each vineyard along the route, sipping on concoctions such as wine cocktails and 'frosé' slushies before jogging off to the next one.

'It's so much fun,' laughs Jennifer Busmann, executive director of Oliver Osoyoos Winery Association, who helped launch the first race back in 2008. 'It's just old-fashioned fun all day.' The BC race is inspired by the Marathon du Médoc in Bordeaux, France, where participants don crazy outfits while running through that region's vineyards. The Half Corked Marathon has grown popular since its humble beginnings; the first edition hosted just 75 runners, but today a ticket lottery allocates between 1200 and 1600 entries. Each year has a distinct theme (examples: Back to the Future or 'That's the '90s') and participants up the ante further by creating outrageous costumes.

When I did the race with a group of friends, entries included a pair of wine barrels dubbed 'The Grape Gatsby' and, my personal favorite, the 'Malibooze Barbies', complete with hot-pink Mattel-box costumes that didn't look easy to run in. For our part, we decided to channel our inner Jane Fonda or

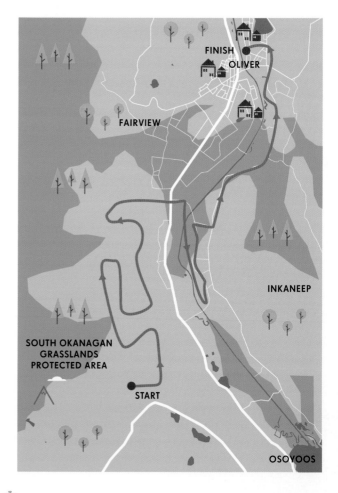

Richard Simmons and run as '80s fitness gurus. Opting for head bands, shorts, and neon-hued sunglasses, our costumes had the benefit of being actual workout attire, and thus suitable for a half-marathon. At least until the arrival of my friend and co-runner, Ryan, who showed up in a thrift-shop wedding dress he'd somehow managed to tug over his 6.5ft/2m (and 300lb/136kg) frame. Racing with another similarly styled friend, Jasmine, this pair of 'runaway brides' made for quite a sight, with Ryan's long veil flowing behind him in the wind.

To beat the heat of the arid Osoyoos desert, buses had brought us to the start line bright and early (we arrived to find wine samples waiting, naturally). After a reminder from an upbeat emcee that none of us should aim to cross the finish line first, the race got underway faster than you can say 'Cabernet Sauvignon'. The course varies each year, taking in between 12 and 16 vineyards. Our course had the full complement of 16 stops, an opportunity for local producers to showcase their best bottles in a highly competitive market.

Offering the chance to impress new visitors in the hope they might become long-standing customers, 'the vineyards like to put their best foot forward,' Busmann explained, presumably with pun intended. 'The more memorable your space, the more likely it is that people will visit you again after the race.'

> *"The underwire in Ryan's dress started poking through the fabric – he might have found it painful were it not for the numbing effects of alcohol"*

As the mid-morning sun rose high in the sky, we ran between wine stations at a decent speed, choosing a slightly faster pace so we could spend more time lingering at each vineyard, chatting with winemakers and asking for seconds when a particularly fantastic vintage was poured. Given its nature, it's hardly surprising the race isn't timed, although participants are given a cut-off of 3.5 hours to complete it. This makes the Half Corked accessible to those who aren't regular runners, with plenty of opportunity to stop and catch their breath along the way.

Each winery is free to serve whatever it pleases, so every tasting is a surprise. Some stick to a handful of varietals, while others go all out, pairing their wines with anything from a Thai barbecue to organic energy bars and even full-buffet lunches, which the Silver Sage Winery generously did during our run. With show-stopping spreads such as these (and the fact that

WINE COUNTRY

With dozens of microclimates and terroir pockets, Oliver Osoyoos Wine Country is a 20-mile (33km) stretch between southern Osoyoos and McIntyre Bluff, north of Oliver. Its 50-odd wineries produce over 60% of BC's wine grapes: Cabernet, Syrah, and Malbec all do well in Osoyoos; Oliver is known for Chardonnay and Pinot Gris; and the cooler areas are ideal for Riesling and Pinot Noir.

Left to right: Jasmine and Ryan, the 'runaway brides'; Osoyoos and its lake are surrounded by vineyards. Previous spread: completing the Half Corked

wine pours are only an ounce), most runners are in surprisingly good shape when they eventually cross the finish line – unless you're wearing a wedding dress, that is.

With about 3 miles (5km) to go, the underwire in Ryan's dress started poking through the fabric and straight into his skin, a wardrobe malfunction he might have found painful were it not for the numbing effects of alcohol. Bringing up the rear, the rest of our group were there to cheer on both Ryan and Jasmine as they waltzed across the finish line. With the Malibooze Barbies close behind them, we were primed and ready to pose for a group photo.

Sporting a bib for the Half Corked Marathon is to do so on one of the more unusual runs out there, but our fun didn't end once the last racer had crossed the finish line. Food trucks and other wineries were there waiting for a post-race party, including live entertainment and, of course, a best-dressed costume contest. Previous winners for best costume have included a KISS tribute band in full make-up and another crew dressed as characters from *Indiana Jones and the Last Crusade* – complete with a giant 'rock' that they rolled over the entire course. With its unique blend of fun, sun, and unforgettable characters, the Half Corked Marathon has to be one of the most memorable runs in North America. **TE**

Start/Finish // Route differs each year
Distance // 12-15 miles (19km-24km)
Getting there // Transport is included both to the start line and from the finish; from/to Oliver, Osoyoos, and Penticton.
When to go // The race takes place on the final Saturday of May, with special dinners the night before and post-race.
What to wear // The craziest costume possible
Where to stay // Watermark Beach Resort in Osoyoos has condo-style suites and beachfront townhomes just steps away from Osoyoos Lake.
Things to know // The ticket lottery for the Half Corked Marathon opens in mid-November. Race-weekend events include the Primavera Party – a long-table dinner with live music the night before the race – and an intimate multi-course feast at a winery the evening following the run.
More info // oliverosoyoos.com/half-corked-marathon

*Opposite: the wine country of
West Kelowna; 3000 runners
take part in the Napa-Sonoma
half-marathon*

MORE LIKE THIS
WINE-COUNTRY RUNS

NAPA TO SONOMA HALF-MARATHON, CALIFORNIA

A wine weekend to savor, during which California's renowned Sonoma Valley hosts both the Rosé 5k, on Saturday, followed by the main event, Sunday's half-marathon. The latter's 13.1-mile (21km) route starts in Napa and winds through rolling hills, ranches and vineyards to the historic Sonoma Plaza where a post-race wine festival awaits, featuring a variety of pours from local producers. If you're after a more leisurely jaunt, the Rosé 5k (3 miles) starts and finishes at the Plaza and includes both on-course and post-race rosé tastings. Participants can then spend the rest of the day enjoying the surrounding wine country. For something more challenging, sign up for 'The Pairing' and run both events.
**Start // Napa (half-marathon);
Sonoma Plaza, 453 1st St East (5k)
Finish // Sonoma Plaza
Distance // 13.1 miles (21km)
More info // runnapatosonoma.com**

TERROIR RUN, PRINCE EDWARD COUNTY, ONTARIO

Like all good ideas, the inspiration for the Terroir Run started over a great bottle of wine. The event's founders, Rebecca LeHeup and Andrew MacKenzie, are both fans of culinary travel and were looking for a fun, wine-themed run without having to go all the way to France. With the beautiful Prince Edward County vineyards on their doorstep, it didn't take them long to get local producers involved. The event, now more than a decade old, partners with a dozen wineries over a 6.2-mile (10km) route, which takes in vineyards and tranquil country roads. Tastings along the course offer wine, as well as beer and cider at the finish line. Transportation and a post-race lunch are included, with costumes encouraged. Like the Half Corked, organizers stress this is not so much a race as a fun, boutique experience. About 100 runners sign up each year.
**Start/Finish // Various
Distance // 6.2 miles (10km)
More info // terroirrun.com**

KELOWNA WINE COUNTRY HALF-MARATHON, KELOWNA, BRITISH COLUMBIA

This annual event is a bit of a rarity among its wine-running counterparts, in that it's actually timed. Welcoming about 2500 runners, the Kelowna Wine Country Half-Marathon (which also offers shorter 5km and 10km routes) is all about soaking up the scenery, from the glistening shores of Okanagan Lake to the surrounding valley celebrated for its top-notch vineyards. The course curves through scenic country roads and along the picturesque Mission Creek Greenway, ending at the city's Waterfront Park in downtown. A big party awaits to toast the finishers, complete with, what else, wine and music.
**Start // Southeast Kelowna
Finish // Downtown Kelowna
Distance // 5km, 10km or 20km
(3.1, 6.2 or 13.1 miles)
More info // kelownamarathon.ca**

TEST YOUR LIMITS ON SEWARD'S MIGHTY MT MARATHON

This short but brutal dash up an ultra-steep mountain has been held annually on July 4th since 1915 and is part of Alaska folklore.

There was a moment halfway up Alaska's Mt Marathon when I started to think that I had bitten off more than I could chew – and I wasn't even taking part in the infamous July 4th race. Electing to tackle the mountain solo on a clear day in June, I had become disorientated soon after the trailhead, scrambling recklessly up a steep ravine before realizing that, even by Alaskan standards, I was entering tricky territory. Trying to correct myself, I diverted into a sloping forest of low bushes and began clawing my way through dense shrubbery, grabbing erratically at devil's club, a mildly toxic plant that left itchy lacerations

on my hands and legs. To get back on the correct path, I was forced to undertake a nervous traverse across an unstable scree slope to merge with the so-called 'race trail' and reach comparative safety. So far, so terrifying. If only I'd watched the race video first.

The Mount Marathon race climbs to the summit of a 2974ft (906m) ridgeline overlooking the Alaskan port of Seward. What it lacks in height, it makes up for in steep, unforgiving terrain. Forget the Hardrock 100 and Barkley Marathons; this is the site of one of the oldest and most fearsome running events in North America.

> ## "It felt as if I was hauling my body up a giant sand dune, trading every two steps forward for one step back"

The event has been held annually on July 4th since 1915. To call it a 'run' is something of an exaggeration. For most mortals, the 3.1-mile (5km) out-and-back course is better described as a short but treacherous scramble to an exposed turnaround point followed by a controlled free-fall back down to sea level. Not that this deters the hordes of masochistic participants who flock to Seward every summer to sign up for the annual pain-fest. For purists, the event might fall short of the 26-mile marathon of Athenian legend, but with its loose rock, slippery shale, and cruel gradients topping out at 60 degrees, it's just as arduous.

The madness began in 1909, when a Seward grocer named Gus Borgen offered $100 to the first person who managed to scramble up and down the town's guardian peak, Mt Lowell, in less than an hour. The first contender, a cocky clerk called Al Taylor, made a valiant attempt but, underestimating the harshness of the mountain's unrelenting slopes, hurtled back to town 20 minutes shy of Borgen's deadline.

Other challengers soon followed, chiseling the time down to a respectable one hour and 16 minutes, but the formidable 60-minute barrier remained elusive. By 1915 there were enough wannabes to merit an official race. James Walters won the first event in a good-but-not-good-enough 62 minutes, but it wasn't until the following year that a gutsy competitor named Alec Bolan finally scooped Borgen's winnings when he completed the challenge in an astonishing 55 minutes. The race promptly became a permanent fixture on Seward's sporting calendar, drawing hundreds of annual competitors – and Mt Lowell was reverently renamed Mt Marathon.

Today, as in 1915, runners line up at an official starting line in downtown Seward, on the corner of 4th Ave and Adams St, to chase a course record that now stands at 41 minutes. For my solo attempt, I decided to skip the asphalt and proceed directly to the base of the mountain. Here, an ominous signboard advertising the race trail doesn't mince words: 'Very strenuous, steep, and grueling route with many life-threatening hazards', it announces, next to a pictorial map of the course decorated with photos of runners descending.

The main quirk of the Mt Marathon race is that there is no single way up. Competitors are permitted to ascend the mountain whichever way they choose. At the base on Lowell Canyon Rd, you are presented with two equally daunting options: the 'cliffs' or the 'roots'. The 'cliffs' comprises a vertiginous wall of slippery rock that is best left to daredevils and mountaineers. The 'roots' is a jumble of hard-to-distinguish paths, half-occluded by thick bushes and covered with mud.

DO YOUR HOMEWORK

Mt Marathon isn't a trail to be taken lightly, even for experienced mountain runners. Emergency rescues are made every year. Choose a fine day with clear, dry weather, take a friend (or tell someone where you're going), and watch the race video first. An easier alternative to the race trail is the 3 mile (4.8km) Jeep trail, which takes you to the summit via switchbacks, an alpine bowl, and a couple of rocky scrambles.

Clockwise from top: starting the big day; the view from the trail; sea level at Seward. Previous spread: it's tough at the top of Mt Marathon

© mhgston / Shutterstock

Neither is easy to find. Heading up what I thought was the 'roots', I got lost within seconds, hence my unnecessary diversion into that precipitous ravine.

Fortunately, after merging belatedly with the race trail somewhere above the 'roots', I was able to continue my slow upward trajectory, ascending a near-vertical path littered with loose stones and slippery shale. With the gradient averaging 34 degrees, it felt as if I was hauling my body up a giant sand dune, trading every two steps forward for one step back.

With lungs gasping and legs aflame, I finally managed to reach Race Point, where I was treated to a Google Earth-like view of the steep-sided Resurrection Bay. With the tiny street-grid of Seward nestled almost vertically below, it was time for the free-fall. Seasoned athletes who ascend the mountain in 35 minutes usually plummet fearlessly back to town in little over six, crashing through an obstacle course of snowfields, ravines, and streambeds. Competition is predictably fierce, and bloody knees, twisted ankles, and dislocated shoulders are common.

After my earlier shenanigans, I decided to play it safe, alternating awkward running with crab-walking and sliding on my backside. It was slow, painstaking work that was alleviated by the bright sunshine and spectacular vistas. Re-entering the mountain's lower forests near the top of the 'cliffs', I swung left and jogged the last quarter-mile down the so-called Jeep trail to the refreshingly firm streets of Seward. With my legs scratched and rubbery but still somehow keeping me vertical, I'd survived what still ranks as one of the toughest runs of my life. **BS**

Start/Finish // 4th Ave & Adams St, Seward
Distance // 3.1 miles (5km)
Getting there // The nearest large airport is Ted Stevens Anchorage International. To get to Seward you can take a bus (daily summer departures), enjoy a spectacular train ride on the Alaska Railroad (alaskarailroad.com), or drive 120 miles (193km) along the Seward Hwy.
When to go // June to September, when the mountain is snow-free.
What to wear // Gloves to protect your hands from the sharp stones and devil's club.
Where to stay // The Harbor 360 Hotel (harbor360hotel.com) is a waterfront property with a restaurant, small pool, and rooms with a view.
Things to know // Watch the course video (mountmarathon.com/for-racer/course) on the official race website before setting out, especially if you are undertaking the course alone.
More info // seward.com; mountmarathon.com

Opposite: beautiful Banff seen from Sulphur Mountain; running in Squamish, BC

MORE LIKE THIS
STEEP MOUNTAIN RUNS

GROUSE GRIND, BRITISH COLUMBIA

The Grind is a super-steep ascent of the southwest face of Grouse Mountain, the 4039ft (1231m) peak that rises above the city of Vancouver. It starts at the mountain's base gondola station and terminates at an attractive resort near the top, replete with restaurants, ziplines and a winter ski area. First built in the 1980s, the Grind has developed into a super-popular fitness test for athletic locals, who race to the top for a personal-best time and a replenishing burger. The path ascends 2624ft (800m) in 1.6 miles (2.5km) and is equipped with numerous steps, signposts, and the occasional boardwalk. Successful grinders can compare times on computer screens in the summit lodge (fastest known time: 23:48), before descending back to the base via the gondola. An annual Grouse Grind Mountain Run is held in late August.
Start // Grouse Mountain Gondola base
Finish // Gondola summit
Distance // 1.6 miles (2.5km)
More info // grousemountain.com

SULPHUR MOUNTAIN TRAIL, ALBERTA

Sulphur Mountain is an 8041ft (2451m) peak overlooking Banff town. It's the source of the national park's famous spring water. There's an observation deck, several eating joints, and an interpretive boardwalk on the summit. While most tourists ascend the mountain on the Banff gondola, it's also possible to reach the summit via a snaking 3.4-mile (5.5km) trail that zigzags up the forested slopes on graded switchbacks. The path is smooth and steady, if unrelenting, making it a perfect ascent for well-conditioned runners. The trail starts adjacent to the Upper Hot Springs pool complex and begins climbing from the get-go, with views of Mt Rundle and Banff flickering sporadically through the trees. Most of the route is forested and the switchbacks become shorter and steeper as you near the top. The total route elevation is 2149ft (655m). At the summit, you can grab an ice cream at the gondola station and hike on a boardwalk to an old weather station.
Start // Banff Upper Hot Springs parking lot
Finish // Top of Banff gondola
Distance // 3.4 miles (5.5km)
More info // banfflakelouise.com/ experiences/sulphur-mountain-trail

SEA TO SUMMIT TRAIL, BRITISH COLUMBIA

The Sea to Summit Trail roughly follows the route of Squamish's Sea to Sky gondola, starting in the shadow of the iconic Stawamus Chief, Canada's premier rock-climbing crag. The tough but mostly runnable trail ascends 3012ft (918m) over 4 miles (6.5km), to a gorgeously integrated summit lodge with spectacular views over the deep-blue fjord of Howe Sound. While there are a couple of steep rocky interludes with ropes and chains for added assistance, the trail is considerably easier than Mt Marathon or the Grouse Grind, with several flattish sections. In its initial stages, the route shares a path with the Stawamus Chief Trail, ascending steeply via a series of wooden staircases.
Start // Sea to Sky Gondola base
Finish // Summit lodge
Distance // 4 miles (6.5km)
More info // seatoskygondola.com/ trails/sea-to-summit-trail

A DEVILISH DESCENT ON WHISTLER'S MUSICAL BUMPS

Brendan Sainsbury takes a gondola to the top of Whistler Mountain and descends back down an exhilarating mix of ridges, meadows, and forest to Whistler Village.

It's a breezy summer afternoon in late August and I'm standing on Flute Summit, hands on knees, sucking in air, after a short sharp sprint from a lofty saddle a few vertical meters below. In the distance, I can see the volcanic spire of The Black Tusk and countless other shapely mountains, some still speckled with snow but no other human beings. The world-famous resort of Whistler, playground to more than three million annual visitors, is just out of sight in a valley to the northwest, but right here, right now, on this wind-blown summit, it's just me, some wispy clouds, and a couple of timid ground squirrels.

Thousands of skiers throng the alpine bowls of Whistler Mountain in the winter but significantly fewer come back between July and September to tackle the dry, snow-free slopes on foot. Here, amid dazzling alpine scenery, it's possible to run for mile after glorious mile on well-maintained interconnected paths to the base station of the Whistler gondola in the busy village below. As a sport, it might not share the same adrenalin rush as skiing, but for a calm-inducing communion with nature, it's hard to beat.

Whistler Mountain is one of two prominent peaks that stand sentinel over North America's largest ski resort, providing access to some of the finest powder on the continent. In summer, with the snow largely melted, hikers and sightseers can take the high-speed gondola up to the Roundhouse, a sprawling lodge located at 6070ft (1850m), and explore the mountain minus its white winter cloak. Several attractions lie in close vicinity, including a chairlift and a skybridge, but my favorite summertime indulgence is to head over to a hump-backed ridge just beyond the immediate tourist area, and test my mettle on the Musical Bumps Trail.

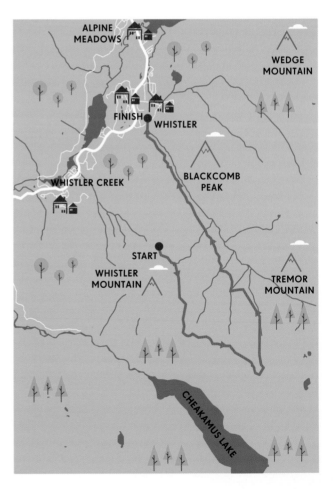

The beauty of the 'Bumps' is its accessibility and close integration with other mountain paths. For amateur middle-of-the-pack athletes like me, this is high-alpine trail running made easy, jogging along undulating paths that mostly avoid the lung-wrenching climbs and overly technical rock-hopping associated with grittier Canadian mountains. The trail, for the most part, is well-marked and simple to navigate, and the protracted descents are refreshingly gentle on the knees. The only real distraction is the views, which in the first half of the run are nothing short of spectacular.

The unofficial starting point is Roundhouse Lodge, whose restaurant complex at the top of the gondola is perched around 1000ft (305m) below Whistler Mountain's craggy summit. This is my go-to place for a pre-trek coffee, which I like to imbibe outside on the panoramic patio, surrounded by the chattering crowds I'll soon be leaving behind.

A significant summer trail network emanates from the lodge with paths graded green (easy), blue (moderate) and black (difficult). I usually start on the gravel Spearhead Loop that leads down to Harmony Lake, a translucent body of water rimmed by willowy trees and a wooden boardwalk. Skirting the lakeshore, I merge with the tougher High

Note Trail, traversing around Harmony Ridge before dipping into the secluded Symphony Bowl, a natural amphitheater beloved by winter skiers for its moguls and advanced runs. This is undoubtedly the narrowest and roughest part of the trail, but still eminently runnable if you stay focused and alert. Fortunately, by this point, the day-trippers have magically evaporated, as the scenery alternates between rocky alpine and luxuriant sub-alpine, with sporadic stands of spruce trees juxtaposed against lush meadows and loose scree.

After passing diminutive Symphony Lake, the path ascends to a saddle where the High Note trail intersects with the Musical Bumps. This is where I do my quick pass-to-peak sprint, making a concerted push up to the rocky plateau of Flute Summit where I rest briefly under a swinging wooden sign that looks like it has been transported over from an English pub.

The next few miles are my favorite part of the run and well worth savoring. Cutting across an open ridgetop, the clear, obstacle-free path drops briefly to another saddle before ascending to Oboe Summit (slightly off the main trail) with fine views over toward Blackcomb Mountain. Thereafter, it's a continuous downward trajectory as I speed through swaying flower meadows and dwarf forest down to Singing Pass, yelling bear warnings as the foliage closes in.

BLACKCOMB MOUNTAIN

Since 2008, Whistler and nearby Blackcomb have been linked by the Peak 2 Peak Gondola, making Whistler the largest ski area in North America. In summer, you can ascend Blackcomb via three conjoined trails (Little Burn, Big Burn, Heart Burn) which end at the Rendezvous Lodge. From here, take the gondola over to the Roundhouse and descend Whistler Mountain via the Musical Bumps.

Left to right: Whistler's resort village in summer; lupins and daisies; Flute Summit is the start of a beautiful stretch of running; more trails at Garibaldi Park. Previous spread: spot wildlife from Whistler's gondola

Singing Pass, just below the tree line, is a backcountry crossroads where a separate trail branches east to Russet Lake, a popular camping spot in Garibaldi Provincial Park. From here, it's 6.8 miles (11km) of gradual descent back to Whistler village, through ever-thickening forest alongside Melody and Fitzsimmons Creeks, with a well-packed trail allowing me to increase my speed without pulverizing my knees.

Halfway down, the trail passes beneath the Peak 2 Peak Gondola that links the summit stations of Whistler and Blackcomb mountains. Here, I usually stop briefly and study the tiny cabins shunting silently across the valley 1427ft (436m) above me. All around, the forest ecosystems continue to morph and change. Tree trunks thicken, bush leaves broaden, and the gushing river, out of sight for much of the journey, gets progressively louder.

Over the final few miles, the Singing Pass Trail cuts across various routes in Whistler's Mountain Bike Park and I try to keep my wits about me as I meet several of the Grand Prix-like runs where helmeted riders dart at rocket-speed out of the forest. The path ultimately delivers me to a trailhead in Whistler Village, a short stroll from the gondola base station and its arc of busy bars. Gratefully, I flop down in one of them and treat myself to a cold beer. It would be rude not to. **BS**

Start/Finish // Top of Whistler Village gondola/ Whistler Village
Distance // 13 miles (21km)
Getting there // The nearest airport is Vancouver International (YVR). Whistler is a 95-minute drive north of Vancouver on Hwy 99, or a two-hour bus journey (yvrskylynx.com)
When to go // July through early October.
Where to stay // Pangea Pod hotel is a chic, modern Japanese-style pod hotel with capsule rooms and shared bathrooms. There's an on-site cafe/bar.
Where to eat // Purebread is a legendary bakery that plies Whistler's finest and sweetest energy-replenishing snacks.
Things to know // Carry bear spray (be sure how to use it).
More info // For trail maps and other details: whistlerblackcomb.com; whistler.com (Tourism Whistler); 5peaks.com (Five Peaks Running Series)

© robcocquyt / Shutterstock

Opposite: be bear-prepared in Sunshine Meadows, Banff National Park

MORE LIKE THIS
RUNS ABOVE THE TREE LINE

HOWE SOUND CREST TRAIL, BRITISH COLUMBIA

This thrilling ridge-route, which cuts across the North Shore Mountains just outside Vancouver, blends exposed terrain with brutal climbs and intermittent scrambling. Due to its difficulty, it's recommended for experienced trail runners only. The route starts in the Cypress Bowl skiing area north of the city and parallels the sparkling waters of Howe Sound for 18 miles (29km), incorporating a succession of craggy peaks above 4700ft (1433m). These include Unnecessary Mountain, James Peak, and a tricky traverse across the imposing face of West Lion. The middle section of the route is rocky and technical, with chains and ropes for extra support. The opening and closing sections are more benign and runnable, with several swimmable lakes if you get overheated. As well as excellent stamina, aspiring runners will need sure feet, a head for heights and plenty of water.

Start // Cypress Mountain
Finish // Porteau Cove
Distance // 18 miles (29km)
More info // bcparks.ca/cypress-park

SKYLINE TRAIL, ALBERTA

The Skyline Trail is Jasper National Park's pièce de résistance and one of the finest backcountry hiking routes in North America. Winding above the tree line for 15 miles (24km) of its total 27 miles (44km), the trail takes you across the rooftop of the Canadian Rockies, revealing the mountains in all their grandeur. Mostly the domain of hikers, who spread the exertion over three days, the Skyline has also developed a cult following among enthusiastic trail runners who try to polish it off in one. This point-to-point trail is best tackled south to north, starting at Maligne Lake. Summer is the best time to go, between July and September, when the path is snow-free. The total elevation is 4593ft (1400m), culminating in a steady but relentless climb to the Notch, at the halfway point. Thereafter, it's mostly downhill. Beware the fickle weather and prepare accordingly.

Start // Maligne Lake
Finish // Maligne Canyon
Distance // 27.3 miles (44km)
More info // parks.canada.ca/pn-np/ab/jasper

SUNSHINE MEADOWS, ALBERTA

Sunshine, Banff National Park's premier ski area, is transformed into a patchwork of wildflower meadows in summer, making it an ideal place for alpine runners keen to stretch their lungs and absorb nature. The joy of running in this area is that it gives you the opportunity to access the vivid lakes and meadows that adorn the Alberta-British Columbia border, by gondola and chairlift, climbing above the tree line without over-tiring your legs or expending gallons of sweat. From the top of the Standish Chairlift, a short trail leads west to a grandstand lookout on the Continental Divide. Watch out for ground squirrels bounding around the pathway as you roll down to Rock Isle Lake, before winding past larch trees and pebble-filled streams en route to Grizzly and Larix Lakes. Skip the chairlift on the return and run back to Sunshine Village via Twin Cairns Meadow and the strategically perched Monarch Viewpoint.

Start // Top of Standish Chairlift
Finish // Sunshine Village
Distance // 5.1 miles (8.3km)
More info // parks.canada.ca/pn-np/ab/banff

FORESTS AND FAR-FLUNG SHORES ALONG BC'S TONQUIN TRAIL

Fiona Tapp finds solitude on an early-morning run on this scenic trail through the beaches, rainforests, and Indigenous lands of Tofino, on Vancouver Island.

The ancient rainforests in Tofino cling to the rugged cliffs as Pacific waves crash below, filling the air with a fresh, salty scent. Here it feels easier, somehow, to connect to the water, the land, and your own body — and what better way to do that than by taking to the trail?

When I am running here, far from home, I slow my pace, stop to enjoy the landscape, snap a photo, or chat with a local about where to go next. I abandon my usual running playlist entirely and instead try to tune in to the sounds all around. Here they include the rush of the waves and children laughing on the beach.

Each time I've come to Tofino, I've stayed at Pacific Sands Beach Resort and have run along Cox Bay, back and forth as the surfers dot the waves. I like to watch them as I run and time my stride with the way they dip below the water and then pop back up to ride triumphantly toward the shore. They have an outdoor barrel sauna here, which is the perfect treat to motivate tired muscles to chug on just a little longer. I've bribed myself many

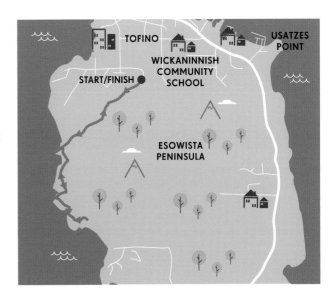

times with the promise of that sauna. When I'm feeling brave, I take it a step further and complete a Scandi-style hydrotherapy circuit by dousing myself in icy water after the heat of the sauna, or even rushing down for a quick wild swim in the ocean.

As much as I love running on the beach, Tofino offers something rare: stunning and contrasting geographical features just steps away from the shore. Running the Tonquin Trail lets you experience the rich variety of Tofino's landscapes, from beach to old-growth coastal rainforest, and the Indigenous Tla-o-qui-aht lands that have been inhabited here for over 5000 years.

It's a looped trail that starts and ends at the Tofino Community Hall, which makes it ideal for running with friends, with a clear meeting point even if you run at different paces. Run along the tree-lined gravel path and first you'll come to Tonquin Beach, via a series of wooden steps set into the forest. Use these for sprints, hill training, or simply catch your breath and look up into those marvelous moss-covered trees. Continue down to the small beach area to run along the sand for some additional resistance, or enjoy the calmer waves here, which are bordered by a rocky shoreline. Retrace your steps to the main trail, then turn in the opposite direction to the Community Hall; here you can run along the coast from above, on the relatively flat gravel forest path. I've never seen anything more than birds on my trips here, but multiple signs alert visitors to the possibility of encountering wildlife such as bears, cougars, and wolves. So, it makes sense to be aware of your surroundings and stay alert to the potential for unwanted running companions.

Along your route, you'll find some spectacular points to stop and enjoy the views of Clayoquot Sound, including the Maze Lookout, where you can spy the lighthouse on top of Lennard Island, and take in Templar Channel and Wickaninnish Island. The latter's name comes from Chief Wickaninnish of the Tla-o-qui-aht, who was a powerful leader controlling the west coast

EVERYTHING IS ONE

The Tla-o-qui-aht First Nation of the Nuu-chah-nulth First Nations uphold values of environmental stewardship known as the principles of Hish-uk ts'a-walk, which means 'everything is one'. Learn more about the Tla-o-qui-aht's guardianship of the land, and the principles of sustainability in this beautiful territory, at their flagship visitor experience, the Big Tree Trail at Wanachus-Hilthuuis (Meares Island) Tribal Park. Here you'll see Western red cedar trees, some as old as 1500 years.

Clockwise from top: Vancouver Island's west coast near Tofino; downtown Tofino; seaplane at Tofino; run through temperate rainforest in the Pacific Rim National Park. Previous spread: Cox Bay Beach and running the Pacific coast of Vancouver Island

© Marina Poushkina / Shutterstock; Elena Elisseeva / Shutterstock

of Vancouver Island in the late 1700s. This is also the site of a shipwreck, from 1811, after a conflict broke out between American traders and members of the Tla-o-qui-aht community, which resulted in an explosion that sank the *Tonquin*, a fur-trading vessel. Later on, walk down Third St toward the harbor and you'll find the anchor from the ill-fated ship on display.

On your run, you'll also pass several creeks and a small wetland before your last beach-stop of the trail, at Middle Beach, which passes through the ha-houlthee (traditional territory) of the Tla-o-qui-aht people. This is your halfway point, so maybe stop for a snack and a stretch before looping back to the start of the trail.

The Tonquin Trail is popular but at many spots, particularly Third Beach, you may well find it deserted, especially if you do as I do and go early in the morning when it feels like you have the Earth to yourself and can enjoy a coastal sunrise.

One of the more surprising aspects of this run is how, at times, it feels so remote, whereas it is, in fact, very central. The Tonquin's start and end are within a 10-minute walk of some of the town's most popular attractions, including the gallery of renowned Indigenous artist Roy Henry Vickers and the popular Wolf in the Fog restaurant. This makes it very accessible even without a car, and a convenient point to meet up with friends for a run or hike before enjoying the rest of your day in Tofino. I also love how it unfolds, beginning just as a path through a forest before revealing glimpses of the coast, the smell of the ocean air, and the sound of crashing waves. As you descend the wooden steps, the appearance of the beach below is like opening a gift. **FT**

Start/Finish // Tofino Community Hall
Distance // 2.2 miles (3.5km) plus half a mile (800m) of boardwalk and stairs.
Getting there // Drive to Tofino from the mainland, crossing on the ferry, or take a seaplane from Vancouver into Tofino Harbor.
When to go // Tofino is popular and well-visited year-round but especially in the summer and the storm-watching season, which runs from November to February.
What to wear // Quick-drying layers that adapt to Tofino's changeable weather.
Where to stay // Pacific Sands Beach Resort (pacificsands.com)
Where to eat // Order a luxury pop-up picnic from Lux.Fino or enjoy wild, foraged, local ingredients when you dine at SoBo.
Things to know // Run the Tonquin Trail at low tide to enjoy even more of the beaches.
More info // tourismtofino.com

Opposite: the Valley of the Five Lakes Trail near Jasper; boardwalk in the Pacific Spirit Regional Park

MORE LIKE THIS
NATURE RUNS IN WESTERN CANADA

PACIFIC SPIRIT REGIONAL PARK, BRITISH COLUMBIA

Located in the north of the park, the Spanish Trail is a picturesque journey through part of this expansive century-old, 1850-acre (750-hectare) second-growth forest. It starts with a steep incline but then plateaus out significantly to a fairly flat path, offering a relaxed run with multiple connecting trails if you want to explore further. Stay alert to other trail users, including those on horseback or riding mountain bikes, as these are shared multi-use paths. The route is well-marked and features hemlock, cedar, and maple leaf trees. You'll follow the route along the Sword Fern Trail before it connects to the Salish Trail and onto the Admiralty Trail, bringing you back around in a loop to the start of the Spanish Trail.
Start/Finish // Spanish Banks Central Parking Lot, Vancouver
Distance // 3.4 miles (5.5km)
More info // metrovancouver.org/ services/regional-parks/park/pacific-spirit-regional-park

VALLEY OF THE FIVE LAKES, ALBERTA

Once you've run from the start of the trail toward the lakes, you'll have a choice: take the clockwise path to see the lakes in order (1st, 2nd, 3rd, etc), or take a right and travel the route counter-clockwise to appreciate the lakes in reverse order, which means you'll save the largest and perhaps most impressive lake (1st lake) for the end of your run. Just a 15-minute drive from Jasper, Alberta, this trail is incredibly popular with good reason – the five lakes are truly stunning, boasting otherworldly turquoise waters that demand you stop and snap a picture or two. You'll cross a footbridge and a marsh during your run, and be sure to keep your eyes out for the sixth, uncounted bonus lake.
Start/Finish // Valley of the Five Lakes, Banff
Distance // 3 miles (4.8km)
More info // jasper.travel/ experiences/valley-five-lakes-everyone

WHITTAKER TRAIL, MT DOUGLAS PARK, BRITISH COLUMBIA

The Whittaker and Irvine Trails are well-maintained paths around the edge of Mt Douglas Park, offering a captivating loop through lush forests, featuring towering Douglas fir and cedar trees. As you get closer to the mountain, you'll need to cross a road and the trail will get steeper here, with some possible scrambling required to reach the 738ft (225m) summit elevation. The incredible views over Victoria are well worth the effort put in on your ascent. Once you've enjoyed your reward, you'll follow the Irvine Trail back down again, connecting with Whittaker to return to the same starting point. Mt Douglas Park is going through a process of name restoration and will be officially known by the Indigenous WSÁNEĆ word PKOLS (pronounced 'p'cawls') which means 'white rock'.
Start/Finish // Cordova Bay Rd, Victoria
Distance // 2.79 miles (4.5km)
More info // saanich.ca/EN/main/ parks-recreation-community/parks/ parks-trails-amenities/signature-parks/mount-douglas-park.html

LAKESIDE LIFE ON THE MARTIN GOODMAN TRAIL

Toronto's favorite outdoor playground dazzles Isabella Noble on this beach-fringed, landmark-lined route around the shores of inky-blue Lake Ontario.

Bringing together silvery, powder-soft beaches, lively lakeside parks, and unmissable urban views, the 14-mile (22km) Martin Goodman Trail (MGT) captures perfectly the spirit of Toronto. From Mimico's Humber Bay Arch Bridge in the west, to the Rouge River at its eastern end, this flat, lake-hugging route is named for a much-loved former *Toronto Star* editor and delivers a slice of local life that will leave even a visiting runner feeling like a real Torontonian.

Lake Ontario might be the smallest of North America's Great Lakes but, no matter the time of year, it's a great tonic for Toronto urbanites. With its blue expanses rippling into the distance toward New York state, on a sunny day it can seem as if half of Toronto hits the MGT to run, walk, cycle or rollerblade, and a whole lot more besides. If you're lucky, you might see paddle boarders or kayakers thrown into the mix, too, just a little way offshore. And even in cooler weather, layers and hats at the ready, hardy Toronto folk just bundle up and get out there.

I've been spending time in Toronto for several years now, getting to know my Canadian partner's hometown, and running along the MGT never fails to help me connect with this sprawling city of almost 3 million people. Some are out jogging a few miles with friends, others taking delighted dogs for strolls, or perhaps in training for serious long-distance runs. Whatever the reason, there's always a warm community spirit, with runners of all kinds greeting each other as they pass.

For today's 4.2-mile (7km), one-way run, my partner and I set off from the Toronto Music Garden. Located at the far south end of Spadina Ave, it begins what for many locals is the loveliest part of the MGT, that section between Harbourfront's Queens Quay and the Humber Bay Arch Bridge. Trails continue on both sides, so you can easily extend the route as far as you like; you might combine it with beautiful High Park (see More Like This, p48), or zip to the bridge and back again for a lengthier itinerary. In fact, the Martin Goodman Trail forms part of the much longer Great Lakes Waterfront Trail, which travels a whopping 2236 miles (3600km) across Ontario and is, in parts, still being developed.

On this late-fall morning, the 550m CN Tower looms behind us and, despite the warm weather forecast earlier, it's now chilly and overcast, so we sprint off through the gardens. Glancing across the water, I spot one of my all-time favorite places in the city, the Toronto Islands. A string of 15 protected low-rise islands characterized by golden beaches and cottage-style homes, it's somewhere I've spent countless fun summer days. As I reminisce, a plane swoops in across the lake to land at tiny Billy Bishop Airport, which sits right on the water at the western end of Centre Island.

Just a few strides further on, the path skirts around Little Norway Park and a spectacular ceremonial pole emerges from the greenery. This is *Dreamwork of the Whales*, carved by a group of Toronto artists in the 1980s, from a single 700-year-old cedar tree. Next up is Coronation Park, which passes in a whirl of dogs racing through earthy-yellow fall leaves; after that, it's the imposing Princes' Gates, a set of monumental arches built in the 1920s and leading, in turn, to Exhibition Place. Every August, this landmark showspace famously hosts the Canadian National Exhibition, yet it was once a key portage spot for local Indigenous people as they traversed the lake by boat. Later, it was appropriated as a French trading post and then a British army barracks.

As the trail meanders past Ontario Place (a former theme park), I catch sight of some distant skyscrapers far across the lake. The city of Niagara Falls flickers out of the haze yet is more than an hour's drive from Toronto (and that's with good traffic). On clear days, you might even be able to make out the famous mist spiraling high above the Horseshoe Falls, the largest of three that make up the Niagara landmark.

SUNNYSIDE

Framed by soaring classical columns and with its intricately decorated arch, Sunnyside Bathing Pavilion is a 1922 Beaux Arts landmark designed by architect Alfred Chapman. At its peak, it was a Toronto summer hub, holding lockers for about 7700 bathers and operating its own streetcar. Swimmers would plunge straight into Lake Ontario or swim in the 'Tank', one of the world's largest heated pools. The pavilion also houses a lake-view cafe.

Left to right: Toronto's CN Tower; Little Norway Park's totem pole by the Ne Chi Zu Works collective; the Humber Bay Arch Bridge. Previous page: Budapest Park's shoreline

"Time your run to catch a flaming Toronto sunset, illuminating the city skyline and the shimmering lake beyond"

From Ontario Place, the MGT becomes its very best self, with lakefront boardwalks meandering past slender beaches, honey-hued fall trees reflecting off the water, and the occasional group of Canadian geese waddling across the path. At Sunnyside Park, a cluster of Muskoka chairs in cheery rainbow colors reminds me of balmy summer days spent cycling here with friends. Today, a handful of people are canoeing on the calm water, while on the sandy shoreline a pair of brave souls brace themselves for a cold-water plunge. It's impossible, too, not to pause for a quick peek at Sunnyside Bathing Pavilion, with its distinctive gold-and-blue arch overlooking the pavement.

Finally, around a tight tree-lined corner, the curving white Humber Bay Arch Bridge swings into view. It was conceived in the 1990s by Montgomery & Sisam, the Toronto-based architects that also gave us the locally loved Tommy Thompson Park. This prize-winning, traffic-free bridge is lauded for its distinctive geometric design which honors southern Ontario's First Nations communities, whose traditional routes northward once commenced here. If you can, time your run to catch a flaming Toronto sunset, illuminating the city skyline and the shimmering lake beyond the mouth of the Humber.

At the end of our run, we head off to find a steaming-hot coffee and wander through nearby High Park, currently awash with fall colors. I stop to soak up the serenity of my surroundings in a place that, thanks to the generous spirit of my fellow runners, has come to feel like a part-time home. **IN**

Start/Finish // Toronto Music Garden/
Humber Bay Arch Bridge
Distance // 4.3 miles (7km)
Getting there // The city's TTC streetcars provide convenient public transport links near both the start and end points and, depending on where you're coming from, the subway is a good option, too. Toronto's Billy Bishop Airport is handily located on the waterfront, though the larger Toronto Pearson Airport has more flights.
When to go // Spring or fall but it's accessible most of the year, weather permitting.
Where to stay // Toronto has a wealth of choices, including the stylish Ace Hotel Toronto (acehotel.com), less than a mile north of the Toronto Music Garden.
Things to know // Weather can vary hugely depending on the time of year, so dress accordingly.
More info // toronto.ca; waterfronttrail.org

Opposite: running Toronto's Waterfront Marathon

MORE LIKE THIS
CLASSIC TORONTO RUNS

TCS TORONTO WATERFRONT MARATHON

Held every October, the lively Waterfront Marathon is generally considered the finest of Toronto's two annual marathons, drawing more than 25,000 participants from across Canada and beyond. The route weaves through The Annex, Little Italy and West Queen West, before tracking west across the lakefront, where it overlaps in parts with the Martin Goodman Trail and eventually loops back east. Then it whizzes past the Distillery District, Riverdale Park and The Beaches neighborhood before hitting the finish line near City Hall. For anyone who doesn't fancy the full 26-mile spin, there are half-marathon and 3-mile (5km) options.
Start // University Ave
Finish // Bay St
Distance // 26 miles (42km)
More info //
torontowaterfrontmarathon.com

HIGH PARK

No matter when you zip through, Toronto's most-loved park is a joy, whether cloaked in springtime cherry blossoms or in red-tinged fall colors. Running (and walking) routes meander along tree-lined dirt paths and over grass-covered hills, all with city views. There are ponds for birdwatching, so dip in and out however you like; a full loop of the perimeter is a 3.2-mile (5km) run, perhaps starting from the convenient High Park subway station at the park's north end. Since it's just north of Sunnyside Beach, High Park also makes a great add-on to the Martin Goodman Trail. The best time to run here is on weekends, when the entire park is closed to traffic.
Start/Finish // High Park subway station (alternative access points are available)
Distance // 3.2 miles (5km)
More info // highparktoronto.com

BELTLINE TRAIL

Stretching across northeast Toronto, the popular Beltline Trail follows the former tracks of the Toronto Belt Line Railway, a failed commuter route that infamously lasted just two years following its opening in the 1890s. The Trail was established in the late 1980s, a tree-shaded running, walking, and cycling path divided into three subsections: York Beltline in the west; Kay Gardner Beltline (the most popular); and Ravine Beltline, where you might spot deer and other wildlife among the forest greenery. The most exciting option is to hop on the Kay Gardner Beltline just east of busy Allen Rd and run around 4.5 miles (7.2km) southeast, to wrap up at the Don Valley/ Evergreen Brick Works (just off Bay View Ave), which hosts markets, cultural events, cafes, and more.
Start // Kay Gardner Beltline
Finish // Evergreen Brick Works
Distance // 4.5 miles (7.2km)

A WINTER WARM-UP IN QUÉBEC CITY

Sometimes the only way to have your favorite city run all to yourself is to do it when the mercury drops below zero and most people are still in bed.

Winter mornings have never been a runner's best friend – unless you happen to live in Québec City. I do live in Québec City for part of the year, and have found that the season is such a part of our culture and landscape, it's actually a time when that internal early morning struggle – the negotiation with oneself for a few more minutes in bed – disappears. In winter, I get up with the alarm, excited to discover how snowy it might be outside, curious about how cold it might be. On go the layers and the four-season running gear – the thermals, the tuque, the YakTrax – and off I go.

Outside, it's always minus a few and my breath steams up in great clouds around me. I never grow tired of what lies ahead: centuries of history and gorgeous natural surroundings along my favorite city run on the planet. It's a run I do a few times a week when I'm here, and it's actually best in the coldest months. However, even in winter, Québec City gets packed with people, which is why early morning is my favorite. A quiet dawn workout is the perfect way to start the day.

Québec sits high on a cape known as Cap Diamant, between the St Lawrence and St Charles Rivers. The old city was built on the site of an Iroquois village, chosen by French explorer and city founder Samuel de Champlain in 1608. Because of its geography, the oldest part of the city is a two-tier affair. The upper city sits high on a promontory with its meandering, history-drenched thoroughfares, imposing ramparts, and the impressive Château Frontenac hotel.

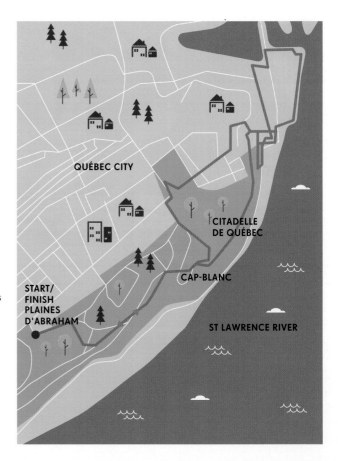

QUÉBEC CITY

CITADELLE DE QUÉBEC

CAP-BLANC

START/ FINISH PLAINES D'ABRAHAM

ST LAWRENCE RIVER

© Wondkun Jia / Shutterstock

The lower part of town is full of impossibly narrow cobbled streets and quaint shops, in what's known as the Quartier Petit Champlain, a neighborhood leading to the Old Port area. I always begin this run near the snowy expanse of the largest city-center park, the Plaines d'Abraham. When it's really cold, say, 5°F (-15°C), I head here first for a warm-up along the flat, green, manicured gardens and tree-fringed lawns. In winter, it's a huge, snowy playground with cross-country ski tracks, a skating rink and snow-running tracks.

Once at the south end of the plains, I pick up some of the off-road trails that lead through the heart of the park. Ice-crusted snow sparkles in the streetlights, early morning skiers glide by and a handful of runners leave trails of frozen exhales in the still air. By the time I reach the Old City though, I'm often the only runner around. There's still fresh white snow on the pavement and no sound other than the rhythmic crunch underfoot. I run over ground where in 1759 the French and British fought the bloody Battle of Québec for control of the city.

Ahead is the nearly 200-year-old Citadelle, one of the best-preserved forts in North America. I jog through one of the city gates, Porte St Louis, opposite Québec's ornate icicle-adorned parliament, before passing more architectural wonders such as the château-esque Hôtel de Ville de Québec (the city hall) and the Notre-Dame de Québec Basilica, first built on this site in 1647. This early, I have these places all to myself and it's wonderful to be able to take them all in, in solitude.

Once at the riverside, I head down the Escalier Casse-Cou (Breakneck Stairs), a steep stone stairway where I hold tight to the railings as I clamber down, being careful not to slip on hidden ice. I then enter the narrow, cobbled streets that run between the squat, stone buildings of Quartier Petit Champlain, the oldest commercial district on the continent. These tiny shops here have been selling their wares for 400 years; today the quartier is a tourist magnet, selling everything from tacky souvenirs to fine art. I often revel in the fact that the cobbles have a fine covering of crunchy snow, which makes them slightly grippier in winter than they are during the summer.

Beyond the cobblestone is the Blvd Champlain at the St Lawrence riverside. The river is wide here – just under a mile (1.6km) across – and steam rises in the early light. Chunks of ice jostle in the turbulent water, catching the low sun as they tumble and bob past the city.

From here, I hit the paved walking tracks that lead me north to the Old Port, before looping south again, back to the Quartier Petit Champlain. This time I'm heading uphill, as I cruise up slender Rue Petit Champlain, which is usually packed with shoppers, many of whom ride the nearby funicular that parallels the street. But not this early. Long before the shops will open, their lit windows paint the untouched snow with a warm, yellow glow.

Eventually, I arrive at the iconic view of the city: the Château Frontenac hotel, towering above me as I duck under the Porte

WINTER WORSHIP

Québec City loves its cold winters so much that the town and its residents celebrate the season with a 10-day-long winter carnival festival every February. The city comes alive with every kind of winter sport imaginable, including sleigh and toboggan rides, as well as snow and ice carvings, music, steaming hot food, and parades. The centerpiece is a vast ice palace, made with thousands of blocks of clear ice, brought to life with cinematic lighting.

Clockwise from top: Québec City's Dufferin Terrace is transformed under a blanket of snow; grippy tread keeps runners on their feet; seeing the Old Town at a more sedate pace. Previous page: an aerial view of Québec City

"The cobbles have a fine covering of crunchy snow, which makes them grippier than they are in summer"

© Jochen Jack / Alamy Stock Photo

Prescott city gate. Built as a hotel in 1893, the château is vast and imaginatively spectacular. Its fairytale turrets, sharp-pointed spires and steep copper roof, sprinkled here and there with snow, make it seem like a magical winter castle. It's florid now in the rising sun. To get even closer, I climb a stone stairway and emerge onto the boardwalk of Terrasse Dufferin, which is a delight underfoot: springy, wooden, flat.

My run ends with an exhilarating climb up 300 stairs to gain the ground I have lost. It's actually several sets of steps, mercifully interspersed with flat sections. I'm careful to tread gingerly and keep an eye on my feet as I ascend the icy steps – doing this run in reverse would require a precarious plunge down the slippery descent.

Finally, I pop out at the top, next to the Citadelle and onto the Plaines of Abraham once again. The city is now awake and my tracks have long been trampled by commuters. There are people now walking – and skiing – to work. There are others out doing their morning runs. But the winter sun still is low in the sky, just enough to warm my face.

With the temperature rising, it's a slushy run back across the park. The tuque comes off and I bask in the last of the cold, clear air for a few final moments.

Of course, this is a run that's brilliant when the snow melts, too. Autumn is particularly beautiful, with the crunch of leaves underfoot. But, for me, this is an early morning winter run, a time when I have it all to myself. **GM**

Start/Finish // Plaines d'Abraham
Distance // About 5.5 miles (9km)
Getting there // Fly into Québec City's Jean Lesage international airport or arrive by train. It's a 3.5-hour train trip from Montréal.
When to go // To experience winter running in Québec City, visit between December and March when there's usually snow on the ground.
Where to stay // The funky C3 art hotel (lec3hotel.com) is just opposite the Plaines d'Abraham, making it the perfect starting place for Québec City running.
Things to know // For cold winter running, bring long running trousers and thermal layers for your top half, including a light windstopper running jacket. Bring a warm hat or headband, windbreaker gloves, waterproof socks, all-weather runners, and snow grips for your shoes.
More info // toursvoirquebec.com/en

Opposite: Montréal's Angel of
Mt Royal

MORE LIKE THIS
WINTER RUNS IN CANADA

MT ROYAL PARK, MONTRÉAL

Just east of Montréal's downtown lies the 280-hectare Mt Royal Park, designed by Frederick Law Olmsted, who also designed New York's Central Park and named the extinct volcano at its center. Mt Royal Park has 62 miles (100km) of tracks and trails to explore, and winter transforms them. There is skating on Beaver Lake, cross-country ski tracks, downhill skiing, and, of course, running tracks. A jog on the packed-snow trails, after a fall of fresh snow with the bare trees dusted in white – and the quad-burning climb to the 764ft (233m) Mt Royal summit – is an essential Montréal experience.

Start/Finish // Le Serpentin Trail, off West Pine Ave
Distance // 3-6 miles (5km-10km)
More info // lemontroyal.qc.ca/en

ST JOHN'S, NEWFOUNDLAND

The 240ft (73m)-high Signal Hill – known for being the site of the first transatlantic radio transmission – is a brutal climb with a breathtaking reward. Start in downtown St John's, where a maze of narrow laneways snake between colorfully painted wooden houses above the harbor. Follow the waterfront northwest to the northernmost head of the Narrows. Here, you climb a series of walkways and staircases to the top. Though St John's gets more than 10ft (3m) of snow a year, the Signal Hill trail is often clear underfoot because of the city's cycle of snow and thaw. Wind, however, can make this a tricky outing, so visit when things are calm. It's 5 to 6 miles (8km-10km) out-and-back from the city center, depending on where you start.

Start/Finish // St John's downtown
Distance // 5-6 miles (8km-10km)

MT TREMBLANT, QUÉBEC

As soon the snow begins to melt on the slopes of Québec's best-known ski resort, local trail runners bust out the running shoes. The classic route is a 10.5-mile (17km) circuit, known as the Johannsen-Sommets-Grand Brule circuit, that starts and ends in Mt Tremblant Village. This hilly, technical trail takes you through gorgeous, deep green forest, across grassy ski trails, over rushing mountain streams, and past gushing waterfalls. You climb over 1950ft (600m) in total and take in killer views over the ski village and surrounds from the summit of Mt Tremblant and Pic Johannssen.

Start/Finish // Mt Tremblant Village
Distance // 10.5 miles (17km)

RUNNING THE TONGASS NEAR PETERSBURG, ALASKA

A run in the Alexander Archipelago immerses you in the extraordinary scenery of southeastern Alaska, complete with bald eagles, muskeg-dotted wetlands, and old-growth rainforest.

Locals will tell you that Petersburg, Alaska, was founded in the late 19th century by a Norwegian immigrant named Peter Buschmann. In actuality, the town was founded by a fish. Or rather many fish. All five species of Pacific salmon flourish in the cold waters surrounding Mitkof Island, and Buschmann knew a good thing when he saw it.

Such thoughts were swimming through my mind as I jogged near the edge of Petersburg's harbor, a dense thicket of masts from commercial fishing boats glinting in the early morning sun. I stopped to stretch along the boardwalk and leaned against the railing. Beyond the gently bobbing vessels, less than a mile away, the verdant slopes of Kupreanof filled the horizon. Like Mitkof, this neighboring island was densely forested but home to only a handful of inhabitants, making Petersburg (population 3100) seem like a comparative metropolis.

Despite the summer sunshine, the morning was chilly, and I set off at a faster than normal pace to keep warm. Today's run would take me through Petersburg's tiny downtown and out into nature. There would be challenging climbs along the way as I went from pavement to trail and tackled one of the closest mountains to downtown: no driving required.

I'd been drawn to this corner of southeastern Alaska ever since I met a Petersburgian named James Valentine, who described the magic of growing up here. 'I didn't have fast food until I went away to college,' he told me. Instead of a typical American upbringing, weekends were spent boating,

hiking and pursuing all things outdoors-related. Here amid the great wilderness, survival skills were built into the curriculum. 'For our final exam in school,' James recalled, 'we were dropped off on an island and wouldn't be retrieved until we'd made shelter, created a water-catchment device and started a fire.'

He also spoke admiringly of the Tongass National Forest, an expanse of wilderness that stretched across the 1100 islands of the Alexander Archipelago. Encompassing some 25,000 sq miles (64,750 sq km) – two-and-a-half times the size of

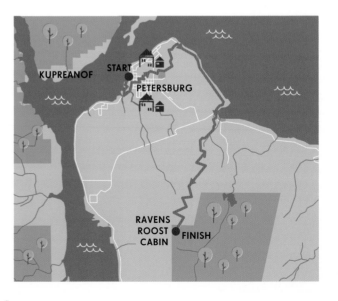

Massachusetts – it was the largest temperate rainforest on the planet. I was looking forward to experiencing one small corner of it on today's run.

Petersburg's main drag, Nordic Dr, was fairly empty at this hour of the morning as I ran along the edge of it. I passed a few inns and restaurants, as well as hardware shops and fish-processing plants: all the essentials to keep this industrious town humming. I stopped for a look at two lofty totem poles outside the Forestry Service office. Made of red cedar, the 35ft (10m) poles were the work of the Tlingit master carver Tommy Joseph who completed them in the year 2000. Each represented the major clans of Raven and Eagle. A showcase of native wildlife, they looked all the more vibrant after Joseph refreshed the poles in 2023.

Zigzagging my way through quiet residential streets, I loped behind an elementary school and found my way onto a boardwalk that traversed a bog-like meadow known as 'muskeg'. I eased into an easy rhythm on this flat stretch fringed by damp peat, wispy grasses, and stumpy trees and shrubs. A marked contrast to the forested slopes in the distance, plunked in the middle of this unusual wetland were several baseball fields. With snowcapped mountains in view, it was the most scenic little league outfield I'd ever seen.

"I couldn't stop thinking about the Tongass: running through this primeval forest felt like entering another realm"

Another half mile (0.8km) further and I was back on pavement, running along the edge of Frederick Sound. The pines grew taller on this winding roadway, and a few massive ravens chortled as I entered their domain. I also heard what sounded like rubber-soled shoes scraping across a squeaky gym floor – the not so glorious cry of the bald eagle. Rounding a bend, I spotted a pair of nesting eagles atop an enormous nest. It looked as though it had hosted countless generations of these iconic raptors.

I stopped for a water break at Sandy Beach. The tide was far out, exposing the mud flats and carefully placed rocks once used as fish traps by Alaska Natives over 2000 years ago. These unknown people left other reminders of their presence too, including several weathered petroglyphs – what appeared to be faces – carved in the dark rocks.

Just beyond, I spotted the sign for the Raven's Roost Trail. From here, I'd be ascending around 1800ft (549m) over the next 3 miles (4.8km). The first section, however, was fairly flat, and I picked up the pace as I bounded along packed gravel, with open muskeg stretching off on either side of me. The path eventually narrowed and grew steeper, while the diminutive shrubbery morphed into ever taller greenery until I was soon ensconced in dense forest. My pace slowed to a jog then a fast walk as the trail ascended wooded slopes, sometimes taking me up metal stairways anchored into the hillsides.

The greenery here was astonishing, with ferns of all shapes and sizes growing amid the damp fecundity of the rainforest. Thick mosses formed a rolling carpet below trunks of hemlock and Sitka spruce, clinging to roots, rocks, and fallen limbs. Periodic gaps through the canopy gave enticing views over the shoreline far below, but it wasn't until I reached the end of the trail, huffing and puffing up a final set of stairs, that a sweeping expanse of Frederick Sound came into full view. From my vantage point above the tree line, I spotted the Sukoi Islets off to the northeast, while the chiseled peaks of Kupreanof Island, just across the Wrangell Narrows, appeared tantalizingly close.

On my way back to the day's starting point, I couldn't stop thinking about the Tongass: running through this primeval forest felt like entering another realm, and I was already daydreaming about other trail runs in the days ahead. With so many islands to choose from, I could spend a lifetime here and never run out of options. **RSL**

FABLED FISH

Like the buffalo to the Plains Indians, the salmon lies at the center of traditional life for southeastern Alaskan Indigenous groups: it features prominently in legends, and often appears in totem pole carvings. In the past, villagers traveled by canoe to summer fishing sites; their smoked or dried catch was packed into great bales that sustained the community over the harsh winters.

Clockwise from top: the temperate rainforest of the Tongass; running the forest trails; under the gaze of a local bald eagle. Previous page: Petersburg's pretty fishing port

Start/Finish // Harbor Way
Distance // 10.6 miles (17km)
Getting there // There are direct flights from Seattle, but it's far more scenic to take the ferry from Bellingham, Washington, operated by the Alaska Marine Hwy System. The 42-hour journey takes you along the dramatic Inside Passage, with plenty of opportunities to see wildlife, including humpback whales and orcas.
When to go // Summer (June through September) offers the best weather, with long days. Come one month before to beat the summertime crowds and also experience the lively Little Norway Festival, held on the third weekend in May.
What to pack // It's not called rainforest for nothing. Be sure to bring a lightweight waterproof jacket and thin layers you can peel off when the skies clear.
More info // petersburg.org

Opposite: an Indigenous totem pole
in Juneau; the Mendenhall Glacier

MORE LIKE THIS
OTHER ALASKAN RUNS

JUNEAU

The capital of Alaska perfectly embodies the ruggedness of this vast, sparsely populated state. It's not uncommon to see bears or even wolves on the outskirts of town, and you can catch a city bus to the magnificent Mendenhall Glacier. Not surprisingly, Juneau has some outstanding trails that offer rewarding and hilly runs with a side of breathtaking scenery. From the center, it's a short jog out to Basin Rd, where you can access well-marked routes like the Perseverance Trail, which takes you past an old mining site and over rushing rivers en route to a scenic canyon. Go in summertime to see wildflowers of every shade and bushes full of salmonberries (a much-needed energy boost along the way). There's a bit of elevation gain (around 1200ft/366m), though you can up the challenge by taking a steep side trail to thundering Ebner Falls.
Start/Finish // Alaska State Capitol, downtown
Distance // 5 miles (8km)
More info // traveljuneau.com

KETCHIKAN

Ketchikan is proud of its Indigenous roots. Though founded in the 1880s, the Tlingit maintained summer fish camps in the area for untold centuries, and the town is home to the largest collection of totem poles on the planet. After taking in these towering beauties at Totem Bight State Historical Park, head to nearby Ward Lake Recreation Area for runs in the rainforest. There are many trails in the area, including an easy-going 1-mile (1.6km) loop around Ward Lake – a nice warm-up before hitting the more challenging Perseverance Lake Trail. This one takes you up through rainforest, across wooden bridges spanning trickling creeks, over muskeg flats, and back into woodlands of spruce and cedar before you finally reach lofty views over the valley. From the top you'll also get a glimpse of the distant Juno and Minerva mountains.
Start/Finish // Ward Lake Nature Trailhead
Distance // 7 miles (11.2km)
More info // visit-ketchikan.com

UTQIAGVIK

Located some 320 miles (515km) north of the Arctic Circle, difficult-to-pronounce Utqiagvik (formerly known as Barrow) is the northernmost city in the United States. Over 60% of the residents have Iñupiat ancestry, and you can learn about age-old traditions at the excellent Iñupiat Heritage Center. Afterwards, you'll want to don sturdy outer layers (the wind howls year round) for a run through town. The best time to go is obviously summer, when you can enjoy 24 hours of daylight and have a chance of spotting snowy owls, eiders, and other birdlife on the lake and waterfront of town. End the day's foray with a run along the beach, overlooking the gently lapping waves of the Arctic Ocean. You can earn serious bragging rights (and a Polar Bear Swim certificate provided by some hotels) by going for a dip in the icy waters afterwards.
Start/Finish // Utqiagvik Whale Bone Arch, Brower St
Distance // 5 miles (8km)

NEW PERSPECTIVES ON THE HOPE POINT TRAIL

Alison Mariella Désir finds camaraderie on a trail-running retreat at Hope Point in Alaska and enjoys gorgeous views of the Kenai Mountains and the Cook Inlet.

For the past 12 years, I've been deeply committed to building movement communities that are racially diverse, welcoming and inclusive. This work began in 2012, when I was going through a period of depression and discovered that long-distance running could be a useful tool to manage my mental health. I trained for my first marathon. What I thought would be a one-and-done event led me to fall in love with running and a deep desire to share its transformational power with other people. In 2013, I created Harlem Run, in Harlem, New York, as a community that would welcome people of all races and abilities to move together.

Road running eventually led to me to try new challenges and, in 2016, I discovered trail running. I immediately fell in love with trail running too, finding it much more exciting due to the heightened opportunity for meditation and connecting with nature. My partner and I began to plan weekends around trail-running adventures and organize vacations based on trail access. In 2021, deep in the pandemic and confined to a 700 sq ft (65 sq m) apartment in the Bronx, my partner and I decided to do what was once unimaginable: leave New York and move to the Pacific Northwest, to offer our family greater access to the outdoors.

It has been one of the best decisions of our lives and brought opportunities I could never have imagined. Not too long after arriving in Seattle, I received a note via my website about the possibility of hosting trail-running retreats in Alaska. Living in New York, Alaska had always seemed completely out of reach. Now, only four hours away and with a tour company to manage the logistics, a trip to the last frontier was closer than ever. I jumped at the chance and decided to host retreats for folks like me, who

may have had limited access, or a limited sense of belonging in the outdoors due to structural racism and a history of hostility to BIPOC in wild spaces.

It was on my first retreat to Alaska with a group of BIPOC trail runners that I got to visit Hope Point Trail, one of the most beautiful I've ever experienced. This run was the culmination of a week of bonding, trail running and taking in the beauty of the Kenai Peninsula.

Hope Point gets its name from the nearby town of Hope, Alaska, home to fewer than 200 residents and just two hours from Anchorage. During the 1890s, Hope was one of Alaska's

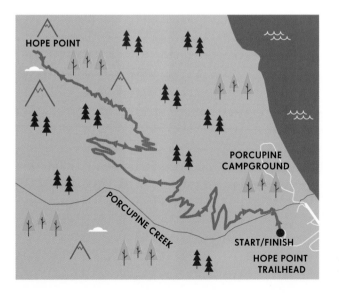

HOPE POINT

PORCUPINE CAMPGROUND

PORCUPINE CREEK

START/FINISH

HOPE POINT TRAILHEAD

"We decided to run the entire way down. Taking care not to fall on loose rocks or roots along the trail, I've never felt more badass"

gold-rush towns and still offers visitors the chance to pan for gold, out of Resurrection Creek. The trail is within the Chugach National Forest, the second-largest national forest in the United States. The lands that make up the Chugach National Forest are home to the Alaska Native peoples, including the Ahtna, Chugach, Dena'ina, and Eyak.

Hope Point Trail begins right from the car park and is well marked. The trailhead is shared with the trailhead for Gull Rock Trail. Hope Point Trail is straightforward, but you'll want to pay attention to a sign that appears pretty quickly and shows a split in the road; Hope Point to the left, Gull Rock to the right. Much of the beginning is through the woods, on a switchback trail. Along the way, you'll see traces of the old Hope Point Trail, which was extremely steep and unforgiving. The switchbacks were put in almost 10 years ago to make the trail more accessible.

We were told by our guides that it would be difficult and that we should pace ourselves. We quickly split into two groups, with the faster group charging ahead and the slower group taking a more moderate pace. We eventually slowed to a run-walk and then, finally, a hike, bracing ourselves for a climb with 3000ft (914m) of elevation gain. The thing I've learned about difficult trails is that they're always better with friends. Within our small group, we each took turns at the front and the rear and exchanged intimate stories that you only feel vulnerable enough to share on a trek like this. The camaraderie gained through this kind of joyful struggle is unmatched.

POOR RELATIONS

The small town of Hope was established during the gold rush of the 1890s. The principal area for prospecting in the region was, famously, the Klondike. Located in the Yukon territory in neighboring Canada, by 1898 most of the best goldfields had been claimed. Searching further afield, major US strikes occurred in Nome, that same year, and also in Fairbanks in 1902. Both went on to become sizeable cities but the majority of prospector settlements, including Hope, did not.

Clockwise from top: soaking in the Alaskan tranquility; the terrain around Resurrection Pass near Hope; footwear assistance; finding camaraderie with a diverse group of runners. Previous page: the author triumphant on the Hope Point Trail

© Hannah Booher

© Amanda Wayne / Shutterstock

As we ran, our guide instructed us to stick together and make noises regularly, in order to scare off any bears – this trail is a favorite of theirs, too. It became a sort of game; whenever we fell into too long a period of quiet, as we sometimes did while catching our breath, one of us would start clapping, singing or shouting, breaking the tension and making our presence known to the wildlife. A few times, we saw what our guide identified as bear scat but it was never fresh and she was prepared with bear spray in case we had an encounter. (We did not.)

After about 2.5 miles (4km), you reach the treeline, the trail widens and you get your first glimpse of Turnagain Arm. As you continue to the summit, it feels as though you are in the clouds and on a clear day you can see Fire Island, Cook Inlet, and Resurrection Creek valley. Wildflowers line either side of the trail, among them fireweed, Alaska's famous pinkish-purple plant.

The route to the very top of Hope Point is a little more than 4 miles (6.4km), the last section requiring you to get on your hands and knees and scramble to the official summit marker. The great news is that if you're afraid of heights (like me), then stopping at around 3.8 miles (6.1km) offers nearly the same breathtaking views. Take your time here, soaking up the sights and sounds. We also paused to refuel and hydrate; be sure to have a pack with adequate supplies to last the duration of the run (4-5 hours). Once those who wanted to had reached the summit, we headed back together. Descending is the easy part and we decided to run the entire way. Taking care not to fall on loose rocks or roots along the trail, I've never felt more badass. **AMD**

Start/Finish // Hope Point Trailhead
Distance // 8 miles (13km)
Getting there // The trail is a 2-hour drive from Anchorage. Take the Seward Hwy and at mile 56.5 (90km), turn west onto Hope Hwy. After 17.8 miles (28.6km), take a left before Porcupine Campground – the trailhead is another quarter of a mile (0.4km).
When to go // Summer, which in Alaska is short, from mid-June through late August.
What to wear // Trail-running or hiking shoes.
What to pack // Water, trail food, sun screen, bug spray, bear spray, plus a spare layer; it will be cooler at the summit and be sure to check the weather before you go.
Where to stay // Bear Creek Lodge offers private log cabins, with wood-burning stoves and modern facilities.
Where to eat // Dirty Skillet is great for a post-run feast, and serves steaks, burgers, and poke bowls.
Things to know // For tours and other information: runalaskatrails.com

Clockwise from top: the Mt Baker Wilderness in Washington's North Cascades range; Deception Pass State Park, Washington

MORE LIKE THIS
RUNS WITH MAGICAL VIEWS

DECEPTION PASS STATE PARK, WASHINGTON

Deception Pass State Park offers beautiful panoramic views, well-maintained hiking trails, and even beach access. Covering 6.4 sq miles (16.5 sq km), it also hosts 35 miles (56km) of trails. Visitors will need a Discover Pass in order to park on-site. There are several trail options, ranging from 1 mile (1.6km) up to 6 miles (9.7km), all offering beautiful views. My favorite is Goose Rock Trail, which is about 2.2 miles (3.5km) long, with 550ft (167m) of elevation gain. If you're afraid of heights, avoid any trails that have you crossing over Deception Pass Bridge. The bridge spans two islands, Whidbey Island and Fidalgo Island, and while it is extremely popular with photographers, it is very narrow and has low barriers on the side of the pedestrian crossing.

TONSINA POINT, ALASKA

This point-to-point run has you traveling on trails, wooden bridges in the forest and ultimately ending at the beach. Located in the Caines Head Recreation Area, the trail is steep in places but if you time the tides right, you'll be able to enjoy the full, 5ish-mile (8km) run; be mindful that if you attempt this trail run and don't make it back before the tide changes, you may well find yourself trapped. The views from the beach are hauntingly serene and you will have the opportunity to see bald eagles and other beautiful birds. The trail can be accessed from Lowell Point Recreation Site, a 10-minute drive from the town of Lowell Point, although the road is unpaved and therefore pretty uneven in sections. You don't necessarily need a four-wheel-drive vehicle but the surface can be quite challenging after heavy rain.
Parking // Caines Head State Parking lot ($5 fee or annual pass for parking). strava.com/activities/9615042480

HEATHER MEADOWS AND ARTISTS POINT TRAIL, WASHINGTON

This is a 3-mile (4.8km) hike/trail run in the Mt Baker Wilderness. The trail is not well marked so I recommend heading to AllTrails (alltrails.com) to download the route beforehand (cell service in the area is notoriously unreliable). The views are beautiful and seem to be pulled straight from a fairy tale, with crystal blue alpine lakes and snow-capped mountain tops. The most prominent peaks are Mt Baker at 10,591ft (3228m), and 9131ft (2783m) Mt Shuksan. I prefer to do this trail in the summer but you can certainly do it year-round, and even in winter if you're prepared to do it with snowshoes. The area is popular with skiers, so you'll need to keep your eyes open, and this also means the trail parking lots fill up early.

© Craig T Fruchtman / Getty Images

BEAT THE HEAT ON THE YANKEE HOMECOMING 10-MILE RACE

Taking place in the August heat and part of a six-decades-old Yankee Homecoming Festival held each summer, this Newburyport, Massachusetts road race is a small-town institution.

It isn't the course that will get you. In fact, under any other circumstances, it's the kind that runners dream about: largely flat with a few fun undulations and one cresting hill at just about the halfway point. It's a race with character, too, wandering through a traditional New England brick-paved downtown (Newburyport's was remastered in the 1970s, the result of a city-wide restoration plan), on toward the Merrimack River and the towering pines of

Maudslay State Park, before ending near the football field of Newburyport High School.

What gets you is the weather. Because, somehow and no matter the year, come race night it is always unbearably hot, a thick, layered heat that is relatively uncommon for New England. The year I ran my best race, it was 90°F (32°C) in the shade, even at 6.15pm, when the runners took off heading east, down stately High St and into the muggy evening.

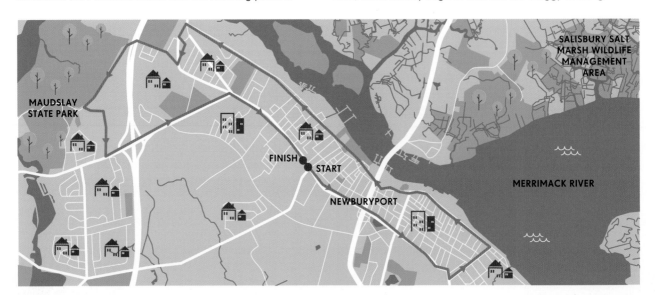

MAUDSLAY
STATE PARK

FINISH
START

NEWBURYPORT

SALISBURY SALT
MARSH WILDLIFE
MANAGEMENT
AREA

MERRIMACK RIVER

"To make it in this heat was to surrender to every part of the road, to charge up the hill, lean into it, and embrace the pain, the heat, and the hollow core of myself"

There's nothing quite like running a race in your hometown. It's like one giant block party, with a familiar face at every turn. On the corner of State St and High St, about 1.5 miles (2.4km) in, I saw friends from elementary school, who hooted and hollered, yelling my name. I waved back. Down broad Marlboro St, people I had once waited tables with at The Grog sprayed me with water from a hose.

Down by the Merrimack, I passed a water station, grabbed two cups – one to toss over my head and one to drink – and saw my old track-and-field coach, the one who told me that my failure at discus was due to my inability to 'dance in the circle'. Now here I was, 15 years later, running faster than he ever could have imagined. Could I even have run one mile at this pace back in the 1990s? Back then, my mile-long 'warm-ups' had been mostly walks. I had been the slowest person on the team, a non-athlete, a non-runner.

But now here I was, not just running but racing. And racing hard. Between miles 4 and 5, I came across the race's primary obstacle, a major hill that loomed large, loud and proud on an otherwise flat course. The July heat hadn't eased, not yet, and I could feel every part of my body moving with the uncomfortable realization of how far I still had to go, of how fast I still had to move to make my goal of a sub 1:15:00 finish. That's what I was going for. But to make it in this heat was to surrender to every part of the road, to charge up the hill, lean into it and embrace the pain and the heat, and the hollow core of myself.

My old running coach wanted me to love hills, but I only liked the part where you got to the top and realized you were coming back down. 'Never look up, only look at your feet,' he told me, a useful ploy for tricking my brain into not knowing how far I had gone or how far I had left to go. It was only one hill on a course that was otherwise flat but, on that night in the stifling heat, that one hill seemed to stretch on forever.

At the top, I acknowledged a modest victory – I'd conquered the climb, yes, but there was still so much running to do. Leaving the hill behind me, I looked back one last time, waving quickly and quietly to that one small achievement. Before me lay the flat pavements that led, eventually, to the State Park. Grateful for the cool shade and soft pine needles, an S-shaped road wound gently through a residential neighborhood, bringing me out near the I-95 overpass. A police car, flashing bright-blue lights and blocking traffic from the off-ramp, awaited the leaders, then the mid-pack, and finally the slower runners who were well behind me.

When I got to that point in the race I stopped checking my Garmin. I stopped looking at the mile signs. I knew that I was having a good race. I made like a metronome and ticked along with the rhythm. You can make it to the Home for Aged Men, I told my brain, and my brain took my feet to that spot on High St. You can make it to Fowles Market, my brain said next and, deep down, I knew I could. Within a few minutes I was there, running faster than I knew possible, digging deep within myself.

My brain kept going, coming up with ever more destinations. Tyng St, where I had grown up, right before the high school, then the gate to the high school itself. Then, finally, I was there, running the last stretch to the finish, uphill of course, and onto the sports field. My feet felt alien, my body soared, so fast I felt as though I could slip right through the finishing posts and disappear.

I stopped my watch and checked my time. I had done it with a little change: 1:14, a goal that had felt unachievable. Even in the heat, even with the hill, even with the thickness of the evening heat upon me. To race like that was a rare and memorable thing, with the wind at your back and feeling like you can keep going forever. I savored every minute. **HS**

YANKEE HOMECOMING

First staged in 1958, Newburyport's Yankee Homecoming Festival is a week-long celebration of the area's history. It's staged to coincide with August 4th when, in 1790, Alexander Hamilton established the Revenue Marine, forerunner to the US Coastguard. The Marine's first vessel, or cutter, was built in Newburyport in 1791.

Clockwise from top: keeping fit in Newburyport; you'll be running along the waterfront; enjoy the town's hospitality afterwards. Previous page: downtown Newburyport

Start/Finish // Newburyport High School, High St
Getting there // Newburyport is a 45-minute drive from Boston. Commuter trains run to/from its North Station
When to go // The race takes place on the Tuesday evening of Yankee Homecoming, held yearly during the final week of July or the first week of August.
Where to stay // Although the city has no major hotels, small venues such as the Compass Rose Inn and the Garrison Inn are ideal for travelers passing through.
Where to eat // Grab dinner outside at the Sunset Club, on Newburyport's Plum Island.
What to wear // Conventional running sneakers, hot-weather running gear, a water belt.
What to pack // Although summer in New England is hot, pack layers, a raincoat, and, of course, bug spray.
Things to know // Despite the evening start, the temperature will likely be high. Water stations are unreliable.
More info // yankeerace.com

Clockwise from top: Dartmouth College, New Hampshire; the towers of Narragansett Pier; trail running in Connecticut

MORE LIKE THIS
NEW ENGLAND GEMS

WEST HARTFORD, CONNECTICUT

In swanky West Hartford, running through chichi neighborhoods is part of the appeal. Yet the district is also home to more than 4.6 sq miles (12 sq km) of forest, along with 30 miles (48km) of paved and gravel trails. For local runners, there are numerous routes in the West Hartford Reservoir recreation area, to the west of the town and just north of Farmington. A popular run (frankly you can take your pick) is the 3.6-mile (5.8km) loop that skirts reservoir no5. Access to this run starts at the public entrance, on Farmington Ave close to reservoir 1. A good number of the smaller reservoir trails connect to the Metacomet Trail, a 62.7-mile (100.9km) route that tracks the Metacomet Ridge and is part of the recently inaugurated (2009) New England Scenic Trail. Obvious perhaps to the point of cliché, the best time to run is the fall, when the leaves turn.
Start/Finish // 1420 Farmington Ave
Distance //3.6-mile (5.8km),
numerous add-ons available
More info // themdc.org/reservoirs

NARRAGANSETT TOWN BEACH, RHODE ISLAND

In a quintessential New England coastal town, this Rhode Island run is definitely one for fall and winter. While in high summer you'll struggle to find room to lay a beach towel, cooler weather brings a host of benefits. The sand is flat and firm, the wind keeps walkers to a minimum and the chill blast off the Atlantic invigorates both body and mind. For a brisk out-and-back, start your run at the eastern end of the beach, at the mouth (more of an inlet) of the Pettaquamscutt River. Follow the beach for 1 mile (1.6km), as it tracks Boston Neck Rd, then leave at the western end to join Ocean Rd. Follow both oceans – the tarmac and Atlantic – until you reach Newton Ave (1.6 miles/2.6km, and also the access point for the Newton Ave Waterfront recreation area). This is your turnaround, from where you can retrace your steps and end by running the beach in the opposite direction.
Start/Finish // Pettaquamscutt River inlet
Distance // 5.2 miles (8.4km)
More info // narragansettri.gov

DARTMOUTH COLLEGE, NEW HAMPSHIRE

Few venues capture the rarefied aspect of New England better than Dartmouth College, the Ivy League institution in Hanover, New Hampshire. Alumni include Robert Frost, several Rockefellers and, for younger readers, David Harbour (Hopper from *Stranger Things*). Whether any were members of the cross-country team is doubtful but most runs around the college are popular with those sporting the Big Green. Take the River Trail; starting at the Green, in the shadow of the library bell tower, head south along Main St. Shortly after passing Granger Circus on your left, you'll see the entrance to the River Trail on your right. The trail follows a zigzag course around Mink Brook, until it connects you to the Connecticut River. Stay with the trail until you reach Maple St, then follow Maple directly until it returns you to Main. Swing a hard left and in a quarter of a mile (400m) or so, you'll be back where you started. For a longer run, go again and, possibly, again.
Start/Finish // The Green, Dartmouth College
Distance // 2 miles (3.2km)
More info // hanovernh.org

ROCKAWAY BEACH SPRING HALF MARATHON

Hannah Selinger competes in this out-and-back run alongside the ocean in Rockaway Beach, Queens, and discovers that this cool and breezy race is great for a personal record.

Mary, who is a much faster runner than I am, has agreed to come pace me for this race. My goal is to break 1:40 on the half-marathon, a goal that has haunted me for a while now, through race after race. I have come close. I have come within minutes, though, if I'm being honest, not within seconds.

I am fast enough for the pacers and fast enough to hang on but every time I get near, my legs start to feel heavy. My coach thinks it's all in my head, which is why he has approved of Mary, my own personal pacer, a cheer-team of one. She

has come to town from Connecticut to stay in my Brooklyn apartment – to rouse me at the vital moment.

Although it is spring, it is a cold morning, made colder by the wind kicking up off the Atlantic. We are running the race in its inaugural year, and everything feels a little thrown-together and haphazard. The volunteers don't quite seem to know where to direct us when we show up, but they do their best. There are only a handful of us mid-April runners, braving the early-morning cold in the interest of a PB. When the gun goes off, we settle into a comfortable pace, sub-8s, solid enough to talk.

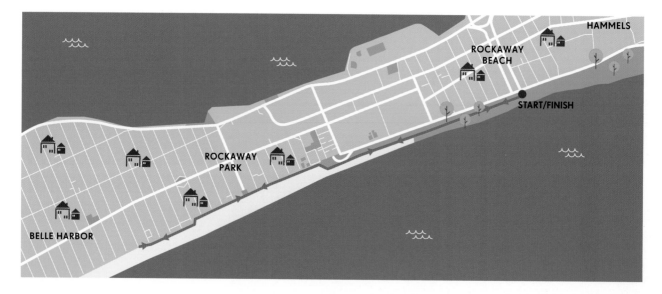

'Give me your watch,' Mary says. I don't want to do it. She wants me to run blind, something my coach loves to torture me with, too. I can calculate the times in my head based on the clocks and the mile signs, a kind of twisted runner-math, even though I am terrible with numbers in everyday life. I hand over my Garmin, as well as my trust, and soon we are flying, through mile markers and through conversation and into a headwind. The beach is to our right, the blue, curling ocean wrapping and unwrapping, not at all inviting.

The boardwalk has not been redone yet. In years to come, it will be a pleasant place to run but, for now, it is a bit dizzying, a bit disorienting, like the old finish of the Brooklyn Half-Marathon – a vertigo-inducing mess. I stare straight ahead but an out-and-back such as this, in a straight line, can be painfully long, nothing to look at but more miles. At the turnaround, where cones delineate the tangent, there is some confusion as to where we must loop. What I'm acutely aware of is how much distance there is ahead of us – exactly the same amount as lies behind.

I feel OK. Not great, but the wind is now behind me. Every runner hopes for a negative split on a perfect race day but I don't feel equipped to run faster on the second leg than I did on the first. Then, Mary kicks into coach mode. 'Keep moving,' she tells me. She clicks in rhythm. One foot in front of the other. We play games at the mile-markers, tempo runs for a few minutes of each mile. It makes the time go faster. We pick up speed. Maybe this will be the day that I shake the numbers off and come away with victory.

'You're going to have to pick this up,' Mary warns, as we get into the double-digits of the race. It's the first occasion I have worried about my time. The first time I have perceived that my race may be in jeopardy. 'Let's go,' she says, but the cold coming

OCEAN'S 13 (KILOMETERS)

A long, languorous (and continuous) view of the Atlantic Ocean defines this half-marathon, which can give New York City runners a crack at a good racing time. Although conditions can vary, it's reliably far from the crowded race fields of the city. This means more runners have an opportunity to place, not just the elites. Organized by the Rockaway Track Club (rockawaytc. org), the 'Spring Half' also serves as a useful marathon tune-up.

Clockwise from top: New York looms behind Rockaway Beach; summer vibes at the Bungalow Bar; swap sneakers for surfboards; if it's a tailwind one way, expect a headwind the other. Previous page: hitch a ride to Rockaway Beach

off the water makes my legs feel like wet concrete. I shake my head. I cannot go faster. 'You can,' she assures me, and for a little while I do – and then I slow down again. I can see the finish and there are few obstacles between here and there.

We play a game of pick-off. She directs me toward other female racers. 'Go,' she says, and I sneak up, catch them and leave them in my wake. I pick off one, two, three racers this way, and then it is only me, the first woman in the pack, with Mary by my side. I do not know how fast I am running or if I am even running fast at all. I just settle in, allow the pace to own me. The miles click by. Eleven. Twelve. Thirteen. Mary tells me to push hard on the final clip and I do, I push hard and then I am through the very last bit, and she hangs back, just enough to allow me to win. I am the fastest female athlete, for five minutes. For one day.

I do not break 1:40 that day but, for the first time, I miss the mark by seconds. I know that when we hit the turnaround, we lost some time circling a series of cones. I also know that I dug as deep as possible – I could not have gone faster if I'd tried. And I did try. I took everything I had and left it on the road. It was enough to win, if not quite enough to win in the way I wanted to.

But there are consolations. As the first female finisher, I get to choose between three different types of cheesecake: apple, chocolate, and plain. I choose an enormous chocolate cheesecake, and Mary gets one, too. We pose for photos with our prizes and while they may not be trophies or medals, they feel precious all the same. The spoils, the fruits of our labor. **HS**

Start/Finish // 94th St Boardwalk, Rockaway, Queens
Getting there // From Manhattan, take a Far Rockaway-bound A train to Beach 90 St
When to go // The race takes place on the second Saturday of April.
Where to stay // The Rockaway Hotel, a boutique hotel, is a great option for those looking to stay in the area. (therockawayhotel.com).
Where to eat // The Bungalow Bar (bungalowbarny.com), a year-round hangout with live music and a formidable brunch, is a great place for an after-race tipple.
What to wear // Conventional running sneakers, cooler weather running gear.
What to pack // Spring weather in New York can be unpredictable, so a little of everything – even a winter coat – is a good idea.
Things to know // Its proximity to the ocean means this out-and-back race can be cold.
More info // runsignup.com/race/ny/rockawaybeach/springhalfmarathonor5k

*Opposite, clockwise from top: starting the
Huntington Beach half marathon; Fort
Lauderdale's beaches; Myrtle Beach's marathon*

MORE LIKE THIS
BEACHSIDE RUNS WITH LOCAL FLAVOR

FORT LAUDERDALE A1A MARATHON, FLORIDA

This popular beachside marathon is staged on Florida State Rd A1A. The 339-mile (545km) highway runs north to south, from Fernandina Beach to Key West, and includes the Scenic & Historic Coastal Byway, a 72-mile (115km) section from Jacksonville to Daytona Beach that locals claim boasts the best of Florida beach culture. Floridians elsewhere might disagree. Continue south, past Cape Canaveral, Palm Beach, and Boca Raton, and you'll reach Fort Lauderdale, location for this classic out-and-back. The race starts (at 6am, to beat the heat) and finishes at the Fort Lauderdale Beach Park. At its southernmost point, the turnaround loops back at Harbor Inlet and past Lago Mar Beach Resort (not to be confused with a certain Mar-a-Lago). There's no official cut-off but the closed-road course reopens to traffic after six hours. More recreationally minded participants may continue on the sidewalks, which are wide, open and frequented by fellow beach-users. At the business end, the event is another qualifier for the Boston Marathon.
Start/Finish // 1100 Seabreeze Blvd
Distance // 26.2 miles (42km)

SURF CITY MARATHON, HUNTINGTON BEACH, CALIFORNIA

The California dream-spot of Huntington Beach is known as Surf City USA. Home, since the 1950s, to the US Open of Surfing, famous winners of America's leading surf contest include Tom Curren, Kelly Slater, and the late, great Andy Irons. Held over the first weekend in February, the marathon named for this wave-riding mecca is run along the Pacific Coast Hwy, on the sun-blissed shores of Orange County. Starting at the intersection with Huntington St, the award-winning course is yet another that dangles the prospect of a much-prized Boston Marathon qualifying (BQ) time. On a route that takes you past the iconic Huntington Beach Pier, the event has a six-hour cut-off (standard across BQ events). Those on a more leisurely trajectory can opt for a half-marathon (21km), a 5k (3.1 miles) or even a Beach Mile (1.6km) run entirely on sand. All routes lead to a finish line at Huntington Beach Central Park. Complete more than one of the four events, a feat dubbed the 'Cowabunga Challenge', and you'll be eligible for a third medal.
Start // Pacific Hwy, intersection with Huntington St
Finish // Huntington Beach Central Park
Distance // 26.2 miles (42km), half-marathon (21km), Beach Mile (1.6km), 5k (3.1 miles)
More info // runsurfcity.com

MYRTLE BEACH MARATHON, SOUTH CAROLINA

Held on the first weekend of March, the largest marathon in South Carolina regularly attracts up to 7500 entrants. First staged in 1997, the event originally coincided with the birthday of George Washington (February 22nd), whose links to the state date back to the War of Independence. The area takes its name from the wax myrtle trees that once lined the beach and was also where the magazine *Sports Illustrated* was founded (by Henry Luce in 1954). As with other beachside marathons, any elevation is notable by its absence. From the start/finish on Robert Grissom Pkwy, just south of Monticello Dr, the total gain is just 110ft (34m, and a mere 20ft/6m over the first 12 miles/19km). This partly explains why the Myrtle Beach marathon ranks in the top 10 Boston Marathon qualifying events. With your BQ bagged, wind down with a walk along the famous Grand Strand beach or, perhaps later, a ride on the SkyWheel.
Start // Robert Grissom Pkwy
Finish // Pelicans Ballpark
Distance // 26.2 miles (42km)
More info // capstoneraces.com/ myrtle-beach-marathon

HUDSON RIVER WATERFRONT WALKWAY

Stephanie Vermillion basks in the Big Apple's glow on this scenic Hudson River run, which pairs northern New Jersey culture with inspiring Manhattan skyline views.

The tangerine sun warmed my face as my running shoes pounded the sidewalk. It was a quiet October morning – just me, some fellow exercisers, and the occasional pier-side angler. I'd jogged this Hudson River route more times than I could count but this golden-hour jaunt felt different. It was day one of the new life I'd dreamed about for more than three years, and much of the planning for this career leap happened right on this inspiring stretch of pavement.

Some rely on mentors to pursue scary career shifts. Others turn to TED Talks, life coaches or networking. For me, inspiration came in the form of the Manhattan skyline. Few cityscapes are as synonymous with hopes and dreams as those of New York City. The Hudson River Waterfront Walkway, a running route I lived just steps from in Hoboken, New Jersey, was the perfect vantage point.

This crown jewel of northern New Jersey is a roughly 18.5-mile (30km) linear track of stitched-together sidewalks, parks, trails, and paved waterfront paths on the Jersey side of the Hudson River. It stretches from Bayonne up to the George Washington Bridge and Palisades Interstate Park in Fort Lee, with myriad tastes of local culture along the way. There's Liberty State Park, lauded for its Statue of Liberty views, as well as restaurants galore in foodie haven Hoboken. You'll also find yacht clubs, fine dining, and great shopping up toward Edgewater and West New York. At the Walkway's northern terminus is Fort Lee Historic Park, where a reconstructed Revolutionary War encampment perched atop sheer cliffs overlooks the colossal GW bridge and Manhattan's Washington Heights neighborhood.

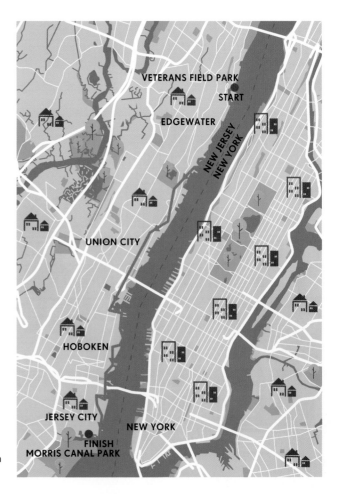

It took decades for this dream of New Jersey's revitalized waterfront to come to fruition. The Hudson River Waterfront Conservancy kicked off the project in the 1980s and, with the exception of a few missing links south of Jersey City, is almost complete.

I'd researched every twist and turn of the path in anticipation of our move to the northeast from Cincinnati, Ohio, in 2015. Google Maps street view had nothing on the real thing. On that initial sunset run – which I took before even unpacking the first moving-box – I watched Manhattan's skyline shift from bright silver to hues of coral and gold. I knew in that moment that this move would change my life. I'd yet to realize this skyline-view running route would play a key role, too.

On a whim, within a month of our move, I attended a meetup for travel-loving women in Central Park. I'd always loved globe-trotting and had once dreamed of pairing my affinity for writing with my enthusiasm for adventure – yet back in Ohio, the career path seemed impossible. Professors and mentors suggested 'communications' as a safer, more secure route.

I happily followed suit for four post-college years, but that 2015 picnic in Central Park opened my eyes. I met travel writers, bloggers, and adventure photographers, and the more happy-hours, parties and hangouts I attended with my new adventure-loving friends, the more I realized my lofty goal was actually within reach.

I spent evenings and weekends meeting with, and learning from, talented travel professionals. My sacred morning runs along the Hudson River Waterfront Walkway were dedicated to puzzling together my career leap. I spent months

"My route felt like an adventure, with the skyline changing at every mile"

brainstorming a side hustle that could help me slowly break into travel media, while simultaneously retaining the full-time job that afforded my half of our apartment. Running in the shadow of that inspirational skyline, I thought through multiple travel-career paths: blogging, filmmaking, writing, and running PR campaigns for travel brands.

I wasn't sure how I'd get from points A to B, but the skyline stood tall as a reminder of what I could achieve – particularly when I could pinpoint milestones in my journey based on skyscrapers. The LEGO-like Central Park Tower near my first travel meetup. The shimmery blue One World Trade Center in lower Manhattan, where a fellow aspiring creative and I met for drinks and dream planning. The colossal Javits Center, where I attended my first travel-media conferences.

Plotting my travel-media career kicked into overdrive when I got accepted into the NYC Marathon, in 2016. Logging miles upon miles, I had more time than ever to think about the future. I woke up early to squeeze in runs before work, from easy ones to watch the sun float above the Empire State Building, to golden-hour speedwork sessions on the track at the Weehawken Waterfront Park and Recreation Center; located on my cherished Hudson River route, the Center is about 1.5 miles (2.4km) north of Hoboken.

LIBERTY STATE PARK

This prime green space along Hudson River Waterfront Walkway holds a century-old railroad terminal and the Empty Sky 9/11 memorial, etched with the names of the terrorist-attack victims. There's also the 2-mile (3.2km) Liberty Walk, which overlooks the Statue of Liberty, and ferries to Ellis Island, which see a fraction of the crowds found on the NYC side.

Left to right: Frank Sinatra on the Hoboken waterfront; the view of Manhattan from Hoboken. Previous page: jogging Jersey City's waterfront

On weekends, I binged podcasts and audio books for career-change advice. My route – mainly runs from Hoboken toward Fort Lee and back, a total of 18 miles (29km) – felt like an adventure, with the skyline changing at every mile. To switch it up, I also ran south to Liberty State Park, an 8-mile (13km) round trip, or added a 5-mile (8km) loop around the Park for inspiration from the Statue of Liberty, too.

The training runs left my legs wobbly but those skyscrapers (along with Jay-Z's *Empire State of Mind* on repeat) ignited my fire. I came home from each Saturday run and went straight into side-hustle mode: penning travel blog posts, writing story proposals for editors and brainstorming documentary and photojournalism projects.

While the Hudson River Waterfront Walkway saw me at my best, during my spirited long runs and enthusiastic life-planning jogs, it also embraced me at my worst. Starting any new craft, particularly in a field as competitive as travel media, comes with heaps of rejection. I earned my fair share and took my stress out on the pavement. A few years later, the Walkway also became a place of solace after my dad passed away from cancer complications, in 2018. I ran, walked, and often sat breathless at the end of a pier staring deep into the Manhattan abyss wondering how to get through.

Several months after my dad's passing, on a rainy afternoon run, the truth hit me. The downpour subsided and a rainbow, which I interpreted as a sign from my dad, arced above my treasured Manhattan skyline. I knew the message. Nothing is guaranteed, I thought, as tears joined the raindrops on my face. Life is short and every second I'm not enjoying it is a second I'll regret. One week later I quit my job and, ever since, I've lived by a motto inspired by that rainy run: If not now, when? **SV**

Start // Fort Lee
Finish // Bayonne
Distance // 18.5 miles (30km)
Getting there // Fly to Newark Airport, then drive, rideshare, or take the train to Hoboken or Jersey City.
When to go // Morning, when the sun rises above Manhattan, or evening, when the sun sets behind New Jersey and casts a golden-hour glow across the skyline.
Where to stay // The W Hoboken sits along the Walkway, with scenic rooms that overlook the skyline and easy connectivity to NYC via the PATH Train or ferry.
Where to eat // End a morning run at Turning Point, Hoboken's go-to brunch spot. Or end your night with high-end bites and local flavor at West New York's Son Cubano, with floor-to-ceiling waterfront windows.
Things to know // Catch a ferry across the river for direct access to another Big Apple run, the Manhattan Waterfront Greenway, which loops around the island of Manhattan.
More info // visithudson.org

Opposite: Atlantic City's boardwalk; serene Cap May Point in New Jersey

MORE LIKE THIS
JERSEY GEMS

ATLANTIC CITY BOARDWALK

Although most come for the casinos rather than the beaches, you can take a run over the boards and along the seafront in Atlantic City. Before the rise of Las Vegas, Atlantic City was associated with a certain style of America at play. The city has hosted numerous examples of what today we might think of as Vegas-style Americana, such as the first Miss America pageant, held in Atlantic City in 1921. The majority of this run, however, takes in grassy sandbanks and residential streets but, once you're in the casino district, you can expect denser crowds as your fellow boardwalkers seek entertainment and deep-fried, sugar-coated treats. Don't be deterred however, for when the hordes clear you'll find the boards are perfect for runners who hate getting sand in their shoes. What's more, the beach is right there if you fancy a barefoot run.
Start // Oscar E McClinton Waterfront Park, Atlantic City
Finish // South Fredericksburg Ave, Ventnor City
Distance // 5.7 miles (9.2km)

LOOKOUT TRAIL LOOP

On the border of New Jersey and New York, Ramapo Mountain State Park is a 6.5 sq mile (17 sq km) green space filled with hiking and biking trails, many of which are also well suited to trail runners. The park is known for its scenic forest trails, most of which come with views of the Manhattan skyline, albeit at a distance. The Lookout Trail loop is something of hybrid concept, allowing you to commune with nature while still feeling like you're on a big-city run (kind of). The route starts and finishes at the parking lot on Skyline Dr; for an added bonus, Ramapo State Park is particularly beautiful in the fall, when the autumn foliage is spectacular.
Start/Finish // Ramapo Lake Trailhead
Distance // 3 miles (4.8km)

CAPE MAY LOOP

A trip to the coast is a summer tradition for many New Jerseyans, and runners in the state are spoiled by miles of Atlantic-front beaches and retro-style boardwalks to help them clock up the miles. However, one of the best routes can be found at New Jersey's southernmost tip, Cape May Point, and where highlights include timing your run to catch a rare east coast sunset. A popular route, the Cape May Point Trail is a 1.8-mile (2.9km) loop that starts and ends at the parking lot near the historic Cape May Lighthouse. You can follow the trail in either direction but if it's an evening run, you might want to follow the circuit in a counter-clockwise direction. This will take you first across the marshes, atop a weathered and windswept boardwalk, delivering you in time to watch the closing of the day on Sunset Beach.
Start/Finish // Cape May Lighthouse
Distance // 1.8 miles (2.9km)

NIAGARA FALLS

*Runs around Niagara Falls are supercharged with spirit-lifting negative ions –
just try not to smile too hard as you trot past America's grandest waterfall.*

The trick to running somewhere truly scenic is to not get too distracted by the views. By all means, acknowledge the terrain while you pound out the miles but save the gawping at the vistas for the end of the run, when you've earned a little resting time to cool off and take in the scenery.

When running beside Niagara Falls, that cooling down is augmented by the misty vapor from 3160 tons of water thundering over the Niagara escarpment every second on the way from Lake Erie to Lake Ontario. When the breeze is blowing in the right direction, it's as refreshing as the spray hitting your top lip on the first sip from a glass of chilled prosecco.

On any list of iconic American locations, Niagara would be up there with Manhattan, Monument Valley, and Yosemite National Park. It's a living embodiment of the notion that everything is bigger in America – or Canada, if you happen to be approaching this legendary cascade from the west. On my personal world map, this was also the spot where Christopher Reeve sprinted for a phone booth to perform a daring rescue in *Superman II* – so an appropriate setting for a few heroic miles of my own.

As someone who likes to christen every new stop with a run, I've clocked up miles everywhere from Cambridge to Kathmandu, but running at Niagara was one circuit where I genuinely felt like I had springs in my heels. I credit the natural soundtrack of the thundering cascades, driving me on with a visceral pulse that the reptile part of my brain couldn't help but respond to. There were certainly points where the roar of the falls and my breath

rate seemed to synchronize, like the run was only partly under my control.

How you run Niagara Falls will mostly likely depend on your immigration status. If you're a US or Canadian citizen, it's comparatively easy to tackle the falls from both sides, presenting your ID when you cross the Rainbow Bridge. For everyone else, it's usually a case of picking the American side or the Canadian side. It doesn't much matter which – both are equally spectacular.

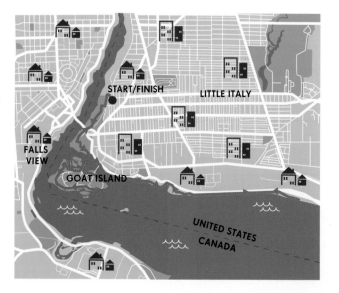

I chose the US side – for no more profound reason than I was already in the US – mapping out a line beside the cascades from the Aquarium of Niagara. A satisfying 7-miler (11km) emerged, tracking the fringe of parkland that hems the American east side of the falls, then continuing for as long as I had energy along the riverside path beside the Niagara Scenic Parkway.

On paper, it ticked all the boxes for an on-the-road run – an easy route to follow, a landmark location, energizing green spaces, and a good distance for a run at pace. And I had time to return later with my camera to take some snaps, so I could run unencumbered by tech and focus on the joy of motion.

With a mid-morning start time, crowds were inevitable, but I'm one of those runners who doesn't mind a bit of creative slaloming to get through busy sections. Paths were wide, with enough green space in between the hand-holding couples, families with strollers and tour groups that I only occasionally had to break my stride.

Indeed, the north end of Niagara Falls State Park was agreeably quiet, apart from a few walkers and joggers heading the opposite way (we nodded cordially in passing). But things got busy around the Rainbow Bridge, with a steady stream of people heading down to the Observation Tower and the riverbank viewpoints gazing over the lip of the falls.

Despite it being a warm summer day, the heat was dampened by the natural air-conditioning effect of tons of constantly refreshed river water, so the conditions were pretty much ideal. I was also reliably informed that the churning water produces huge amounts of negatively charged ions, said to have a positive effect on mood and wellbeing.

FALLS RIDERS

Running beside the falls is one thing, but Niagara also has a long tradition of going over the falls. The most famous waterfall rider of all time was schoolteacher Annie Edson Taylor, who in 1901 survived the 512ft (156m) drop with only bumps and bruises. Not everyone has been so lucky – following the untimely demise of Canadian daredevil William 'Red' Hill Jr in 1951, anyone entering the water near the falls faces a fine of up to $25,000.

Clockwise from top: both sides of Niagara Falls; welcome to the state park, Goat Island; watching from the Rainbow Bridge

Maybe there was something in that. I definitely felt like I had something extra in the tank as I zigzagged in and out of pockets of sightseers to reach the pedestrian bridge to Goat Island, crossing the accelerating water about to plunge over both the American and Bridal Veil Falls.

Up close, the falls are seriously loud. The sound of the cascades can reach 95 decibels, equivalent to a jet on takeoff. Looping around this triangular wedge of greenery, I had to resist the temptation to slow to a walk to admire the roaring white water on either side – but there'd be time enough for that on the return leg. For now, it was back over the bridge, and out onto the multi-use path beside the Niagara Scenic Parkway, where ambling selfie snappers were replaced by the comradely company of more committed joggers, skaters and cyclists.

It's possible to continue for another 4 miles (6.4km), to LaSalle Waterfront Park, but I turned around after two, by the modest remains of British-built Fort Schlosser – enough distance for muscles to feel well used, but not so much as to impact sightseeing the following day.

Returning to the falls, I felt I'd earned the luxury of a proper pause to let my heart slow to its resting rate and goggle at the views from Luna Island, a precarious aerie perched on the very lip of the Bridal Veil Falls, off the edge of Goat Island.

It's hard to imagine a better spot to cool off after a run – enveloped by mist-laden breezes and buffeted by the heavy-metal noise of thundering water. I think I did feel a little super. **JB**

Previous spread: more than 3000 tons of water flow over Niagara every second

Start/Finish // Aquarium of Niagara
Distance // 7 miles (11km)
Getting there // Fly into Buffalo in the US or Toronto in Canada and pick up a hire car to explore – few useful flights serve tiny Niagara Falls International Airport.
When to go // Niagara is bitterly cold in winter; stick to the warm summer months from June to August and avoid crowded weekends.
What to wear // In summer, not much – shorts and a tee will be plenty. At other times, bring layers.
What to pack // A jogger's mobile phone holder and running app on your phone, so you can record the event!
Where to stay // On the US side, the stylish Giacomo (thegiacomo.com); on the Canadian side, try retro Cadillac Motel (cadillacmotelniagara.com).
More info // niagarafallsusa.com; niagarafallstourism.com

*Opposite: running in Yosemite
National Park; the Jefferson
Memorial on the National Mall*

MORE LIKE THIS
RUNNING AMERICAN ICONS

YOSEMITE NATIONAL PARK, CALIFORNIA

These days, you're as likely to see ambling empty-nesters as grizzled prospectors in Yosemite National Park, but you'll also find a committed community of trail runners, tackling some of the most thrilling circuits in the Americas. To get started, lace up your jogging shoes and board the valley-wide Yosemite Shuttle Bus for easy access to a string of Yosemite trails; just bring plenty of water and avoid the incendiary summer months. The Valley Loop Trail is a Yosemite classic – an agreeably level dirt track following sections of the original wagon trails, taking in views of mighty granite buttresses, pounding falls, forests, talus slopes, and green meadows. Come in spring or fall to beat the crowds and this running track can feel like heaven on Earth.
Start/Finish // Lower Yosemite Fall shuttle bus stop
Distance // Up to 11.5 miles (18.5km)

BIG SUR, CALIFORNIA

The Beat Generation saw the open road as the ultimate symbol of freedom, but there's no obligation to drive. The central coast of California overflows with epic running trails that mirror some of the state's most iconic driving routes. To get the best out of the coast, you'll need a hire car – public transport is limited and most trails are drive-in, drive-out. For full-scale scenery, try the Old Coast Rd, a dirt track that was once the main access road to the Big Sur coast. Starting near the Bixby Bridge, you can weave through the hills, escaping the hordes and taking in some highly memorable landscapes along the way. Pick a distance to match your energy levels – runs range from a few gentle miles to an epic 20-mile (32km) round trip to Andrew Molera State Park.
Start/Finish // Bixby Bridge, State Rte 1
Distance // Up to 20 miles (32km)

NATIONAL MALL, WASHINGTON, DC

Few running locations have such a powerful sense of history – and quite as many movie cameos – as the National Mall in Washington, DC. As you trot the tracks around the Washington Monument, the Lincoln Memorial, and the Capitol, you'll be treading in the footsteps of American presidents, civil rights protesters, anti-war activists, and of course, Spiderman, the X-Men, and Forrest Gump. The classic Mall run traces the cinder paths between the Capitol and the Lincoln Memorial, taking in a bumper crop of national icons in the capital's favorite green lung. An easy add-on is the loop around the Tidal Basin, visiting the memorials to Franklin D Roosevelt, Martin Luther King Jnr, and Thomas Jefferson. However you tackle the Mall, you'll finish with a powerful sense of America's pride in its national story.
Start/Finish // Capitol Building
Distance // 4 miles (6.4km)

THE RUGGED SHORES OF ACADIA NATIONAL PARK

The mountains meet the sea in Acadia National Park, where a run that blends road and trail takes you along one of the most dramatic coastlines in Maine.

Waves lapped the golden sands as early-morning sunlight sparkled on the topaz waters. If I didn't know any better, it would've been easy to imagine myself gazing across a stretch of Caribbean seascape. Except it wasn't palm trees fringing the beach but rather dense pine forest. And – in an even bigger giveaway – to my back, the craggy slopes of Champlain Mountain still held patches of snow. It was late spring in Acadia National Park and balmy skies and summer wildflowers still seemed a distant prospect. The lower-elevation trails, however, were mostly free of snow, and the welcome lack of visitors made it an enchanting time to go for a run in New England's only national park.

My starting point for the day's 6-mile (9.6km) loop was Sand Beach, a breathtaking, if unimaginatively named, stretch of shoreline overlooking Newport Cove on Acadia's eastern shore. The day would start with a relatively short trail run, followed by some road mileage along the oceanside, passing the craggy shores for which Acadia is famous.

With the sun hanging low over the eastern sky, I could still see my breath, and the salty air mingled with the scent of pine forest. From the beach, I jogged the length of the golden shoreline and found the rocky steps leading to the start of the trail along Great Head, a bluff jutting out into the water.

My pace slowed as I headed up the incline and I was soon immersed in the pines, with ferns lining the way. Clearings gave views over the beach and back to the Beehive, a low-slung mountain that was carved by glaciers some 30,000 years ago. I continued along the path, which was fairly level, though

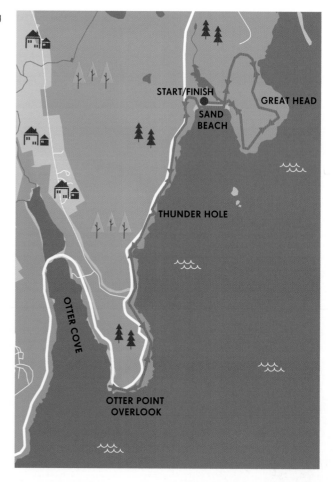

plenty of rocks and roots slowed my pace. It was a delight emerging from the cool shade and out onto the sun-drenched promontory at the trail's southern end. Seagulls winged past as a panorama of the eastern shore stretched out before me; the forest-covered mountains sloping to the water, with the frothy surf swirling around several islets offshore.

Around a quarter-mile further, the path ascended to the highest point on the headland, where it was a steep 145ft (44m) drop from the cliffs to the sea. With warm sunshine on my face, I lingered a few moments longer and then eased into a run, following the trail as it headed north. The last stretch plunged me deeper into Acadia's woodlands, a mix of spruce, birch, and the occasional hemlock. It's hard to believe that all this had been burned to the ground during the devastating fire of 1947, when 2000 acres (809 hectares) of Great Head were destroyed along with more than 170 homes, hotels, and estates in the nearby town of Bar Harbor.

Back at Sand Beach, this time I veered closer to the water hoping to catch sight of a harbor seal offshore. Alas, no marine mammal, whiskered or otherwise, poked its head above the waves so I headed to the Ocean Path Trailhead. Running parallel to the Park Loop Rd, this route – paved in places and

> *"With the sun hanging low, I could still see my breath, and the salty air mingled with the scent of pine forest"*

smooth gravel in others – allowed me to pick up the pace as I ran south. After a mile, I reached a set of stairs that led down to a fenced overlook of the so-called Thunder Hole. The winds had clearly picked up; in contrast to the calm waters off Sand Beach, here, the frothing sea bashed against the granite cliffs. As I stood listening to the howling wind, foaming waves rushed into a narrow channel below and blasted icy seawater 30ft (9m) into the air. Coated in spray, I quickly hustled back to the upper deck, where I watched a few more cycles of oceanic eruptions before continuing the run.

The dramatic views kept getting better as I ran south. Another few minutes along, I ran past the spur to Monument Cove, named for the granite pillar standing guard over a small rocky beach. Once attached to the cliffs behind it, the unusual formation is a favorite sunrise spot when the rocks take on an auburn hue.

THE BEEHIVE

In some places Acadia's geological history is literally written in stone. Visible from Sand Beach, the Beehive has a gently slanted north slope; its steep south face (home to the park's most extreme, via-ferrata-esque hikes) was worn down by glaciers, as they arrived from the north. The thick layer of overlying ice that extended past the peak ultimately broke off huge chunks of the Beehive's south side as it continued its journey.

Left to right: views over the coast from the Beehive Trail; Sand Beach in summer, viewed from Great Head Trail; Boulder Beach lives up to its name; the trailhead. Previous page: the Beehive scramble, Acadia National Park

After another bend in the road, I loped past Boulder Beach, yet another little-known spot for watching the first light of daybreak. I shifted into a slow jog as I teetered across the grapefruit-sized rocks, worn smooth by the ceaseless energy of the seas. Back on the path, it was a quick hop to an overlook of Otter Cliff, its craggy features looming some 110ft (33.5m) above the sea. In fact, it is one of the highest coastal headlands on the Atlantic lying north of Rio de Janeiro.

My turnaround point arrived a few minutes later as I reached the similarly named Otter Point. This was as far south as I could go on this stretch of narrow peninsula. I stopped to take a drink of water while enjoying the meditative quiet over the seaside. Off to the west stretched Otter Cove, with near mirror-like shorelines on either side of it; dense forests rose above rocky shores, while a span of mountains rolled off into the distance.

My mind was cluttered with the beauty of Acadia as I headed back up the trail to my starting point. As I finished the loop, I was already making plans to return by night. Picturing myself walking on Sand Beach under a great swath of the Milky Way amid the pollution-free night skies, I was reminded that the wonders of Acadia extend well beyond the boundaries of coastal Maine. **RSL**

Start/Finish // Sand Beach
Distance // 6 miles (9.7km)
Getting there // Most people drive to Acadia; the small Bar Harbor Airport (BHB) has direct flights to Boston. Coach Lines buses run to Bar Harbor from Bangor, with onward connections from there. From late June to early October, the free Island Explorer bus loops around the park and also connects to Bar Harbor and the airport.
When to go // Crowds are thickest and prices highest during the warm summer months of June through September. May and early October have cooler but pleasant temperatures and fewer visitors.
Where to stay // Book well ahead for the two Mt Desert Island campgrounds. Bar Harbor has abundant options, including charming B&Bs like the Moseley Cottage Inn.
More info // nps.gov/acadia

Opposite: Daicey Pond in Baxter State Park

MORE LIKE THIS
OTHER MAINE RUNS

QUODDY HEAD STATE PARK

Anchoring the easternmost point in Maine (and thus the contiguous United States), Quoddy Head State Park is best known for its jagged sea cliffs that offer dramatic views along the coast – at least when the weather is co-operating. Fog often blankets this lush peninsula, making for some cinematic shots of the historic, red-and-white striped West Quoddy Head Lighthouse. There are various trails in the 541-acre (219-hectare) park, most of which are fairly level but require constant vigilance while negotiating the uneven, sometimes slippery terrain. One of the area's best runs parallels the rocky shoreline along the Coastal Trail, then loops back through conifer woods, rich in lichens and mosses along the Thompson Trail. It's worth making a short detour to the Bog Trail, a boardwalk that passes arctic and sub-arctic plants rarely found this far south.

Start/Finish // Trailhead for the Coastal Trail
Distance // 4.3 miles (6.9km)

BAXTER STATE PARK

If Baxter State Park were plunked down in any other part of the US, it would undoubtedly be named a national park. The reserve's 327 sq miles (847 sq km) encompass mirror-like lakes, rushing streams and some of the highest peaks in the state, including Mt Katahdin, the terminus of the Appalachian Trail. But Maine residents like Baxter just the way it is, with unpaved roads, minimal infrastructure, and strict limits on visitor numbers. You need to plan ahead to reserve a day-use parking pass. Once inside, you'll find over 200 miles (322km) of trails. Steep ascents can make for challenging runs, but there are plenty of options to keep elevation gain moderate. One stretch of the Appalachian Trail near Katahdin Stream Campground takes you past two scenic ponds amid the lush northern forests. You can circle around Daicey Pond for a rewarding out-and-back trail run.

Start/Finish // Katahdin Stream Campground
Distance // 5 miles (8km)
More info // baxterstatepark.org

CAMDEN HILLS STATE PARK

It's easy to fall in love with Maine while running the rugged paths of Camden Hills State Park. Set in Mid-Coast Maine, the 9 sq mile (23 sq km) park has 30 miles (48km) of trails that wind through thick woodlands, past shimmering lakes, and up to the slopes of flat-topped mountains. The park's highest point, Mt Megunticook, affords sweeping views over island-studded Penobscot Bay as well as the coastal town of Camden and the distant mountains in Acadia National Park. Though short in mileage (2.7 miles/4.3km), the out-and-back trail to the top offers plenty of challenge as you ascend nearly 1000ft (305m) along the way. Take care traversing the loose rocks and slick-wet tree roots. Aim for a weekday summit to beat the Saturday and Sunday crowds.

Start/Finish // Mt Megunticook trailhead on Mt Battie Rd
Distance // 2.7 miles (4.3km)

THE BOSTON MARATHON

Qualifying for the world's oldest and most iconic marathon is a milestone in itself. Running it, however, transcends athletic accomplishment.

Hopkinton, Massachusetts is a quiet town of about 17,000, with all the hallmarks of an old New England village – historic buildings, a grassy common, and a farmers' market. One day every spring, however, this quiet town goes absolutely bananas. That day is the third Monday of every April. Though it happens to be Patriots' Day, commemorating the first battles of the Revolutionary War, that's not what all the commotion is about. For this is also the day that 30,000 or so runners from all over the world show up to compete in the Boston Marathon, a race that begins on Hopkinton's Main St and ends 26.2 miles later in Copley Sq, Boston.

No other marathon can match Boston in terms of history. Held annually since 1897, it's the world's oldest, and few can touch it in terms of prestige. Apart from the Olympics, Boston is the only major marathon to impose qualifying times. (The toughest, for men ages 18 to 34, is 3hr, an average pace of under seven minutes per mile.) For many runners, a Boston qualifier, or 'BQ', is the Holy Grail.

Runners begin arriving early in the morning, in a caravan of yellow school buses. 'Welcome to Hopkinton, it all starts here' reads a large sign. It does indeed. I ran my first Boston Marathon in 1999 and when I saw that sign it hit me like 26.2 tons of bricks. Wow! This is really happening. On the morning of my ninth Boston

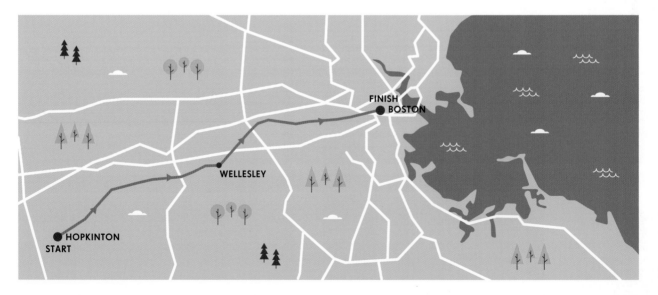

Marathon last year, that feeling hadn't changed one bit. The first half-dozen times I ran it, Boston was, for me, all about racing. Then, the year of the bombings in 2013, in which three people were killed and 260 were injured, I was actually home on paternity leave with my newborn son. I vowed to return the following year, in solidarity and defiance. And I did. That year was transformative – I felt grateful and more connected to the race.

A couple of years later, my friend Tim, who is registered blind, asked me to guide him in the 2017 race. Afterwards, it was clear Boston had become something much bigger for me. And Tim was hooked. We agreed we would do it again the following year.

So there we were in Hopkinton in 2018, beneath that sign once again, beneath a cold, steady rain that would make this year a bone-chilling slog. 'You know,' I told Tim as we walked through puddles. 'This is not that bad.' It was that bad, of course, and would only get worse. Nonetheless, Tim – who was clearly in denial – agreed that the weather wasn't a big deal. Tim and I each grasped an end of a short elastic band as we slowly moved toward the hand-painted startline.

We cruised the first mile, a downhill stretch that's easy for adrenaline-juiced runners to take too fast. In fact, the first several miles are almost completely downhill. Seductively so. Runners who blaze these early miles hammer their quads and pay for it later. Tim and I kept cool. We enjoyed easy conversation, which included occasional cues: 'Here's a guy walking, move left to pass him... Rough road up ahead... Timing mat coming up in 3... 2...'

Here's the thing about the Boston Marathon: even your first time here, the course can feel familiar. After leaving Hopkinton, the race wends east through towns and villages that, if you've been a runner for any length of time, you'll recognize by name alone: Ashland, Framingham, Natick, Wellesley, Brookline. Same goes for the landmarks: the red-brick Newton Firehouse, its tall garage doors flung open, music blaring; the Chestnut Hill Reservoir around mile 22; the CITGO sign, looming high above Kenmore Sq.

Around three miles in, Tim and I passed a golden retriever in a raincoat, sitting on a wooden box. The dog had two blue-and-gold BOSTON STRONG flags clenched in his teeth – a typical Boston spectator insofar as there is no typical Boston spectator. Everybody turns out, lining the roads, cheering their heads off.

For me, the next 9 to 10 miles, through Framingham and Natick, are all about getting to Wellesley. No offence to Framingham and Natick, which are fine towns. But Wellesley is home to the Scream Tunnel, which you can hear long before you can see it. Tim and I picked up the din a good quarter-mile away. Soon after we were passing hundreds of women leaning over steel barriers, cheering and holding signs like 'Kiss me, I'm a mathematician', and 'I won't tell your wife'.

After Wellesley, the crowds thin and the course dips into Newton Lower Falls. The Newton hills, as much as anything, have come to define Boston. Heartbreak Hill, between miles 20 and 21, gets most of the attention, but Heartbreak is actually the last in a series

TORTOISE OR HARE?

Despite its prestige and reputation, the Boston Marathon is not world-record eligible. For one, Boston's course is a net downhill, starting at 490ft (150m) elevation and ending at 10ft (3m). It's also a point-to-point, meaning a tailwind could give competitors an unfair advantage. Meanwhile, slower runners with little chance of qualifying, take heart: if you can raise at least $5000 for one of the marathon's official charities, you're guaranteed a place on the starting line.

Clockwise from top: challenging weather is the norm in Boston; triumphant runners celebrate finishing; people run for all reasons. Previous page: more than 30,000 runners starting the historic race

"After the bombing, I vowed to return in solidarity and defiance – that race a year later was transformative"

© Icon Sportswire / Getty Images

of climbs. No single one is that bad – Heartbreak itself climbs just 91ft (28m) – but the fact that they come in rapid succession, and so late in the race, makes them feel like Alpine passes.

Tim and I put our heads down, grinding our way upward. The rain, perhaps sensing an opportunity to destroy what was left of our good cheer, lashed down harder than ever. The only good thing about the Newton hills is that once you're past them, it's almost entirely downhill to the finish. Still, unless you've done everything perfectly, it doesn't matter. By then, you're running on empty.

But it's Boston and things conspire to keep you moving. The crowds grow denser and louder with each stride. Nothing prepares you for that turn on to Boylston St, the grandstands full of roaring spectators, the 120-year-old finish line. In the blink of an eye, all the suffering and pain and doubt – not just from that day, but from the months or years you spent working to get there – all of it rushes up and out. Then, bliss. There was nothing but me, Tim, and the big, blue-and-yellow finish line, four-tenths of a mile away.

Many people cry at this point. I usually do, at least a little.

In 1999 I crossed that finish line for the first time, in under three hours. I crossed it with Tim in five and change. As we trudged toward the finishers' medals and space blankets, I found myself shaking uncontrollably from the cold. 'You OK?' a volunteer asked. I wasn't, but I lied. In fact, 130 runners were treated for hypothermia that year. But I'd be warm and dry soon enough. To paraphrase an old motivational quote: Hypothermia is temporary; Boston is forever. **MR**

Start // Hopkinton, Massachusetts
Finish // Boston's Copley Sq
Distance // 26.2 miles (42km)
Getting there // Logan Airport (BOS) offers easy access to all parts of Boston; because of limited space and narrow roads around the start, taking private vehicles is strongly discouraged – the buses provided are much less stressful.
When to go // Race day is the third Monday of April.
Where to stay // Demand for hotel rooms is very high, especially those near the finish line in Copley Sq. Consider an Airbnb or hotel further away, but near a T line.
What to wear // Weather is a wild card, varying from scorching heat to freezing rain and snow.
Things to know // There is a 5km race on the Saturday before Marathon Monday, giving companions of visiting marathoners a chance to do some racing themselves.
More info // baa.org/races/boston-marathon

*Opposite: runners pass through
Manhattan's Times Sq during the New
York City Marathon*

MORE LIKE THIS
BUCKET-LIST US MARATHONS

NEW YORK CITY MARATHON, NEW YORK

Like NYC itself, the New York City Marathon is big – the biggest in the world, in fact, with a field size north of 50,000 – and pulsing with an energy that no other marathon can replicate. Held on the first Sunday of November, the race is a 26.2-mile tour of the city's five boroughs. Runners start in Staten Island and then, in a scene that's become iconic, stream across both levels of the Verrazano-Narrows Bridge into Brooklyn. The race winds through Queens, Manhattan, and, briefly, The Bronx, before returning to Manhattan, where runners sail down Fifth Ave and then slingshot around the southern edge of Central Park to the finish line, near the famed Tavern on the Green restaurant. Each borough has its own personality, but the one constant is the crowd – an estimated two million spectators turn out, and they aren't shy about expressing their enthusiasm.
**Start // Fort Wadsworth, Staten Island
Finish // Central Park West at 67th St
More info // tcsnycmarathon.org**

CHICAGO MARATHON, ILLINOIS

Another tremendously popular fall race, Chicago (in early October) is one of the six World Marathon Majors – along with Boston, New York, London, Berlin, and Tokyo. It's big, too, with a field size of around 45,000. The course begins and ends in Grant Park, in the city's downtown business district, and sends runners north on LaSalle St, parallel to Lake Michigan. Between miles 7 and 8 the course doubles back and runners return downtown before heading west and passing the halfway point. The remainder of the course is a series of Etch-A-Sketch turns that lead runners, gradually, south of downtown before turning north one final time, to the finish line. This race is pancake-flat and famously fast – four world records have been set here. If you're looking to PB, Chicago may be the race for you.
**Start/Finish // Grant Park, Columbus Dr
More info // chicagomarathon.com**

DISNEY MARATHON, FLORIDA

Hey, don't laugh. Traditionalists may sneer or scoff, but the Walt Disney World Marathon is all about over-the-top fun. With a course that snakes through the Disney World resort – yes, that includes Cinderella's Castle – you'll find it hard not to smile right along with the costumed characters you'll see along the way. It's all a little trippy, though the organizers would likely prefer the word magical. The marathon is just one event, by the way, of a weekend-long whirlwind of running: there's also a 5km, 10km and half-marathon, plus a series of short kids' races. Ambitious runners can also take on the Goofy Challenge (half-marathon and full marathon) or the Dopey Challenge (5km, 10km, half-marathon and full marathon). One thing: be prepared for some godawful wakeup calls – each race starts at 5.30am, sharp. Fun!
**Start/Finish // Epcot Parking Lot
More info // rundisney.com/
disneyworld-marathon**

SOUTH USA

JOIE DE VIVRE
IN NEW ORLEANS

A springtime run takes you through the Big Easy's most enchanting neighborhoods,
with river views, rattling streetcars, and verdant green spaces along the way.

The sidewalks glisten from last night's rainstorm and the palm trees lining Canal St look gilded in the early morning light. A lone saxophone player runs through a spirited, Coltrane-esque rendition of *My Favorite Things* as a bright red streetcar trundles past. It's Sunday morning and the scent of spring hangs in the air. I'm about to head off on my favorite run in my hometown: a meandering route that will take me through photogenic neighborhoods and along the river, passing the people and places that remind me what it means to live in New Orleans – and why there's no other place like it on Earth.

I start my watch as I cross Canal and turn up Royal St. At this hour the French Quarter feels surprisingly quiet. Few people are out, and there's so little traffic that I can run in the street – all the better to take in the scenery on both sides of the pavement. Antiques stores, galleries, and famous Creole restaurants like Brennan's roll past as I ease into a moderate pace. Like most other parts of the Quarter, Royal is awash with wrought-iron balconies and 19th-century facades, and it's easy to imagine elegantly dressed gentry of another era window-shopping along the lane. This is quite a contrast from Royal's raucous neighbor one block up. Lined with strip clubs and neon-lit bars, Bourbon St is the first – and often last – port of call for a certain kind of visitor, eager to drink up every last drop of debauchery the city can pour forth.

The streets are no longer empty when I reach the edge of Jackson Sq, which is always a hub of activity. Fortune tellers

and tarot-card readers call out to me from folding tables, while several artists are setting up their paintings for sale against the park's wrought-iron fence. Another busker, trumpet tucked under his arm, sits at a park bench, waiting for the plaza to fill with visitors.

My run slows to a halt as I wait for a break in traffic at Decatur St. A minute later, I'm running up two flights of steps and then catch my first glimpse of the Mississippi. Though no one would describe this muddy-brown waterway as lovely,

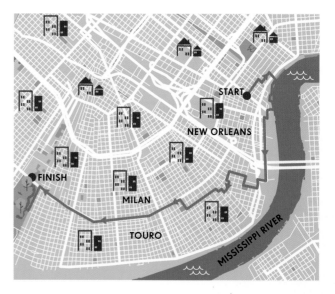

I've always taken comfort in its wide, ever-flowing presence. The breezy views over the open expanses of water and sky must have felt restorative to early inhabitants, crammed in the densely populated streets nearby. With the sun now blazing, I pick up the pace. With a smooth brick promenade underfoot, I'm speeding by cast-iron street lamps, statues of forgotten figures, and grassy lawns that will later gather picnickers. Up ahead a slow-moving riverboat glides under the twin bridges connecting New Orleans with communities of the Westbank.

The river views soon come to an end but I'm reminded once again of the great waterway to my left when I pass under the twin spans a mile (1.6km) on. Later, I zigzag through quiet backstreets and across small leafy parks as I make my way onto St Charles Ave, one of the most scenic thoroughfares in the city. Centuries-old live oak trees dripping with Spanish moss stretch their finger-like branches over the avenue, casting welcome shade above the sidewalks. This being St Charles though, I've left the curb behind and am running down the grass-lined median in the middle of the street – better known as 'the neutral ground' in these parts. Clattering green streetcars – in service since 1835 – also trundle along St Charles but move slowly enough that you can easily dodge out of the way before they draw near.

I tick off another 2.5 miles (4km) before I reach Audubon Park, which is named for the famous naturalist and painter who lived off and on in New Orleans in the 1820s and '30s. Audubon, who illustrated one of the greatest ornithological

> *"My favorite run is a meandering route, passing the people and places that remind me what it means to live in New Orleans"*

POTIONS AND POISONS

In a former 19th-century apothecary in the French Quarter, the Pharmacy Museum is an eye-opening tour of the past. Self-taught pharmacists sold 'love potions' here, administered opium (an oft-prescribed sedative), and gave mercury injections for venereal diseases. When yellow fever and cholera outbreaks devastated the city, afflicted patients were subjected to bloodletting, purgatives, and nefarious cure-alls, which sometimes contained arsenic and other neurotoxins.

Clockwise from top: Royal St recitals; the St Louis cathedral dates from the 18th century; catch a brass band in New Orleans; skip the heat on an early morning run. Previous page: the beating heart of the French Quarter

works of all time, would undoubtedly be pleased to lend his name to this 350-acre (141-hectare) green space. The long narrow lagoon is noisy with the sound of birdsong. I run along the water's edge and spot a pair of anhingas perched on a log, drying their slick, outstretched wings in the sun. Near the riverbank, a great blue heron stands motionless, its dagger-like bill poised over the water while patiently waiting for its next meal to swim past. Nearby, a small flock of ibis are needling their way across the grass, their long, curved beaks working feverishly in the soil.

My run comes to an end as I round the lagoon and slow to a walk near the Gumbel Fountain. Though I've run past it frequently over the years, I've never paid it much heed. Pink foxgloves ring the circular base, which looks more like a small watery stage for the elegantly poised water nymph, who holds a dove in her outstretched hand. Entitled *The Meeting of Air and Water*, it seems an appropriate symbol for a city so often dominated by the elements. For New Orleans is a place not just of hurricanes and flood-prone streets but also of astonishing bird life, rich Gulf seafood, blaring Mardi Gras trumpets, and welcome downpours bringing relief from the heat. And yet for all this, New Orleans is also a place that defies breezy, watered-down classifications. It's a place with countless stories, and dense layers of history and culture woven into its moldering streets. It's a place where you can run the same route dozens of times but it's never the same. That's the magic of New Orleans. **RSL**

Start // Corner of Canal & Royal streets
Finish // Audubon Park
Distance // 8 miles (13km)
Getting there // Take the slow but scenic Amtrak train to reach New Orleans, which has rail services to Chicago, Atlanta, and Los Angeles among other major cities. Once in town, hop aboard the streetcar to reach the edge of the French Quarter.
When to go // Spring (March through early May) brings lovely weather, and you can also time your visit to hit Jazz Fest, which kicks off in late April.
Where to stay // Most people stay in the French Quarter, but you'll find a more local vibe by staying in other appealing neighborhoods, including the Marigny (which puts you close to the jazz clubs on Frenchmen St), the Bywater, the Garden District, and Uptown.
More info // neworleans.com

Opposite: the Forsyth Park fountain in Savannah; timeless Charleston in South Carolina

MORE LIKE THIS
OTHER RUNS IN THE SOUTH

SAVANNAH, GEORGIA

History lurks around every corner in Savannah, the oldest city in Georgia – and the state's first capital. Founded by the British in 1733, Savannah is packed with icons from its past, including grand Greek Revival homes, colonial cemeteries, and the oldest African American church in the country. The epicenter of town is the aptly named historic district, which encompasses some 2 sq miles (5.2 sq km), one of the largest in the country. You can get in some decent mileage zigzagging your way along the tree-lined streets and passing through Savannah's famous 22 squares en route. End your run at Forsyth Park, an elegant expanse of verdant lawns, oak-lined promenades, and a much-photographed fountain. If the humidity hasn't gotten to you, add a run along the River Walk, a promenade that stretches for half a mile beside the Savannah River.

Start // Franklin Sq
Finish // Forsyth Park
Distance // 5 miles (8km)
More info // visitsavannah.com

CHARLESTON, SOUTH CAROLINA

Wedged between two rivers near the mouth of Charleston Harbor, South Carolina's oldest city embodies both the beauty and the heartache of the Deep South. The locals' kindhearted welcome and genteel manners feel like something out of a Victorian novel, while the centuries-old buildings lining the historic district evoke an even older era. And yet the city itself was built on slave labor, which is thoughtfully addressed in places like the International African American Museum, which opened in 2023. You can get a taste of Charleston's complicated history on a run that loops around the south end of the peninsula, passing through the neighborhoods of South of Broad, Harleston Village, and the French Quarter. You'll run by early 18th-century homes and elegant plazas as well as harrowing vestiges from the past including the Old Slave Mart Museum, where men, women and children were auctioned off in the mid-1800s.

Start/Finish // Joe Riley
Waterfront Park
Distance // 4 miles (6.4km)
More info // charlestoncvb.com

NASHVILLE, TENNESSEE

Country stars know they've made it big when they play on the brightly lit stages of Nashville. Music City, as it's sometimes called, is famous for its hallowed concert halls, ramshackle honky-tonks and legendary recording studios, but it's also a draw for outdoor activities. When it comes to running, the options are nearly limitless thanks to an expansive network of 'greenways' – nearly 100 miles (160km) of paved, multi-use, off-street paths – as well as 40-plus miles (65km) of dirt trails for more rugged runs and hikes. A rewarding loop through downtown takes you through the Bicentennial Capitol Mall, past the music-themed Walk of Fame Park, across the John Seigenthaler Pedestrian Bridge and along the Nashville Riverfront with its fine views. If you're not ready to call it a day, you can continue on to the Cumberland River Greenway, which hugs the river for some 6 miles (9.7km) all the way to Ted Rhodes Park.

Start/Finish // Bicentennial
Capitol Mall
Distance // 6 miles (9.7km)
More info // visitmusiccity.com;
greenwaysfornashville.org

DISCOVER
DAUFUSKIE ISLAND

This relatively untouched barrier island near Hilton Head, South Carolina, offers a mellow run through natural beauty but with reminders of the South's darker history.

Located just a short hop across Calibogue Sound from Hilton Head, the only way to reach this remote, barrier isle in South Carolina is by boat. And that's the beauty of it. The concerns of the world drift away as you chug across glistening waters, arriving at Freeport Marina after 45 minutes watching soaring sea birds, spotting dolphins (if you're lucky), and examining the marshy coastline as you lean into the salt-tinged breeze.

Such natural delights are a foreshadowing of the run to come. To land on this petite island, measuring just 5 miles (8km) long and 2.5 miles (4km) wide, is to enter a seemingly bygone world. Waiting to greet you are oaks draped in Spanish moss, a crab-shack restaurant, colorful bungalows for rent, and a general store. From the marina, sandy lanes grant access to the rest of the island, occupied by 400 or so year-round residents and few cars – most people get around by golf cart.

Today, it's an idyllic place for a run, but it wasn't always so. Daufuskie Island was inhabited for thousands of years by numerous Native American peoples, including the Yemassee, before the English conquered them in a series of bloody raids and divided the island into indigo and cotton plantations. Enslaved African American laborers subsequently worked the fields, undergoing brutal conditions in what was punishing work. Union troops occupied Daufuskie during the Civil War, chasing away the residents. Freed from enslavement, the Gullah people returned after the war and purchased small tracts of land for themselves and their families. Due to Daufuskie's isolation, they maintained their dialect – a mixture of English and African languages – and culture.

Sallie Ann Robinson, whom I met on the island, is a sixth-generation Daufuskian, born in her grandmother's house, who now offers guided tours that shed light on the Gullah way of life. 'The voices of the ancestors started saying "you got this",' she tells me, 'and I'm having a blast sharing the history.' From the marina, I decide to run a wandering loop that takes in the island's most interesting sights, although really, the thing to do here is mosey and see what you discover along the way.

To take my run, follow Copper River Landing Rd to Old Haig Rd to find the Billie Burn Museum – housed in the old Mt Carmel Baptist Church No. 2, it dates from 1940. This small space, run by the Daufuskie Island Historical Foundation, has artifacts depicting island history, including Native American arrowheads, military buttons (courtesy of various invading soldiers, particularly during the Civil War), and an 11.5ft (3.5m) stuffed alligator.

"I decide to run a wandering loop – the thing to do here is mosey and see what you discover along the way"

From here head south, wandering along dusty lanes until you pass the Daufuskie Island Rum Company, a renowned distillery that uses all-American products in its handcrafted rums, including sugar and glass bottles. Onward and you'll spy the two-room Mary Fields School, on School Rd, built in the 1930s, primarily for the island's African American children. It was immortalized in *The Water is Wide* (1972), the memoir by Pat Conroy, who taught students here for one year, including Sallie Ann. She has a lot to say about the experience, too, such as how Conroy encouraged students to explore the world 'off-island'. A tiny exhibit commemorates Conroy's time here, comprising mostly newspaper and magazine clippings.

Today, the school building houses Daufuskie Blues, a textile studio owned and run by Leanne Coulter and Rhonda Davis. In addition to selling indigo-dyed scarves, shirts and other fabrics, they offer dyeing workshops. They can also tell you how indigo was successfully cultivated to obtain the coveted blue dye; during the Revolutionary War, indigo made up more than one quarter of all exports from the American colonies. While you're mulling over this history, School Grounds Coffee in the back has amazing iced-caramel lattes and berry muffins.

OYSTER STORIES

Oysters have played a major part in Daufuskie history. Opened in 1894, LP Maggioni cannery made island oysters famous around the world – Gullah men collected them from flat-bottomed *bateaux* during low tide, while women and children shucked them. The cannery closed in 1956, after a paper mill contaminated the oyster beds, but efforts to create new habitats are ongoing.

Left to right: the Daufuskie Ferry from Hilton Head; a great egret at home on the island; the Moses Ficklin Cottage, a restored Gullah home. Previous page: Daufuskie's wetlands; Lowcountry cuisine

Next door is the white-painted First Union African Baptist Church, dating from 1884. Sallie Ann's grandfather helped build the structure, which still holds Sunday services. Another mile (1.6km) brings you to the tiny Silver Dew Winery, which has been making wines since 1953 in a building dating back to 1883. A public beach awaits down the street, where green-blue waters lap against an empty stretch of golden sands.

Continuing on, you can visit Chase Allen at his Iron Fish Gallery on Benjies Point Rd, where he displays colorfully painted mermaids, sea turtles, and crabs (and fish) made from iron. You can buy his pieces on the honor system although, if he's in, you're welcome to watch him work. Chase is also very chatty. When I visited (not on a run), he told me how to find the best deviled crab, the local specialty, and gave us a tour of the next-door bungalow, which he has converted into a charming Airbnb.

What I like most about this run is the quiet, and the chance to admire the island's traditions. Along the way, you'll spot historic cottages tucked beneath giant oaks, many of which belong to the Gullah people. A light 'heaven-blue' is painted on the doors and shutters of many, to keep away the haints (evil spirits). Also keep an eye out for the remains of plantation dwellings built with tabby, a type of concrete made from burning crushed oyster shells to create lime, which was then mixed with sand and water. History lurks everywhere. My run ends back at Freeport Marina, where Old Daufuskie Crab Company Restaurant offers deviled crab appetizers and Lowcountry oysters, the perfect ending to another Daufuskie day. **BNK**

Start/Finish // Melrose Landing
Distance // 10.5 miles (16.8km)
Getting there // By ferry from Hilton Head (Daufuskie Island Ferry) or Bluffton (May River Excursions). The nearest airport is Savannah, an hour's drive to/from the ferry landing.
When to go // Spring and fall are best, when it's not too hot or cold (and the bugs are at bay). Businesses generally are open Tuesdays through Saturdays.
Where to stay // VRBOs and Airbnbs (including Chase Allen's Oyster Cottage), plus colorful cabins at Freeport Marina.
Where to eat // Lucy Bell's Café and Old Daufuskie Crab Company.
Tours // Sallie Ann Robinson offers the Sallie Ann Authentic Gullah Tour (sallieannrobinson.com)

Opposite: feral horses roam
Assateague beaches; miles of sand
on which to run on Jekyll Island

MORE LIKE THIS
IDYLLIC ISLAND RUNS

ASSATEAGUE ISLAND, MARYLAND

A gorgeous barrier island, Assateague lies about 10 miles (16km) south of bustling Ocean City – and a world away. Starting from the Assateague Island Visitor Center, follow the paved multiuse path paralleling the Verrazano Bridge across Assateague Channel to the island. From here, a 3.6-mile (5.8km) paved bike path follows Bayberry Dr, with mile markers every quarter mile. Along the way, take in serene views of dunes, waving grasslands, the roaring Atlantic surf and, if you're lucky, wild horses. The Chincoteague pony (technically they're not ponies) is stout and small thanks to its salt-marsh diet. You can add on additional half-mile loops on the Life of the Dunes Trail, Life of the Forest Trail, and Life of the Marsh Trail. There are miles of empty beach to run on as well.
Start/Finish // Assateague Island Visitor Center, south side of Rte 611 before the Verrazano Bridge entrance into park
Distance // 9.2 miles (15km)

JEKYLL ISLAND, GEORGIA

Once the exclusive retreat of the wealthy (including JP Morgan, William K Vanderbilt, and Marshall Field), Jekyll Island was acquired by the state in 1947, permitting only 1600 of the island's 8.5 sq miles (22 sq km) to be developed. Today, the wild, sultry barrier isle is webbed with marshes, maritime forests, ocean views – and 25 miles (40km) of paved trails, perfect for a run. One of the prettiest pathways is the 1.75-mile (2.8km) Ocean View Trail, striding alongside the beach and populated by friendly bikers and dog walkers. Midway, you can turn inland on Shell Road Trail to extend your run, exploring the historic district punctuated by historic cottages and moss-draped oaks. The Jekyll Island Club National Historic Landmark here, comprising the former club grounds with 34 structures, is one of the Southeast's largest ongoing restoration projects. Or, just run on the beach, barefoot... 10 miles (16km) of nearly continuous sands await.
Start/Finish // Village Green
Distance // 3.5 miles (5.6km)

SUNKEN FOREST TRAIL, FIRE ISLAND, NEW YORK

This large, wild barrier island along Long Island's south shore offers wide, open beaches, pristine forests, and buzzing towns – but that's not all. You'll also find several good trails for running, including the Sunken Forest Trail. This 1.5-mile (2.4km) wooden boardwalk loops through one of the world's only preserved maritime forests, dominated by hollies hundreds of years old. Protected by a secondary dune system, none of the trees grow taller than the dunes, making it, in effect, a sunken forest. Deer, red fox, coyote, butterflies, and birds (especially migrating songbirds) abound. Even on the hottest summer days, the thick canopy ensures that the trail remains cool and shaded, though the mosquitos can be beasts. Along the way, a network of staircases drops to the beachfront, where miles of empty sands inspire more running.
Start/Finish // Sailors Haven Visitor Center; take the Sayville Ferry from Sayville, Long Island, to Sailors Haven (closed November through April)
Distance // 1.5 miles (2.4km)

IN THE FOOTSTEPS OF MUHAMMAD ALI

Learn about the civil rights struggle and one of America's most famous sportsmen on this riverside run across the state lines of Kentucky and Indiana.

Horns honk and SUVs flash by in a seemingly endless parade of traffic. It's not the most picturesque location but it is one of the most important spots in the history of the US Civil Rights struggle. In fact, it should be marked with a permanent plaque. Here in 1960, halfway along the 2nd St Bridge and exactly on the state border between Kentucky and Indiana, a young Muhammad Ali threw his Olympic medal into the gushing waters of the Ohio River, 50ft (15m) below, in protest at both his personal treatment and that of all African Americans in the US – especially the nation's Black athletes. This spot is a milestone in sports history.

The acceptance and coming dominance of African American athletes in so many modern sports in America can be traced back to Ali's influence. It's fitting, then, to celebrate Ali and his contribution the wider civil rights struggle with a run which passes right over this spot. The 2nd St Bridge runs from downtown Louisville to downtown in neighboring Clarksville. Ali was proud of his home town, despite its historically racist attitudes. He made it known all over the world that he was a son of Louisville, the most famous in fact, and it's no surprise the city's airport is named for him (there's also a Muhammad Ali Blvd, among others).

My run starts at the Louisville end of the bridge and heads over the Ohio River past the famous 'drop spot'. Ali won gold at the 1960 Rome Olympics and instantly became a boxing icon. But, on his return, he was refused service at a Louisville lunch counter and the experience made him so angry that he ran out to the bridge and flung his medal into the water. Of course, there is a chance the story might be apocryphal, given Ali's oratorial style was often quite cryptic. Either way, in 1996 Ali lit the flame at the Atlanta Olympics and was presented with a replacement gold for that which supposedly went into the Ohio.

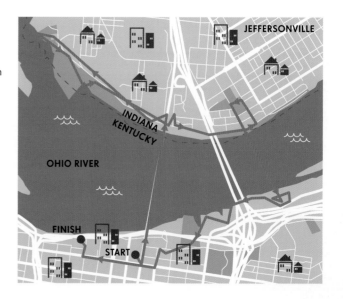

I head onwards toward the Indiana side of the bridge and turn west. I know I'm approaching the Falls of the Ohio thanks to the thunderous sounds of the water. The Falls were once a significant obstacle to Ohio River shipping, until the completion of a dam and subsequent canal in the 1960s. They are still a dramatic sight though. I clamber down a steep cliff to the river beach, which is a renowned fossil-hunting site. Despite my best efforts I fail to locate an anemone, although in the small museum by the Falls I learn more about the wildlife and history of this area.

Turning 180 degrees, it's time to head back east along the Ohio shore, past picnic tables and squawking birds. I spy signs for the Ohio Valley Scenic Drive, which reminds me of Orlando Bloom's Kentucky road trip in the movie *Elizabethtown*. Moving on, I head in the direction of Clarksville, past what remains of the Colgate-Palmolive factory, with its giant clock. At the northern end of the 2nd St Bridge, I pop into the Falls of the Ohio visitor center and chat with Megan Paz, a guide, who tells me they don't get many English visitors.

I pass under the I-65 bridges (named for Abraham Lincoln and John F Kennedy) and reach the start of the Big Four Bridge. The 2nd Street Bridge was built primarily for cars but the Big Four was constructed for trains and named for the now defunct Cleveland, Cincinnati, Chicago and St Louis Railway. Abandoned for years, it reopened in 2013. And where once freight cars clattered along here, the deck is now a dedicated route for pedestrian and bicycle traffic; unsurprisingly, it is

> *"I can see the entire route of the journey I've just made, as the fog and cloud begin to roll in down the Ohio Valley"*

LEWIS & CLARK

Clarksville stakes a claim as the starting point for the famous expedition undertaken by Merriwether Lewis and William Clark in 1804. Part of Thomas Jefferson's plan to explore territory west of the Missouri, the expedition proper began in St Louis, but it was in Clarksville that the two men agreed terms. A statue of the two explorers can be found at the Falls of the Ohio Interpretive Center, but the city was named for William's older brother, Revolutionary War officer George Rogers Clark.

Clockwise from top: Louisville's Muhammad Ali Center; Waterfront Park, near the Big Four Bridge; Muhammad Ali in 1960; the Ohio River Falls. Previous page: the Big Four Pedestrian Bridge opened to the public in 2013

incredibly popular with joggers and cyclists and nothing short of a runner's dream. The Big Four carries you high above the Ohio while information boards in the style of old-time newspaper pages tell of the bridge's torrid history and the fact more than 30 workers died during its construction. Unused and unloved for decades in the 20th century, today honky-tonk jazz, played through speakers, accompanies visitors. It's quirky and fun.

I now trace my route back toward downtown Louisville, along the southern side of the Ohio. Passing the Yum Brands Arena and some historic hotels and office buildings, my final stop is the Muhammad Ali Center. A museum and education center dedicated to the life and times of the mercurial heavyweight known forever as 'The Greatest', it also hosts regular events intended to keep the spirit of Ali alive. Inside you'll discover just how Ali learned to float like a butterfly and sting like bee, and you'll gain numerous other insights into Louisville's most charismatic son. Access between the center and surrounding area has improved significantly thanks to the opening, in 2023, of a $1m pedestrian bridge.

After my exertions, I head for a well-earned drink. But before that, inspired by Ali (a man whose training sessions alone played to packed audiences), I make one final stop – the rooftop gym at the nearby Galt Hotel, a venue equally associated with the annual Kentucky Derby horse race. From this vantage point I can see the entire route of the journey I've just made, as the fog and cloud begin to roll in down the Ohio Valley. **CB**

Start // Yum Brands Arena, 2nd St Bridge
Finish // Muhammad Ali Center
Distance // 6.2 miles (10km)
Getting there // Greyhound buses or Louisville Muhammad Ali International Airport, which has services to hubs such as Chicago, New York, and Atlanta.
When to go // Spring or autumn is best, to avoid the sticky southern summers.
What to wear // Nothing too specialist, a t-shirt, shorts and sneakers is fine.
What to pack // A camera for Falls photos, plus a light picnic; there are tables outside the Falls visitor center at the halfway point of your run.
Where to stay // Hotel Distil is a suave, design-led hotel in the heart of Old Louisville.
More info // alicenter.org; fallsoftheohio.org

*Opposite: the steps of the
Philadelphia Museum of Art;
Central Park's Jacqueline Kennedy
Onassis Reservoir*

MORE LIKE THIS
SPORTING SORTIES

CENTRAL PHILADELPHIA, PENNSYLVANIA

Who could forget that great, albeit fictional, boxer Rocky Balboa? Thanks to one of the most famous cinematic sports montages of all time, it's no surprise that even today you will spy fans taking photos on the Rocky Steps, in front of the Museum of Art in Philadelphia. One of the city's key landmarks, there's also a Rocky statue and footprints to photograph. Continue your run along the Schuylkill River to East Fairmount Park, which teems with fellow joggers. Then cross the river and head to the grassy expanse of the Belmont Plateau.

Start // Philadelphia Museum of Art
Finish // Belmont Plateau,
Fairmount Park
Distance // 3 miles (4.8km)
More info // visitphilly.com

BRANTFORD, ONTARIO

Wayne Gretzky rose from small-town suburbia to become one of the most celebrated ice-hockey players in history. His easy charm and everyman upbringing were among the reasons he is so beloved (that and being the NHL's all-time leading goal-scorer). In his home town of Brantford, Ontario, start from the Wayne Gretzky Sports Centre, running south-west through residential suburbs and down to the Grand River. Turn east and follow a trail through Waterworks Park, leading you to downtown, where you can finish by grabbing a drink at the Earl Haig Family Fun Park.

Start // Wayne Gretzky Sports Centre
Finish // Earl Haig Family Fun Park
Distance // 7 miles (11.3km)
More info //
waynegretzkysportscentre.ca;
brantford.ca

YANKEE STADIUM, NEW YORK CITY

In the 1970s, Pelé lit the fuse for American soccer when he arrived in NYC to play for the fledgling New York Cosmos. The Brazilian legend, christened Edson Arantes do Nascimento, helped pave the way for the modern MLS and its ever-growing retinue of imported (albeit fading) stars. That US soccer continues to go from strength to strength owes much to Pelé's enduring popularity, so why not start your run at his former house, at 54th and 2nd. Head up through Manhattan by taking in Central Park (of course), including a loop of the Jackie Onassis reservoir. Continue north to the Bronx and the iconic Yankee Stadium, playground of such other sporting luminaries as Babe Ruth, Mickey Mantle and Joe DiMaggio.

Start // 54th and 2nd
Finish // Yankee Stadium
Distance // 7 miles (11.2km)

ART DECO MILES IN MIAMI

A run beneath the palms and past the pastel-colored Art Deco frontages of the Miami Beach Architectural District is exercise reinvented as time travel.

When compiling a playlist for a run in Miami, you can go one of two ways. The easy option would be to line up the classics – *Welcome to Miami* by Will Smith, *Goin' Back to Miami* by Wayne Cochran, *Crocket's Theme* by Jan Hammer... But the historic Miami Beach Architectural District deserves something a little more sophisticated.

Lined with Art Deco hotels and apartments, this 2-mile (3.2km) stretch of Florida's most iconic beachfront was the setting for jazz-era beach parties, Cuban political meetings, and illicit liaisons between politicians and stars of stage and screen; not to mention backroom deals by the middlemen who laundered the profits of Prohibition for everyone from Lucky Luciano to Al Capone.

The playlist I created for the Miami Beach Architectural District made me almost wish I was jogging in spats. Gypsy jazz from Django Reinhardt and Stephane Grappelli, Fontainebleau Hotel-era Frank Sinatra, segregation-busting proto-doo-wop from the Ink Spots, breakthrough Latin fusion from Machito and his Afro-Cubans – so, songs in the key of Miami's golden age, rather than songs specifically about Florida's first city.

The gorgeous southern portion of the sandbar island that houses Miami Beach is the world's most definitive Art Deco quarter. Squeezed into a few square miles of cityscape are more than 800 apartments, villas, theaters, cafeterias,

hotels, and more, all executed in a classic Deco fusion of pastel paintwork, vintage neon, and stucco geometry.

To run here is to be carried along by a wave of architectural optimism. Most of these exuberant edifices were built after the painful years of the Great Depression, inspired by a national belief that things were going to get better, in a future filled with elegant motor cars and elegant homes.

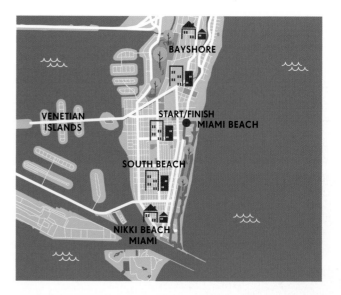

That these buildings are still here today is a lucky fluke. Developers in the 1970s had ambitions to demolish dozens of the city's 1940s masterpieces, before concerned citizens mounted a grassroots campaign to save Deco Miami.

Now, while I'm an enthusiastic Deco fan, I should confess that I was drawn to Miami by the weather, visiting from the Midwest, snowbird-style, in the depths of winter. Even in December, daytime highs of 75°F (24°C) meant perfect running weather. Not baking, but still warm enough to run in shorts and a tee, maximizing the vitamin D-promoting effects of sunshine on exposed skin.

But the architecture came a close second. Running here was a chance to tick off two great loves – early 20th-century design and outdoor exercise – and all of this in the depths of an American winter. Who could ask for more from an active vacation?

I anchored my route around Ocean Drive, Miami Beach's signature beachfront boulevard. Among other perks, this meant a choice of running surfaces – pink pavement facing the Deco strip; green lawns fanned by swaying palm trees; and open sand, hemmed by waters that were just about warm enough for a dip, even in winter.

Kicking off from the junction of Collins Ave and Lincoln Rd, I quickly made my way past more recent condos and hotels to the top of Ocean Drive, tracing the salmon-colored pavement with leaning palm trees to my left and a gorgeous sweep of vintage Deco facades to my right.

Indeed, with every blast of brass on my earphones, another Deco wonder rolled into view, each with an evocative name picked out in an achingly nostalgic font – the Crescent, Winter Haven, the Carlyle, the Avalon Hotel, the Colony Hotel.

In the bright morning sunshine, the pastel frontages radiated jazz-era elegance, and I vowed to return with my camera after dark to capture the razzmatazz as hotels and apartment buildings fired up their neon signs.

In the meantime, I settled in to enjoy the architectural mood music, with the warm rays melting away the lingering tension left behind by the northern winter. With no pressure to rush and no great distance to cover, I took my time, dropping into a gentle pace that seemed to fit the holiday vibe.

Two relaxingly flat miles (3.2km) took me the length of Ocean Drive, spitting me out at South Pointe Park, where Miami Beach screeches to a halt amid a sprawl of manmade islands occupied by the exclusive homes of such Miami bright lights as Don Johnson, Gloria Estefan and – formerly – Al Capone.

For the return leg, I shifted east to the waterfront, picking up the multiuse path running parallel to Ocean Drive, tracking a green sweep of palm-dotted lawns. Southbound, my attention was focused on the buildings; heading north it was all about the people.

DECO DELIGHTS

Running the Miami Beach Architectural District is just a taster. To fully appreciate the backstory of these optimistic edifices, you need to slow to a walking pace, on a guided tour led by genuine Art Deco aficionados from the Miami Design Preservation League. While you walk, learning about such landmarks as the Carlyle Hotel and Cardozo South Beach, you'll be helping to fund the preservation, restoration and protection of Miami's rich Deco heritage.

Clockwise from top: South Beach's Art Deco district; enjoy a run in the sun; Ocean Drive. Previous page: the Avalon Hotel and a vintage Ford Thunderbird

"To run here is to be carried along by a wave of architectural optimism"

With morning getting underway, all of Miami Beach seemed to be on the move: gym dudes striding in blindingly white cotton shirts; committed joggers and rollerbladers with arm-strap phone holders and CamelBak water bottles; beautiful bodies playing beach volleyball; retirees sitting and absorbing the rays. A profusion of holidaymakers in tropical shirts and shades slid by – fellow snowbirds, making the most of the balmy winter weather in America's southernmost state, but also stopping unexpectedly for selfies, meaning some abrupt evasive maneuvers!

Uplifted by this taste of summer in midwinter, I decided to finish up with a last mile (1.6km) along Miami Beach's eponymous strands, abandoning the greenery for the soft-packed sand along the tideline. I flicked out my earphones to let in the sounds of surf, seabirds, and sea breezes swooshing among the palm fronds. In the end, it wasn't quite warm enough for a post-run swim. I made do with a paddle, kicking off my shoes and wading knee-deep into the bubbling surf. But my mood was undeniably buoyant – infused with a transfusion of positivity from America's most optimistic architecture, and its sunniest, sandiest seafront. **JB**

Start/Finish // Corner of Lincoln Rd and Collins Ave, Miami Beach, FL
Distance // 4 miles (6.5km)
Getting there // Fly into busy Miami International Airport and transfer downtown on the Miami Beach Airport Express bus.
When to go // Come in the cooler winter to escape the summer humidity and peak holiday crowds.
What to wear // In winter, you can run comfortably in shorts and a tee. In summer, you'll swelter even in a vest or bra-top.
What to pack // A lightweight towel and jogging pack, should the stars align for a post-run swim.
Where to stay // Stay in the Betsy Hotel for Ocean Drive glam, or the Winter Haven Hotel or Marlin Hotel for boutique Deco charm.
More info // mdpl.org

Opposite: San Antonio's Mission San Jose; jog with a jazz soundtrack in New Orleans' French Quarter

MORE LIKE THIS
RUNS WITH HISTORY APPEAL

PHILADELPHIA'S HISTORIC HEART, PENNSYLVANIA

Few places in America cram in as much of the national story as downtown Philly, and the historic sights of downtown also make for a highly rewarding running route, stringing together green spaces, Independence landmarks, national treasures, and more. Kick off in Franklin Sq – one of the five original squares of Philadelphia, laid out by William Penn in 1682. From here, a rewarding 3-mile (4.8km) loop leads through green parklands past the Christ Church Burial Ground – final resting place of Benjamin Franklin – to the Liberty Bell, Independence Hall and the Philosophical Hall, and on to Washington Sq. It's the ultimate 'America's founding story' trot – or, alternatively, a chance to mull over the gaping plot holes in Nicolas Cage's excruciating *National Treasure* during an enjoyable few miles around Pennsylvania's most historic quarter.
Start/Finish // Franklin Sq, Philadelphia
Distance // 3 miles (4.8km)
More info // visitphilly.com/areas/philadelphia-neighborhoods/philadelphias-historic-district

NEW ORLEANS FRENCH QUARTER, LOUISIANA

Running the French-flavored streets of downtown New Orleans is an experience best savored in the spring or fall, rather than the steamy-as-a-pot-of-fillet-gumbo months of the Louisiana summer. Time it right, and you can appreciate the unmistakably European-influenced architecture and leafy balconies in relative cool and calm, while you meander between small, shady parks and the banks of the mighty Mississippi River. With just a little more effort, you can tag on 2.6 bonus miles (4.2km) of greenery on the Lafitte Greenway, or the 1.4 landscaped miles (2.3km) of Crescent Park – perfect bookends to a downtown run that pounds streets made famous by *Live and Let Die*, *Easy Rider*, *Wild at Heart* and *A Streetcar Named Desire*. Whichever route you follow, aim to finish by the water, watching steamboats ferry sightseers along New Orleans' Old Man River.
Start/Finish // Jackson Sq, New Orleans, Louisiana
Distance // 3 to 6 miles (4.8km to 9.7km)

SAN ANTONIO RIVER WALK MISSION REACH TRAIL, TEXAS

The story of how the West was won – and lost – lives on in San Antonio, Texas. The River Walk Mission Reach Trail daisy-chains through peaceful parklands alongside the oft-fought-over San Antonio River, visiting World Heritage-listed Mission Concepción, Mission San Jose, Mission San Juan, and Mission Espada. Some hike, some bike, and others run through this living history map of the American frontier. Starting in Roosevelt Park, you can track the San Antonio River for 8 miles (13km) in each direction, with handy waymarkers indicating how far you've come. Follow the Acequia Park Trail to the I-10, then the River Walk Mission Reach Trail along the green riverbanks to Mission Concepción to begin this run through American history. The full route is a 16-mile (26km) out-and-back, taking in four missions and 300 years of Texan heritage.
Start/Finish // Roosevelt Park, San Antonio, Texas
Distance // Up to 16 miles (26km)
More info // sariverauthority.org/be-river-proud/parks-trails/san-antonio-river-walk-mission-reach

THE LIGHTHOUSE TRAIL IN PALO DURO CANYON, TEXAS

Head off on a memorable run amid age-old rock formations and a surprising array of wildlife inside the second largest canyon in the US.

The sky was a deep shade of blue when I stepped out of the tent and breathed in the cool morning air. A slender crescent of moon hung low in the west, while off to the east the first glimmer of dawn appeared as a faint pink glow above the juniper trees. It was early May in the Texas Panhandle, and with the temperature still hovering in the low 60s (16°C), I felt lucky to be lacing up my running shoes on such a promising day.

Sometimes called the 'Grand Canyon of Texas', Palo Duro stretches some 120 miles (193km) in length and spans 6 miles/9.6km in width (up to 20 miles/32km in places). Unlike its better-known sibling in Arizona, Palo Duro feels much more accessible – at least if you want to venture beyond the rim. A road winds down to the bottom, and trails inside the canyon meander through a sunbaked wilderness full of striated cliffs and pinnacles. The most famous of all is Lighthouse Rock, an unusual formation that's become a symbol of the surrounding state park. It's also the terminus for the canyon's most famous trail, a 2.8-mile (4.5km) path that, as well as runners, draws hikers, mountain bikers and horseback riders. On this morning, however, the lot was empty and for the moment at least, I had this corner of the canyon all to myself. Or almost to myself.

Standing at the trailhead, I refilled my water bottles and had a final look at the map before sliding it back into my pocket. I was just about to set out when something caught my eye. Padding down the road off to my right was a bristly tailed coyote. He glanced at me with little interest then turned into the brush and disappeared, leaving only the early-morning silence (and my astonishment) in his wake. As I set off, I couldn't help

wondering if he was part of the pack I'd heard howling during the previous night.

Now mindful of other creatures inhabiting this wilderness, I decided to take things slowly as I eased into a run. With hard-packed red dirt underfoot, this trail seemed made for running. On either side of me, the parched landscape of the high plains stretched off to the horizon, with prickly yucca and sand sage sprinkled amid the twisting trunks of fragrant mesquite and Rocky Mountain juniper. Rising up before me was Capitol Peak, a multi-hued dome-topped formation, its geologic history stacked in horizontal layers above the prairie. The morning sun bathed the

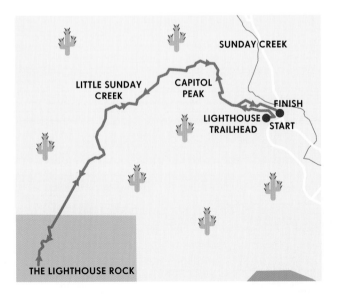

© IrinaK / Shutterstock

lower slopes in an orange-red glow. Dating back to the Permian age, these rocks were formed over 200 million years ago. Higher up, the colors meld into lavender and darker hues, punctuated with white gypsum, like cake frosting between the layers.

My pace was dragging as the trail headed gradually uphill and skirted the north side of Capitol Peak. Luckily, there was soon reason to take a break. Nearly halfway into the run (mile 1.4; 2.3km), I caught my first glimpse of Lighthouse Rock and I stopped to admire the view. From this distance it resembled a weathered carving from the ancient world, like some long-lost relic from, say, the city of Petra. The view soon disappeared as I rounded a bend lined with cottonwood trees. Up another slope, and down, the trail ribboned along to the south. I was pushing the pace a bit when I heard rustling up ahead. Two mule deer grazing near the trail looked up and, a split-second later, were bounding off. I saw only the tops of their oversized ears as they disappeared among a thicket of junipers.

A bit further along, I reached the edge of Little Sunday Creek, which on this day was as parched as the rest of the landscape. I grabbed a bottle to rehydrate and scanned the smooth, sandy creek bed nearby. Crouching down, I spotted tiny prints leading up to a small critter with an emerald green carapace. I watched as the fingernail-sized rainbow scarab worked industriously – possibly at a bit of dung that she would carry back to her burrow to lay her eggs in.

The level terrain came to an end when I reached a small clearing with a picnic table and bike rack, along with mesquite trees that doubled as a hitching post. From here, it was a steep ascent to the base of the Lighthouse, meaning you'd have to leave bikes, horses and any whining companions in the comfort of the shade before making the climb. I chugged some more water then set out, my stride slowing as I wound up the narrow trail. After a short but exhausting climb, I rounded a bend and caught sight of it. The towering monolith of Lighthouse Rock was even more impressive as I drew close. I marveled at the combination of wind, rain, and gushing rivers that had, over millions of years, created this 312ft (95m) icon. The surrounding view was equally awe-inspiring, a panorama that took in the sage-dappled canyon floor and the eroded slopes of rock formations in nearly every direction.

On the run back, I passed a few other hikers, most of whom seemed energized to travel amid such untouched wilderness. I also came across a diamondback rattlesnake sunning itself on the trail. Feeling my vibrations, it slithered off the path, and I watched it from a respectable distance. Although I've never had much love for serpents, I was delighted to see yet another resident species on that fine morning. As I finished my run, I felt happy to have shared this landscape with the creatures big and small that I'd seen, and to be part of their world – if only briefly – in this extraordinary and little-known corner of northern Texas. **RSL**

PEOPLE OF THE CANYON

Indigenous peoples inhabited the Palo Duro region as far back as 10,000 BCE, when Clovis and Folsom cultures hunted mammoth and giant bison in the canyon. In more recent times, the Kiowa and Apache hunted herds of bison here, as did the Comanche, the 'lords of the plains'. No other tribe matched their skill on horseback, which they used to formidable effect while ruling a vast territory.

Clockwise from top left: watch out for prickly purple thistles in the canyons; stay hydrated here; run this way; a lizard basks on the red rock. Previous page: the Lighthouse in Palo Duro Canyon State Park

Start/Finish // Lighthouse Rock Trailhead
Distance // 6.3 miles (10.1km)
Getting there // There's no public transportation into (or inside) the park, so you'll need to rent a car. Amarillo has the nearest airport, a mere 35-minute drive to the park entrance.
When to go // Summer is the hottest and busiest time to visit. Beat the heat and the crowds by coming in spring (April to May) or autumn (late September through early November).
Where to stay // There are four campgrounds in the park as well as glamping tents, and rustic wood and stone cabins. Reserve well ahead, especially in summer.
Where to eat // The Palo Duro Trading Post serves sandwiches, burgers, and ice cream, and also stocks groceries and camping supplies.
More info // tpwd.texas.gov/state-parks/palo-duro-canyon

*Opposite: rugged running in Big
Bend National Park; the Canyon
Loop Trail in Caprock Canyons
State Park*

MORE LIKE THIS
OTHER TEXAS RUNS

BIG BEND NATIONAL PARK

The old saying 'Everything is bigger in
Texas' rings true when you reach the
edge of Big Bend National Park. Tucked
in a remote corner of the state, Big Bend
encompasses some 1252 sq miles (3243
sq km) of rugged wilderness. It's the only
national park that contains an entire
mountain range, the Chisos, within its
boundaries. Apart from challenging trail
runs up these craggy peaks, aquatic
activities include rafting the Rio Grande,
or else look for shooting stars in the
world's largest dark-sky reserve. With
150 miles (241km) of trails, you won't
lack for running options. Desert and river
trails keep steep ascents to a minimum.
A good way to immerse yourself is to
run the Chimneys Trail, which takes you
across desert grasslands. Most people
turn around at the Chimneys, a rock
formation covered with Native American
pictographs, but you can keep going all
the way to Old Maverick Rd, making for
a 15-mile (24km) round-trip excursion.
**Start/Finish // Chimneys Trailhead
Distance // 4.8 miles (7.7km)
More info: nps.gov/bibe**

CAPROCK CANYONS STATE PARK

Not as well-known as Palo Duro,
Caprock Canyons State Park is another
north Texas beauty that offers the same
opportunities to see wildlife amid steep,
red-rock escarpments and short-grass
prairie. The canyon is home to prairie-
dog towns and bobcats as well as road
runners, red-tailed hawks, and other
abundant birdlife. The park's best-known
species are the bison that freely roam
the park's 15.6 sq miles (40.4 sq km).
You could spend a few days running the
trails here or make an epic ultra-outing
on the 64-mile (103km) Caprock Canyons
Trailway (a former rail line) that links
to the park. If time is limited, make the
big loop around the northwest corner
of the park, connecting the trails of
Upper South Prong, Upper North Prong,
and the North Prong Spur. Along the
way you'll see some striking hoodoos,
panoramic views from the canyon rim,
and your fair share of critters as well.
**Start/Finish // South Prong Tent
Camping Area
Distance // 7 miles (11km)
More info // tpwd.texas.gov/state-
parks/caprock-canyons**

AUSTIN

The captivating capital of Texas is
a dynamic hub of creativity, with a
legendary music scene, cutting-edge
festivals and a global palate. Austinites
also have a serious love for the outdoors,
which is perhaps not surprising given the
wealth of green spaces woven into the
urban landscape. Runners in particular
have some outstanding options. There's
the 10-mile (16km) Ann and Roy Butler
Hike-and-Bike Trail that loops around
Lady Bird Lake, while just out of town
is the River Place Canyon Trail with
its scenic overlooks. For sheer natural
beauty it's hard to beat the Barton Creek
Greenbelt, a 7-mile (11km) stretch of
greenery that follows the eponymous
waterway past rock walls, wildflowers,
and seasonal waterfalls. After a day on
the trail, cool off with a dip in Barton
Springs Pool, a massive (3-acre/1.2
hectare) swimming pool fed by springs
that keep the water chilly even on the
hottest summer days.
**Start/Finish // Barton Creek
Greenbelt east trailhead, off
William Barton Dr
Distance // 5 to 14 miles
(8km to 23km)
More info // austintexas.org**

A RUN THROUGH FREE-SPIRITED KEY WEST

Plot a route through the colorful streets of Florida's southernmost island town, which is home to wild roosters, six-toed cats, and a captivating arts-minded community.

There ought to be a sign above the road that says, 'Now leaving the United States of America'. Key West has always seemed a world removed from other parts of the country, let alone Florida – and not just because you have to drive over many miles of bridges and across an overseas highway to get here. In fact, back in 1982, the state's southernmost town did secede, sort of, from the Union. On a single action-packed day in April, 'Prime Minister' Dennis Wardlow (aka the local mayor) announced the creation of the Conch Republic micronation, declared war on the US, surrendered 60 seconds later, then requested $1 billion in foreign aid. US officials mostly shrugged and went about their business.

On many levels the cheeky publicity stunt was a roaring success (and it's still going strong: merch available at conchrepublic.com). Among other things, the media coverage helped spread the word about the Conchs (pronounced

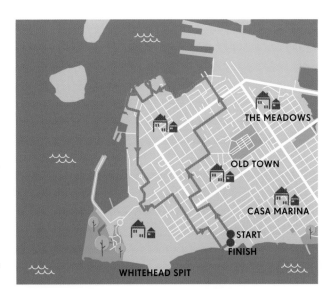

'conks') – what locals have been calling themselves since the 19th century – as a free-spirited, independent-minded community espousing the virtues of tolerance and inclusivity, while openly brandishing their eccentricity.

That anything-goes spirit was on full display as I laced up my running shoes and headed onto Duval St, Key West's most vibrant thoroughfare. With the sun still low overhead, I relished the thought of a meandering run that would take me by some of the city's iconic spots – both famous and not so well known. I started off at a slow pace and soon passed La Te Da, a restaurant, piano bar and cabaret that hosted Key West's best drag Sunday show. Not to be confused with 801 Bourbon or Aqua Bar, which also held frequent drag performances and nightly revelry. Further along loomed the Garden of Eden, where imbibers could strip down to the buff while enjoying breezy views from the clothing-optional rooftop bar.

Vestiges of Key West's wild side appeared in other, more surprising forms as well. As I rounded a corner, I came upon a preening rooster – one of the most extravagantly plumed creatures I'd ever seen, at least on a sidewalk in Florida. After passing its cold clinical eye over me, the bird turned tail and strutted away. Beloved by locals, 'gypsy chickens' (as they've been dubbed) roam freely around town. They are descendants of hens once raised as a food source by cigar workers back in the late 1800s, then set free when the industry went bust in the early 20th century.

I picked up the pace as I headed along Whitehead St. Looming up ahead was a photogenic 19th-century lighthouse,

"The temperature was rising and the humidity enveloping me like an overcoat"

which guided countless ships over the years thanks to Barbara Mabrity. During a time when it was unheard of for a woman to hold such a post, Mabrity kept the 15 oil-fueled lamps lit around the clock through devastating storms and hurricanes (including one that took nearly everything she owned), while also raising her six children. She kept watch for over three decades, until 1864 when she reluctantly relinquished the post at the age of 84.

I jogged onto the road to dodge the crowds gathering nearby at the 1851 home where the writer Ernest Hemingway lived for much of the 1930s. Running past, I peeked through the entrance gate and caught a glimpse of a furry tail and hindquarters skittering across the walkway. Hemingway's home was ruled not by chickens but felines. I could only imagine the author's astonishment upon learning that, nearly a century after his receiving a six-toed cat from a sailor, the feature lived on in dozens of her descendants that pranced about the property.

The temperature was rising and the humidity quietly enveloping me like an overcoat as I paced my way northwest. Luckily the tree-lined streets provided welcome shade, while lush gardens containing the vibrant blooms of flame trees filled the air with the scent of the tropics. I'd ticked off another mile by the time I reached the end of Grinnell St, the waterfront stretching before me. A dense cluster of sailboats, motorboats,

© Joe Dube / Shutterstock

WRECK EFFECT

Storms and coral reefs caused many shipwrecks hereabouts, and in the 19th century the cottage industry of 'wrecking' was born. After sailors were rescued, scavengers laid claim to salvageable goods and auctioned them off, earning huge fortunes. By 1850 Key West was one of the richest US cities per capita. Bounty from the wrecking boom days is displayed at the Key West Shipwreck Museum, near Mallory Sq.

Left to right: start your run from laidback Duval St; the many roosters and hens have become local celebrities. Previous page: Mallory Sq; downtown Key West's lighthouse

and multi-masted yachts bobbed next to one another in the Key West Historic Seaport. I maintained my pace while finding my footing on the creaky boardwalk skirting the water's edge. Flashing past on my left were wooden-sided seafood eateries, open-air bars, and surf shops, along with outfits touting cruises and jet-ski tours.

The shade had disappeared as I zigzagged my way around a trio of waterfront resorts and passed a hidden pocket of sandy shoreline (tiny Simonton Beach). Eventually I reached Mallory Sq. The town's most famous late-afternoon gathering spot was fairly quiet at this time of day. Key West sunsets are legendary – all the more so on this wide plaza where busking banjo players, acrobats, and fire twirlers put on a show for the always sizable crowds.

I admired the view of nearby islands then headed off to complete my loop. My mind was cluttered with visions of Key West's eye-catching beauty and near-constant surprises. Yet, I was also daydreaming of post-run activities. Namely, breakfast. Blue Heaven served up legendary fruit-covered pancakes in a setting that was pure Key West; tables scattered across a ramshackle backyard, tropical almond trees overhead, and a small wooden stage where musicians played. Of course, the picture wouldn't be complete without a rooster or two. They roamed the grounds, drawing nearly as much attention as the resident artist selling her work. I could think of no better spot to complete my run. It was a place that perfectly embodied the delicious creativity of this iconoclastic little island – an island that felt like a (micro)nation all its own. **RSL**

Start/Finish // Corner of Duval & South sts
Distance // 4.5 miles (7.2km)
Getting there // Whether traveling by Flixbus, Greyhound or your own car, the 167-mile (269km) drive from Miami makes an epic road trip. Key West Airport also has flights to a dozen or so cities in the eastern US.
When to go // To beat the sky-high winter prices (and the crowds), come in the springtime, from March through May.
Where to eat // Key West has many outstanding restaurants, particularly when it comes to seafood. BO's Fish Wagon looks like a maritime wreck and serves mouthwatering conch fritters, soft-shell crab sandwiches, and fish tacos.
Where to stay // The aptly named Gardens Hotel has elegant guest cottages set amid lush tropical greenery.
More info // keywest.com

Opposite: the pier at St Petersburg

MORE LIKE THIS
OTHER FLORIDA RUNS

TAMPA

At first glance, Tampa might seem an unlikely destination for travelers with running on their minds. As part of Florida's second-largest metropolitan area (after Miami), Tampa has a dense urban center, ample traffic, and perhaps most damningly – this being Florida, after all – no beaches. It does, however, have the Hillsborough River and the glorious Riverwalk, a 2.6-mile (4.1km) multiuse path along the left bank that skirts the edge of downtown Tampa, travels under bridges and expressways, and reaches up into Tampa Heights. Much loved by locals and out-of-towners alike, the Riverwalk yields impressive views of Tampa icons – like the glittering towers of the former Tampa Bay Hotel – and takes you past waterfront parks and historic sites. Time your run to take advantage of Armature Works, a massive food hall that anchors the northern end of the Riverwalk.

Start/Finish // Riverwalk East End at Channelside and Beneficial Drives
Distance // 5.2 miles (8.4km)
More info // visittampabay.com

ST PETERSBURG

Near Florida's Gulf Coast, St Petersburg is home to the architecturally striking Dalí Museum, colorful murals, and ample galleries crowding two different arts districts. The city also has an attractive setting overlooking the west side of Tampa Bay, and sandy barrier-island beaches are easily reached by public transportation. All of this makes for some vibrantly diverse areas for a run, and it's easy to mix urban culture with nature on a route that combines city streets with bayside scenery. Start off in the Grand Central District, home to eye-catching murals created by talented artists from across the globe. Continue east for 2 miles (3.2km), then turn north when you hit the waterfront. You'll run your way past expansive parks and revitalized spaces – like St Pete Pier, with playgrounds, eating and drinking spots, and yet more intriguing art. Just be sure to get an early start to avoid the humidity.

Start // Central Ave & 25th St North
Finish // Flora Wylie Park
Distance // 5 miles (8km)
More info // visitstpeteclearwater. com

ST AUGUSTINE

Leave it to the Europeans to design one of America's most pedestrian-friendly cities. Founded by the Spanish in 1565, St Augustine has a compact cobblestone center that exudes history. Like other runs in Florida, you'll want to go early or late in the day to avoid the worst of the heat. This being the northeast part of the state, though, the winters are cooler here. St Augustine's best-known landmark – the 17th-century fortress of Castillo de San Marcos – is also a great starting point for a run that takes you through some of the city's highlights. From the fort, head south along the waterfront past the Lion Bridge, with its imposing felines sculpted form Carrara marble. Turn inland and loop around the St Augustine National Cemetery, then head back north along narrow lanes passing Spanish-colonial homes, an 18th-century cathedral, and various vintage buildings transformed into museums.

Start/Finish // Castillo de San Marcos
Distance // 2 miles (3.2km)
More info // visitstaugustine.com

THE BARKLEY MARATHONS

Stephanie Case runs this secretive and mythical ultramarathon in Tennessee, where even the entry process is designed to be difficult and the course itself will downright crush you.

I t was night, pouring with rain, and the water droplets were making it hard to read my compass. I had been crashing through the brush in the Tennessee wilderness for over 15 hours and, even though I had covered the same terrain just a few hours prior, I was now running in the opposite direction and nothing was recognizable. All I knew was that I needed to run in a southeasterly direction, down the steepest part of the hillside to the river below, where navigation would, hopefully, be easier.

I grabbed tree branches to keep me from falling over in the mud, and I strained to hear the sounds of running water. Then, when I did finally reach it, it was flowing in the wrong direction. I pulled out my map. At this point, I didn't even care about finishing the Barkley Marathons ultra. I just wanted to make it back to camp in one piece.

If you haven't heard of Barkley Marathons ultra, that's because you're not really supposed to. The entry process is a closely guarded secret and the more you research it, the more questions you have. The website tells you to submit an essay on 'Why I Should Be Allowed to Run the Barkley'. It doesn't tell you when the entry period is or even to whom you should send your essay. When I first heard about the race almost 10 years ago, I could never have imagined actually competing. However, for me, ultrarunning has always been about pushing my comfort zone. So after completing almost all of the major races on my bucket list, all roads seemed to be leading me to the Barkley. Though I knew I was physically capable – I had placed well in some seriously tough mountain ultras over the years – I had zero navigational experience.

You see, the mysterious registration process is the easy part of the Barkley. The course consists of an unmarked loop through Frozen Head State Park near Wartburg, Tennessee, which runners must

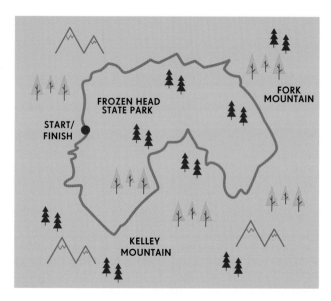

complete five times in 60 hours or less – in opposite directions. Watches, GPS devices and phones are strictly forbidden. To prove that the course has been correctly followed, runners tear pages out of books hidden along the way that match their bib numbers. Runners have been known to spend hours just searching for the hidden books.

Every year around April Fool's Day, 40 invitees from all over the world line up at the yellow gate, in the hope of just finishing. In the 30-plus years the race has been going, fewer than 20 people have finished it. In the year I ran, no one even came close finishing. In fact, if or when someone does finish, they just make the course harder.

The event is the crazy brainchild of local distance runner Gary Cantrell, better known as 'Lazarus Lake' (or 'Laz'). Back in the 70s, Cantrell had heard of the escape of James Earl Ray – the man who assassinated Martin Luther King Jr – from Brushy Mountain State Penitentiary. After a 55-hour manhunt in the woods, Ray was found just 8 miles (12.8km) from his starting point, defeated by the harsh terrain. To Cantrell, this was a rather unimpressive performance. He figured he could run at least 100 miles (160km) during that same time. And so runners have been attempting to do just that ever since the inaugural Barkley (today's course even passes through a tunnel under the very penitentiary from which Ray escaped).

The day before the race, I found Cantrell ceremoniously hanging up license plates from former competitors. The race registration fee was $1.60 and, for virgin racers like me, a license plate from their home state or country. My hands were sweating as I handed over the plate that I'd had specially made, which was emblazoned with the words 'BKLYVIRGIN'.

Laz's eyes twinkled as he passed me my race bib and an emergency device, warning me that it could only be activated once; he implored me to handle it carefully. Then I realized that the device was completely fake; on my race bib it said 'help is not coming'.

I spent the next few hours marking my map and memorizing each line, squiggle, and dot before heading to bed. Instead of a start time, runners are given a 12-hour window in which the race could start. I slept in my race clothes.

At 8.33am, after a restless night of tossing and turning, the sound of a conch shell reverberated ominously throughout the camp. This signals one hour to start. At 9.33am, Laz lit his cigarette – the Barkley version of a start gun – and we were off.

I spent the first few hours stumbling around like a squirrel on a competitive acorn hunt, running back and forth between trees and twitching with confusion as I stared at my map. Everything looked the same and it was difficult to get my bearings. Though none of the climbs were longer than about 2500ft (760m), the

RACE HAZING

The Barkley Marathons is probably the one race in which you do not want to be wearing the number 1 race bib. Rather than singling you out as a favorite to win, it actually marks you as the 'human sacrifice' and the runner most likely to fail first. In Laz's opinion, if he gives you the number 1 bib, you have no business being out on the course. If you do get the number 1 bib? Well, it's best to deal with it Barkley style and try to prove him wrong.

Clockwise from top: founder Gary Cantrell; first-timer license plates; organized chaos; pulling an all-nighter. Previous page: the race's many travails

"In the 30-plus years the race has been going, fewer than 20 people have finished it. And when someone does, they make it harder"

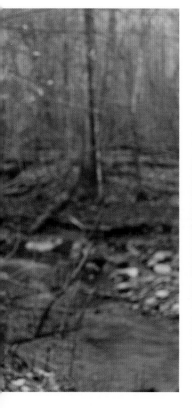

gradients were beyond anything I had imagined for Tennessee. My calves were in agony.

I latched on to a couple of veterans whose course knowledge outweighed their slower speed. They methodically navigated their way through the brush, pointing out landmarks as hints for the next loop. As we discovered each new book, the titles never failed to disappoint: Let's Pretend This Never Happened, 61 Hours, and Left Behind...

I was faring pretty well until I got to a descent called 'Leonard's Butt Slide'. Not realizing the name is also advice on how to get down, I attempted to run it. After ending up facedown in a tangle of limbs and hiking poles, I realized I needed to change my strategy.

The first few hours of the Barkley were as disorienting as anything I had ever experienced. I only really got into a groove once I fully embraced the chaos. What took over was a determination to simply stay out on that course until I found all of my pages, even if it took me days.

A lot happened during the subsequent loops. Though, in the spirit of the race itself, I'll leave some of it to the imagination. Let's just say I did not finish and I returned to the yellow gate far more beat up than I had hoped. But I had finished two whole laps and, the truth is, I couldn't have felt more proud. I hadn't quit. Only two other women made it that far and the strongest men only finished one more loop. Once again, The Barkley had won. But that's just how it should be. **SC**

Start/Finish // Big Cove Campground, Frozen Head Park, TN
Distance // 100 miles (160km), 60,000ft (18,000m) of elevation
Getting there // Fly into Knoxville (50 miles/80km away) or Nashville (150 miles/240km away) and drive to the park.
When to go // Around April Fool's Day (the date changes).
Where to stay // In tents, vans, or motor homes in the park, or a hotel in Oakridge in the days before the race.
What to wear // Sturdy gloves and pants, or shin guards for surviving the briar patches.
Things to know // Bring laminating sheets or clear packing tape to protect your map from rain and mud. And bringing treats for Laz – favorites include Dr Pepper and Camel unfiltereds – is never a bad idea. Documentary film *The Barkley Marathons – the Race that Eats its Young* shows the mental and physical challenges of the race.

*From top: the loneliness
of the Self-Transcendence
ultramarathon; braving the
Barkley Fall Classic*

MORE LIKE THIS
EXTREME RUNNING CHALLENGES

SELF-TRANSCENDENCE 3100-MILE ULTRAMARATHON, NEW YORK CITY

Founded in 1996, the 'world's longest footrace' started life as a paltry 2700-miler (4345km). The event was the brainchild of Sri Chinmoy, an Indian spiritual leader who immigrated to NYC in the 1960s, advocating self-improvement through 'athleticism'. In its current form, runners must complete 3100 miles (4989km) over 5649 laps of an otherwise nondescript city block in Queens, NYC. Regulations include a maximum 52 days to cover the distance, which can only be undertaken while the streets are deemed to be in use by fellow city-dwellers (between 6am and midnight). The idea, presumably, is to negotiate an arduous physical challenge amid the hubbub of everyday life, and in so doing achieve some sort of transcendence. Finish it, however, and you'll be part of a pretty exclusive club. At the 2023 edition, only six of the 14 starters completed the course. The winning time, posted by Italy's Andrea Marcato, was 43 days, 13 hours, 33 minutes and 23 seconds.
**Start/Finish // Joseph Austin Playground, 84th Ave, Queens
Distance // 3100 miles (4989km)**

BIG DOG BACKYARD ULTRA, TENNESSEE

Another one of Lazarus Lake's concoctions, this October race challenges competitors to run a 4.167-mile (6.7km) loop within an hour at whatever speed they choose – and then to repeat this as many times as they can until there is only one runner left. All eating, sleeping, and bathroom breaks must be squeezed in during the moments of downtime every hour, so there is not a lot of room for error. During the day, runners follow a dirt trail in Laz's own backyard in Tennessee, while at night they run out and back on a country road near Laz's house, reportedly to avoid the many snakes in the area. In 2014, the last two runners finished together after 49 hours, stopping at just over 204 miles (328km). However, as they violated the 'Last Man Standing Rule' – dictating a single winner – Laz gave them both a DNF and declared no winners that year.
**Start/Finish // Millersburg Rd, Bell Buckle
Distance // As far as you can go
More info // ultrasignup.com**

BARKLEY FALL CLASSIC, TENNESSEE

Often called the 'Barkley for Beginners', this September race is a shorter and easier version of the Barkley Marathons, also held in Frozen Head State Park. Like the Barkley, runners do not know the course until the night before the race and GPS equipment is strictly prohibited. There is a 9.5-hour cutoff at 22.1 miles (35.5km), at which point runners must decide whether to run just 0.7 miles (1.1km) to end their race or continue on for another 9 miles (14.5km) to finish the full 31-mile (50km) race. Male and female runners are awarded guaranteed spots in the Barkley Marathons, should they choose to accept them after getting a taste of some of the deceptively steep ascents and descents hidden away in Frozen Head.
**Start/Finish // Frozen Head State Park
Distance // 31 miles (50km)
More info // ultrasignup.com**

A PATRIOTIC PATH AROUND THE NATIONAL MALL

*Washington, DC's spread-out monuments can leave you drained. But for a runner,
it is perhaps the most fascinating city park workout in the world.*

Celebrated documentary filmmaker Ken Burns once described Washington, DC's National Mall as 'America's Front Yard'. Indeed, this manicured stretch of parkland surrounded by some of America's most important monuments has been the site of everything from presidential inaugurations to fierce historic demonstrations. The memorials and monuments surrounding it celebrate both the nation's bold achievements and its tragic losses.

Some 24 million people visit the Mall each year. But spanning a half mile in width and more than 2 miles end to end, it presents obvious logistical challenges to those exploring on foot. On any

given day, you'll find throngs of out-of-towners sitting down to nurse sore legs and resign themselves to the disappointment of missing a few things, after grappling with the great expanses between sights. Some give up after the long slog between the US Capitol and the Washington Monument.

I decided instead to tour the Mall during a well-planned run – it was a surprisingly fun and fast way to take it all in without spending most of my day walking. Suddenly, landmarks like the Washington Monument become an essential marker on an interval-filled dash from the Lincoln Memorial. Most importantly, you can see it all – and in less than 40 minutes flat if going at a decent clip. On an

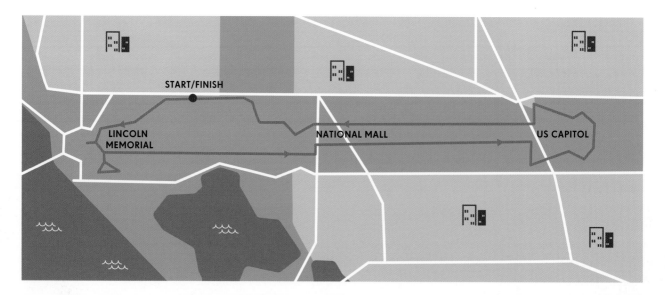

inspiring but efficient 4.5-mile (7km) loop, you can tick off every single monument and memorial, while mentally mapping out sights warranting further attention on a more in-depth visit later in the day.

It was late March, the cherry blossoms were just appearing on the trees and the morning was crisp and clear, with the promise of a warm day ahead. All was surprisingly quiet as I crossed Constitution Ave and headed into the Mall itself. In the pre-dawn light, I began the day's run along a winding path around the pond at the heart of Constitution Gardens, a 50-acre (20 hectare) expanse that forms a park within a park.

My body was still waking up as I passed graceful willow trees along the water line and a wooden bridge leading to a tiny island. The gardens are among the lesser-visited serene spots hidden in quiet corners – things you might skip touring the highlights. At the end of the pond, I merged onto a curving lane beneath shady elm trees and ran past the entrance to the Vietnam Veterans Memorial. If it were later in the day, it would have been crowded with both tourists as well as relatives of Vietnam vets. But at 6.30am, no one was out, and I had the space to myself. I followed the black polished granite wall as it descends into the earth. Towering columns of row after row of names – some 58,200 who never returned – flashed past, no less powerful at a distance.

As I rounded the corner, the Lincoln Memorial came into view. One of the grandest monuments in the world, it anchors the western

"I couldn't help but imagine Martin Luther King Jr standing atop these steps delivering his famous speech"

end of the Mall. I couldn't help but imagine the famous black-and-white images of Martin Luther King Jr standing atop these steps before a crowd of 200,000 onlookers for his 'I Have a Dream' speech. I picked up the pace and made a dash up the famous steps, enjoying the burn in my quads. At the top, I came eye-to-eye with honest Abe himself, seated on his marble throne, five times the size of the real man.

Before galloping back down the steps, I soaked in the view – it's one of the best in Washington. From here, I could see across the full length of the Mall to the Capitol on the eastern edge, and I got a full view of the soaring Washington Monument shimmering on the pool in the foreground.

Back in my stride, I charged past a platoon of motionless soldiers who appeared to be on patrol. In the early morning light, these larger-than-life stainless-steel figures take on a ghostly gray cast, their forms vaguely reflected in a long black granite wall to their south flank. Leaving behind the Korean War Veterans Memorial, I set my sights on the 555ft-high (170m) Washington Monument, DC's tallest building. For the next three-quarters of a mile, it loomed

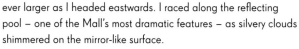

THE 'SWAMP'

Despite the commonly made claim, neither the National Mall nor Washington, DC was actually built on a swamp. DC's most famous patch of green was actually laid out on low, flat land near three waterways (the Anacostia, the Potomac and Tiber Creek) and was prone to flooding during heavy rains, not only creating marshy areas, but also inspiring that politicians' cry to 'drain the swamp'.

From left: Washington, DC's Vietnam Veterans Memorial; the city's famous cherry blossom bloom; the US Capitol Building. Previous page: the Washington Monument

ever larger as I headed eastwards. I raced along the reflecting pool – one of the Mall's most dramatic features – as silvery clouds shimmered on the mirror-like surface.

At this point, I decided to slow down as I neared the Washington Monument, which is roughly the midpoint of the Mall. Even at a clip, it's hard not to feel the majesty of this surprisingly simple structure, which was modeled on the obelisks of Ancient Egypt and is a strange homage to a man who wanted to be forever done with hero-worshipping monarchies.

I tried to not lose my footing on the downhill slope at the monument's base. From here, it was a flat mile along a wide gravel path to the US Capitol Building. This long straightaway is slow-going for non-runners – many complain that the domed building just keeps moving back as they walk forwards. Not for me. I relished this open stretch, picking things up a notch, leaning into an exhilarating high-intensity pace, determined to reach the grand building in less than seven minutes.

By the time I arrived at the edge of the reflecting pool, I felt as if I was flying. There's something inexplicably satisfying about racing along the edge of a vast field ringed by the great power centers in the heart of a nation's capital. As I looped around the pool and began the return journey, it really did feel like America's collective 'front yard'. Few other places in the world can evoke so much on such a short run. **RS**

Start // 18th St NW & Constitution Ave
Finish // Constitution Gardens, near 18th St NW & Constitution Ave
Distance // 5 miles (8km)
Getting there // The metro is convenient. There's also Capital Bikeshare, which has hundreds of stations.
When to go // April to October.
Where to stay // For lodging, great restaurants and nightlife, stay near Dupont Circle. Woodley Park has classy B&Bs along leafy streets, while Georgetown is home to upscale guesthouses tucked along cobblestone lanes.
Things to know // Crowds can be a real issue in summer if you want to get up close to any monuments you pass. In the early morning, you'll have them all to yourself.
More info // nps.gov/nama

Opposite, clockwise from top: plenty of space for pedestrians in Sugar House Park; marathoners in Ottawa; Little Rock, Arkansas

MORE LIKE THIS
RUNS IN NATIONAL AND STATE CAPITALS

ARKANSAS RIVER TRAIL/PFEIFFER LOOP, LITTLE ROCK, ARKANSAS

Part of the Arkansas River Trail, this out-and-back run starts at Two Rivers Park Bridge, the rivers in question being the Arkansas and Little Maumelle. Run east until you reach Big Dam Bridge (1.7 miles). Completed in 2006, at 0.8 miles (1.3km) it is the nation's longest bridge built specifically for cyclists and pedestrians (ie not repurposed from rail or vehicular use). Crossing Big Dam will bring you to Campbell Lake Park, where you can hook up with the Pfeiffer Loop, a 2-mile (3.2km) trail you can run clockwise or anti, before heading back whence you came. If you're in need of even more miles, the start/finish of Two Rivers Park Bridge also marks the beginning of the Arkansas River Trail Grand Loop, an 88-mile hard-top route that will take you deeper into the state, through North Little Rock, Maumelle, and Conway.
Start/Finish // Two Rivers Park Bridge
Distance // 7 miles (11.3km)

SUGAR HOUSE PARK, SALT LAKE CITY, UTAH

Located in the Salt Lake City district of the same name, Sugar House Park was developed on the site of Utah's first state prison. With 110 acres (44.5 hectares) of beautifully maintained green spaces, it is a year-round attraction for runners, not least because of its spectacular views of the Wasatch Mountains. Runners can choose between two circuits: a paved, inner loop of around 1.4 miles (2.3km) and which offers rolling terrain (not quite hills); or the grassy outer loop, slightly longer at 1.8 miles (2.9km). On both routes, you'll periodically cross Parleys Creek, the 20-mile watercourse that originates in the mountains, terminates in the park, and is popular with fishers. The clean, crisp air is ideal for runners – Salt Lake City is 4327ft (1319m) above sea level – while the various grand pavilions available for hire mean you might also find yourself as 'background' in the occasional wedding photograph. In summer the park is open from 7am through 10pm daily, closing at 9pm in the winter.
Start/Finish // Sugar House Park, any entrance
Distance // 1.4 miles (2.3km); 1.8 miles (2.9km)

OTTAWA, ONTARIO

Canada's capital is great for running, with more than 100 miles (160km) of pedestrian paths. Like DC, Ottawa has some grand buildings and monuments, which you can see easily on a 5-mile (8km) out-and-back run, starting near Rideau Hall, the official residence of the Governor General of Canada. From here, a tree-lined lane passes the prime minister's residence and then follows the Ottawa River. At Green Island, you can loop past monuments such as the Commonwealth Air Forces Memorial. Eventually, you'll reach the castle-like Royal Canadian Mint, with the spectacular National Gallery of Canada and the soaring towers of Notre Dame Cathedral Basilica just beyond. Nearby is the grand Parliament of Canada, the gothic revival Confederation Building, and the Supreme Court of Canada building. From here, you can loop back along the waterfront, taking a leafy pedestrian-biking path on the return to the starting point.
Start // Rideau Hall
Finish // Supreme Court of Canada
Distance // 5 miles (8km)
More info // ottawatourism.ca

MIDWEST USA

THE DETROIT RIVERWALK

Allison Burtka discovers that Detroit's Riverwalk has transformed previously inaccessible spaces into a vibrant, inviting stretch along the Motor City's river – and a beautiful place to run.

Detroit is going through a renaissance. Until about 20 years ago, the city's riverfront was barely usable, or even accessible. It certainly wasn't a destination. But over the years, the riverfront has been transformed into a beautiful path that connects several parks and other popular spots in the city, and now it's an ideal location for people to walk, run, and bike.

Across the city, all manner of greenways have been created or revitalized in recent years, reconnecting neighborhoods once separated from each other; and also, crucially, making Detroit's car-centric culture more navigable on foot or by bike. Running

on the Detroit Riverwalk is the perfect way to appreciate these changes – and also an opportunity to cast your eye towards Canada, on the opposite side of the Detroit River and less than a mile away.

Research has shown that simply being near water can have a calming effect. Running next to the blue-green Detroit, along a path lined with parks and foliage only amplifies that feeling. And if you consider that, not too long ago, some of the land beneath your feet was industrial wasteland, it's pretty inspiring.

A good starting point is the east end of the Riverwalk, at Gabriel Richard Park, running west for 3.5 miles (5.6km) and then

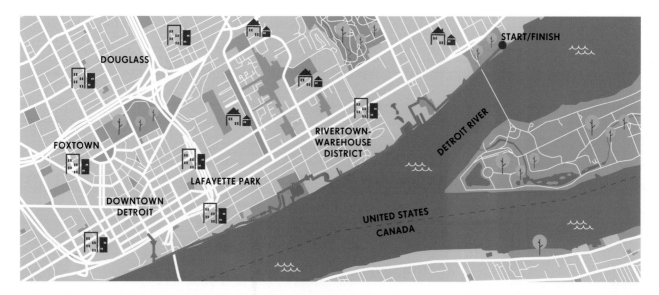

"Running the Riverwalk and Dequindre Cut is special because it connects us to people from all walks of life and the Detroit community"

back. (Fun fact: although Canada is north of the US generally, at this point the city of Windsor, Ontario, is south of Detroit.) The path takes you under the MacArthur Bridge that leads to Belle Isle, and on to the newest stretch of the Riverwalk. Called the Uniroyal Promenade, it opened in October 2023 after a long process of cleaning up contamination from the former Uniroyal car tire plant that operated there until 1985.

The Promenade completed the long-term plan of the Detroit Riverfront Conservancy, the organization behind the regeneration, to build the Riverwalk. That the area was out of reach for many years makes the wide path there now genuinely exciting to run on. This route goes through parks and by marinas, past a lighthouse at William G Milliken State Park and Harbor, and also past the appositely named Renaissance Center, a major Detroit landmark and General Motors' headquarters. In 2003, it was here that GM built the first section of the Riverwalk.

Just past the 'Ren Cen', cars are crossing the border in the underground Detroit–Windsor Tunnel. Despite so much activity beneath your feet, it's something you might not realize if you don't spot the border station. Next, the path comes to the International Memorial to the Underground Railroad. Turning away from the river here, you can run through Hart Plaza and cross Jefferson Ave to get to *The Fist*. An imposing sculpture, its official title is the *Monument to Joe Louis*, honoring the pioneering boxer whose family moved to Detroit in the 1920s. It is also a good turnaround spot to begin your run back. Alternatively, on the opposite side of the street is the *Spirit of Detroit*, a statue dedicated to all those who live and work in the city, and worth stopping to appreciate before you turn around.

While many of these landmarks have been here for decades – the first of the Renaissance Center's seven towers was built in 1976 – a typical pre-Riverwalk running route would have taken you far away from the water as you negotiated the city streets. It is true that pedestrians have long been able to cross the MacArthur Bridge on foot, but the bridge was not connected to the riverfront as it is today. It's a detail that makes Belle Isle Park even more popular. Known as the 'Jewel of Detroit' thanks to its beautiful lakes and woodlands, Belle Isle's 985 acres (399 hectares) are also home to an aquarium and golf course.

The city's renaissance still has a long way to go but running on the Riverwalk is certainly a good way to celebrate the success thus far. And, aside from the significance of improving Detroit's urban spaces, the Riverwalk is very pretty. The route has been plotted to bypass works of public art and also areas that are

THE JOE LOUIS FIST

Joe Louis was the world heavyweight boxing champion from 1937 to 1949, and Detroit is where he started boxing as a kid. Louis became an American hero, in part for his 1938 defeat of Max Schmeling, a German boxer Hitler claimed was an example of Aryan superiority. The *Monument to Joe Louis*, also known as *The Fist*, was created in 1985 by Robert Graham and given as a gift from Sports Illustrated to the people of Detroit.

Clockwise from top: downtown Detroit; running the Riverwalk; the Gateway to Freedom International Memorial to the Underground Railroad by Edward Dwight

home to native plants. In 2023, the Detroit Riverwalk was named the best riverwalk in America by the *USA Today* 10 Best Readers' Choice Awards – and for the third year in a row.

If you're looking to extend this run, taking the bridge across the river to Belle Isle is one option. Another is to turn away from the river at Milliken State Park, next to the Outdoor Adventure Center, at the start of the Dequindre Cut. The Cut is another revitalized greenway, opened in 2009, a thoroughfare that was previously home to a line of the Grand Trunk Railroad. It is a notably wide path, running mostly below street level and lined with murals, and which extends for a further 2 miles (3.2km), to Eastern Market.

A familiar presence here is WeRun313, a Detroit run club, whose weekly runs include routes along the Dequindre Cut and Riverwalk. The club's mission is to use running to bring together like-minded people and in turn build a healthier and happier community. WeRun313 co-founder Lance Woods says the Riverwalk helps the club further that mission. 'Running along the Riverwalk and Dequindre Cut is special because it connects us to people from all walks of life and the Detroit community,' Woods says. 'Even before Detroit had the best riverwalk in the USA, the area had been a meeting place for our group runs since the inception of the club, in May 2019.'

The Riverwalk draws people, from both Detroit and further afield, for good reason. Located next to a bustling downtown and with an international border, the beautiful green spaces and celebrated landmarks along the route all add up to a memorable urban run. **AB**

Previous page: the Monument to Joe Louis by artist Robert Graham

Start/Finish // Gabriel Richard Park
Distance // 7 miles (11km) round-trip
Getting there // Detroit still lacks the robust public transit that many other American cities have, but you can take the QLine from certain areas of the city to get to the Riverwalk, and the city's buses are an option, too. The closest airport is Detroit Metropolitan Wayne County.
Where to eat // Dime Store, 719 Griswold St (eatdimestore.com).
Things to know // If you want to fall in step with a welcoming local group, WeRun313 (werun313.com) welcomes new runners and also hosts weekly runs along the Riverwalk.
More info // detroitriverfront.org

Opposite: Point State Park and Fort Duquesne in Pittsburgh

MORE LIKE THIS
URBAN RIVERFRONT TRAILS

PITTSBURGH'S THREE RIVERS HERITAGE TRAIL, PENNSYLVANIA

This riverfront trail system goes through and around Pittsburgh's downtown, where the Monongahela, Ohio, and Allegheny Rivers converge. The trail covers 33 miles (53km) in total, with sections along all three rivers, so you have plenty of route options. Pedestrian-friendly bridges enable you to begin your run on the side of one river before crossing to carry on along another. If you start at Point State Park and run via the south side of downtown, along the Monongahela, you'll go by the revitalized Monongahela Wharf; or, you can go north along the Allegheny, toward the convention center. Like the Detroit Riverwalk, the trail includes areas that once were industrial sites and have since been rehabilitated. The trail is part of the larger Great Allegheny Passage, which connects Pittsburgh to Washington, DC.
Start/Finish // Point State Park
Distance // 33 miles (53km) total
**More info // pittsburghpa.gov/
citiparks/three-rivers-heritage**

BOSTON'S CHARLES RIVER ESPLANADE, MASSACHUSETTS

The Charles River Esplanade is a popular park and trail that runs along the Boston side of the Charles River for 3 miles (4.8km), from the Museum of Science to the Boston University Bridge. Running along the river is a good way to watch the boats and rowers going by and along the route are gardens, docks, the Hatch Shell amphitheater, as well as public art and other landmarks. You can get to the Museum of Science by public transit, taking the T to Science Park.
**Start/Finish // Boston Museum
of Science**
Distance // 6 miles (9.7km) round-trip
More info // esplanade.org

CHATTANOOGA RIVERWALK, TENNESSEE

On the south side of the Tennessee River, the Chattanooga Riverwalk goes for 16.1 miles (25.9km) and is connected to other trails as well. You can take your pick of starting points but a good one is Ross's Landing, near the Tennessee Aquarium. If you run east from there, the riverwalk will take you by the Hunter Museum of American Art, sculpture gardens, and through green spaces, some of them shaded. The path is paved and marked every half-mile. At Walnut St, you can take a pedestrian bridge across the river to explore Coolidge Park and Renaissance Park.
**Start/Finish // Ross's Landing, near
the Tennessee Aquarium**
Distance // 16.1 miles (25.9km)
**More info // visitchattanooga.com/
things-to-do/outdoors/chattanooga-
riverwalk**

THE CHICAGO SHORELINE

After decades in development, the Windy City's Lakefront Trail is an impressive network of city parks and adventure playgrounds.

Chicago's 18-mile (29km) Lakefront Trail passes plenty of the city's trophy sights: splashy beaches along Lake Michigan, world-famous museums, downtown's mighty skyscrapers, and one very big Ferris wheel. But more importantly, the opening of this continuous path that spans Chicago's entire sprawl provides a tour of local life in all of its disparate glory, from struggling forgotten communities to mansion-lined streets, from oppressive urbanity to breathtaking wilderness.

On balmy days it seems the entire city makes a dash for the waterfront and it doesn't matter how fit – or not so fit – you are. The Lakefront Trail has a way of showing you that this city of 2.7 million people somehow remains small-town and neighborly. Heartland values reign supreme here, strangers wave to strangers along the way. Fast runners politely pass slower runners.

It begins – or ends, depending on which direction you're traveling – outside the South Shore Cultural Center, a former country club where the Obamas held their wedding reception. The flat, paved trail hugs Lake Michigan, one of the world's largest freshwater expanses. It's an inland 'sea' vast enough to sink 1500 ships over the years. Its frothy waves ripple over the horizon with no end in sight. For locals who feel hemmed in by the asphalt jungle, the lake is powerfully restorative.

You can run the Lakefront Trail in either direction, but starting in the less traveled south means more legroom for the early miles. That's my way. I take a bus from downtown, passing through a jumble of working-class neighborhoods, past low-slung apartment buildings and the occasional vacant lot.

FINISH

LINCOLN PARK

CHICAGO

JACKSON HARBOR

START

"The Lakefront Trail has a way of showing you that heartland values reign supreme here – strangers wave to strangers; fast runners politely pass slower runners"

I exit the bus and walk a few minutes to a sign on an obscure street corner that marks the start. At first the trail is just an unremarkable sidewalk skirting a public golf course. But after just a half mile, I round a bend and the turquoise lake appears, stretching out to meet the sky, while the trail unfurls elegantly along its shores.

In the first few miles, the path takes me past Jackson Harbor, where sailboats wobble in the water and old men cast for bass off the docks. Here, locals from the surrounding neighborhoods gather outside, tailgating-style, blasting hip-hop and tending to grills that sizzle with sausages.

But not much further along is another strand of sand popular with students from the University of Chicago, whose ivory towers loom a few blocks west. Also nearby is the Museum of Science and Industry, the largest science museum in the western hemisphere – MSI visitors often wander down to the shoreline once they're done.

For the next few miles, the path travels between the lake to the east and cars whizzing by on busy Lake Shore Dr to the west. But there is still plenty to distract me from the sounds of the city. When the water is low you can actually see a shipwreck offshore from 49th St; the *Silver Spray* ran aground on a rocky outcrop called Morgan Shoal, in 1914. Today, its iron boiler pokes

out of the lake. At 41st St Beach, muscled dudes do pull-ups and crunches at the outdoor fitness station.

Suddenly, I'm in the middle of nowhere. Gone is the hum of traffic and the exhaust fumes. The sound of birdsong and the sweet smell of grasses tells me I've entered the Burnham Centennial Prairie. Tall buildings fall away and busy roadways disappear. They are replaced by butterflies and swaying coneflowers that buffer the trail. It's as if I've passed through a portal and onto a trail run in the grasslands of Nebraska.

Once on the other side of this wild section, I enter yet another one of Chicago's iconic urban cores. Bronzeville is the historic heart of the city's African American cultural scene, the neighborhood where Louis Armstrong and Gwendolyn Brooks once lived. The neighborhood's pride is 31st St Beach. Often crowded with happy, tight-knit families, it also has some of the city's best public recreation facilities for a population that loves outdoor living.

Next up is a burst of famous Chicago landmarks: Soldier Field, Shedd Aquarium, and Buckingham Fountain, which marks the trail's halfway point. Meanwhile, deep-dish pizzas, margaritas and an insanely tall Ferris wheel wink from Navy Pier. This is commercial Chicago on steroids. Love it or hate it – most locals feel both – it sets the tone for the next few miles through the posh, consumerist

ALFRESCO ART

Chicago is an international center for public art, and there are always great sculptures along the Lakefront Trail. Notable pieces to have been exhibited on the trail include Tom Friedman's *Looking Up*, a fairy-tale-like giant made of aluminum foil and pans (near 48th St), and John Henry's *Chevron*, a 52ft-tall (16m) windmill-esque piece (Diversey Pkwy). The artwork changes every few years.

From left: Lincoln Park on the North Side of Chicago; Chicago's Museum of Science and Industry. Previous page: some sections of the Lakefront Trail cut through the city, others escape it

neighborhoods of Streeterville and an area known as the Gold Coast. The path here fringes Ohio St Beach, a favorite open-water swimming training ground for triathletes. In fact, it stays close to the shore all the way until reaching Oak St Beach.

Flashy high-rise buildings keep things interesting until North Ave Beach, Chicago's most expansive shore. It's chock-full of watersport vendors and volleyball courts, giving it a southern California vibe.

Toward the end, the trail enters leafy Lincoln Park. Urban planners have praised this 'green lung' as one of America's great public spaces for its zoo, theater, and gardens. But really, Chicago's entire Lakefront Trail is now the city's most impressive public space. Chicago's forefathers mandated that the shoreline remain forever open and free of development. It's thanks to their vision I can run through this city end-to-end.

Finally, the trail swings north through more parkland, then into the communities of Uptown and Edgewater. Young toughs shoot hoops on basketball courts, Latino teams collide on soccer fields, and elderly Vietnamese couples rest on trail-side benches. This far north, the lakefront is once again more a window into daily life than a show for visitors. At Osterman Beach, the end of the line, I decide to grab a Coke at the snack bar and blend right back in with the rest of my fellow Chicagoans. **KZ**

Start // 7100 S South Shore Dr
Finish // W Ardmore Ave, just east of N Sheridan Rd
Distance // 18 miles (29km)
Getting there // From downtown, take bus 6 (Jackson Park Express) to the South Shore Dr/71st St stop. Walk east a few blocks on 71st St to the Lakefront Trail Mile 0/18 sign.
When to go // Spring; weekdays are least crowded.
Where to stay // The Loop and Near North neighborhoods.
Things to know // It's easy to get on/off anywhere along the trail and run a shorter distance. Abundant restrooms and water fountains are available at the beaches and parks.
More info // chicagoparkdistrict.com/park-facilities/lakefront-trail. Check activetrans.org for updates on trail conditions.

*Opposite: New York City's
Brooklyn Bridge*

MORE LIKE THIS
SUPER SHORELINE RUNS

BROOKLYN BRIDGE, NEW YORK CITY

Yes, it's mobbed most of the time, but
it's worth the crowds. Start among the
skyscrapers of lower Manhattan, make your
way up the slow rise toward the bridge's
towering crisscrossed cables, pass through
the granite towers, and eventually drop into
Brooklyn's groovy waterfront district known
as DUMBO (an acronym for 'down under
the Manhattan and Brooklyn Bridges').
Once over the span, Brooklyn Bridge Park
rolls out a waterfront path that makes it
easy to add more miles, with stellar views
across the East River, toward the high-rises
of Wall St, One World Trade Center, and
even the Statue of Liberty, further out into
the harbor.
Start // City Hall, Lower Manhattan
Finish // Pier 6, Brooklyn Bridge Park
Distance // 2.5 miles (4km)
More info // nycgo.com

EMBARCADERO, SAN FRANCISCO

San Francisco's Embarcadero is a
promenade that wraps around the city's
eastern edge, following the Bay north. A
run here lets you breathe the salt air and
soak up maritime views, including a close-
up of the hulking Bay Bridge. The route also
passes by the Giants' gorgeous baseball
stadium and hipster foodie hangout the
Ferry Building, as well as the more touristy
Fisherman's Wharf. The entire area draws
a crowd, both local and from out of town,
but don't be put off: the path is wide
and flat, with views clear to Berkeley and
Oakland in the distance the entire time.
Pier 39 makes a fine stop for clam chowder,
a microbrew, or a bucket of mini donuts as
your post-run reward.
Start // AT&T Park baseball stadium
Finish // Pier 45
Distance // 3 miles (5km)

WEST RIVER PARKWAY, MINNEAPOLIS

The Mississippi River churns right through
downtown Minneapolis, and the West River
Parkway hugs its storied shore. The trail
starts at the foot of the hip Warehouse
District and zips by vintage bridges, spooky
old flour-mill ruins, and the famed Guthrie
Theater, with its cobalt-blue Endless Bridge
that seems to dangle in mid-air. Onwards,
it passes the University of Minnesota
campus and swooping silver Frank
Gehry-designed Weisman Art Museum.
Minnehaha Park is an oasis of trees,
verdant knolls of grass and bluffs above
Old Man River, and a poetry-inspiring
waterfall. The trail is part of the Grand
Rounds, a 51-mile (82km) network that
loops around the city, connecting several
other scenic routes for longer runs.
**Start // Plymouth Ave, opposite
Boom Island**
**Finish // Ford Parkway at Minnehaha
Park Distance // 8.9 miles (14.5km)**
More info // minneapolisparks.org

TRAVERSE CITY'S BAYSHORE MARATHON

Kick off summer by racing alongside breathtaking views of Lake Michigan, says Cindy Kuzma, then celebrate with a scoop of cherry ice cream in a charming coastal community.

Few marathoners want their race to end with a sprint finish. But if you have to pick up the pace in the final meters – whether it's to surge past a competitor, or to beat the clock – it helps to make your final push on a soft, cushy track.

That's exactly the pot of gold that runners will find at the end of the Bayshore Marathon, held the Saturday of Memorial Day weekend in Traverse City, Michigan. But make no mistake, the entire 26.2-mile journey holds magic.

The course takes you out and back along the eastern edge of the Old Mission Peninsula, hugging the shoreline of gorgeous Grand Traverse Bay. Then, in the final 200 meters, you enter a stadium and surge down the straightaway of the Traverse City Central High School track. It's a set-up that can bring out the sports star in even the most fatigued athlete.

The first time I experienced Bayshore's enchanting powers was in 2007, not quite halfway through the race's four-decade history (2024 marked its 42nd running). As a late-blooming runner low in natural talent, it took me six marathons to break the four-hour barrier. But in the fall of 2006, I finally did it, clocking 3:57:21 on my hometown course in Chicago.

After that, I set my sights on the holy grail of amateur runners: qualifying for the Boston Marathon, a feat often referred to as a 'BQ'. I'd need to take nearly 18 more minutes off my time – back then, runners in my 18-to-34 age group needed a 3:40 or faster to earn a spot on the starting line in Hopkinton. Once you train hard for a while, progress is usually incremental, so I wasn't expecting it to happen in one race. Still, a mostly flat, scenic course within driving distance of my Chicago apartment sounded like an ideal place to start.

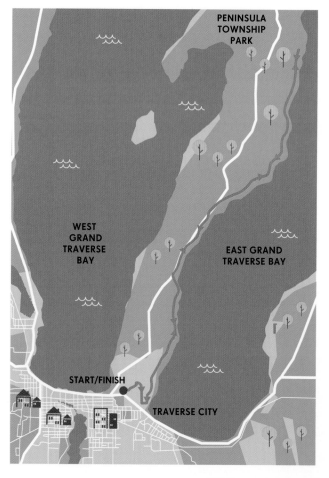

PENINSULA TOWNSHIP PARK

WEST GRAND TRAVERSE BAY

EAST GRAND TRAVERSE BAY

START/FINISH

TRAVERSE CITY

© Andy Wakeman Photography

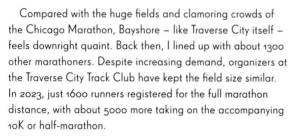

Compared with the huge fields and clamoring crowds of the Chicago Marathon, Bayshore – like Traverse City itself – feels downright quaint. Back then, I lined up with about 1300 other marathoners. Despite increasing demand, organizers at the Traverse City Track Club have kept the field size similar. In 2023, just 1600 runners registered for the full marathon distance, with about 5000 more taking on the accompanying 10K or half-marathon.

The first section of the race is ever-so-slightly downhill, winding through neighborhood streets en route to the eastern flank of the peninsula. Once you turn left onto East Bay Blvd, not long after the one-mile mark, it happens – Lake Michigan, your constant companion for the next 24 miles (38.6km), emerges to your right.

Like many performance-minded runners, I'd experienced some anxiety about achieving my goal. But as soon as I found myself nestled between the lake and the cherry orchards to my left, I felt a sense of calm.

The day was slightly warmer than I'd have liked – nearing 60°F (15°C) – but most of the course was shaded by a canopy of pines, oaks, birches, and spruce. As if on cue, each time I felt things heating up, a blanket of fluffy white clouds floated

through, or a cool breeze drifted over the water to refresh me. Given the scenery, the small bands of enthusiastic spectators, and a relatively straight route up the peninsula, it was easy to lock into a pace and stay there.

I largely ignored my watch until I hit the turnaround, halfway through. There, a tight horseshoe curve points you directly back south on the opposite side of the road you came in on. When I did glance down, what I saw shocked me. I'd run 1:49:10 – a pace of 8 minutes, 20 seconds per mile. If I kept it up, I'd earn a BQ by about a minute and a half.

The second half of the race wasn't exactly easy – what endurance event ever is? But this course is tailor-made to maintain momentum. The trees still offered protection from the rising sun; the sparkling waters, now to my left, remained a soothing distraction. And instead of seeing speedier runners fly by on the west side of the road, I got – and offered – plenty of high-fives and encouragement from those still heading north behind me.

The miles clicked by until about 25, when – call it marathon physics – that small downhill in the first mile transformed into a more significant upward swell. But just when I feared I might slow, I hit the track. As my parents and husband watched from the grandstands, I pushed across the line in 3:37:26.

CHERRY CITY

With the first Montmorency cherry orchards planted on the Old Mission Peninsula in the 1850s, Traverse City is Michigan's cherry central. Peak season isn't till later in the summer, but you'll find plenty of opportunities to enjoy previous years' bounties. Visit Cherry Republic's flagship location on Front St to load up on jam, salsa, wine, and tart cherry juice – rich in anti-inflammatories, and the perfect post-run recovery beverage.

Left to right: yachting in Grand Traverse Bay; the Old Mission Point Lighthouse; running the Bayshore; a fresh fruit stall in Michigan. Previous page: racing beside Grand Traverse Bay

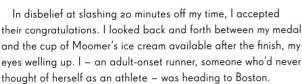

In disbelief at slashing 20 minutes off my time, I accepted their congratulations. I looked back and forth between my medal and the cup of Moomer's ice cream available after the finish, my eyes welling up. I – an adult-onset runner, someone who'd never thought of herself as an athlete – was heading to Boston.

A decade later, I'd return as a journalist, producing a *Runner's World* podcast episode. David Willey, the editor-in-chief at the time, was also aiming for his first BQ – an accomplishment that had eluded him despite years of attempts.

This time, I traveled the same distance by car, hopping out with my recorder and mic at several points to catch David in action. As we waited for him to appear near the halfway mark, I interviewed his son Tristan, who noted the picturesque scene and proclaimed it perfect for his dad. 'He takes natural beauty and turns it into energy,' the thoughtful 12-year-old told me. 'It's amazing.'

So, I wasn't surprised when, despite mid-race hamstring pain that caused him to walk four times, David burst onto the track and crossed the line in 3:28:55, a BQ by over a minute. That track finish is the icing on top. But it's the scenic splendor along the way that, through a special sort of running alchemy, turns athletic dreams into reality. **CK**

Start // Northwestern Michigan College
Finish // Traverse City Central High School track
Distance // 26.2 miles (42km)
Getting there // Drive about 325 miles (523km) from Chicago, or 250 miles (402km) from Detroit; Cherry Capital Airport is just 4.2 miles (6.75km) from the start line.
When to go // Race day is the Saturday of Memorial Day weekend.
What to wear // The average low is 41°F (6°C), and the average high is 66°F (19°C) – layers are your best bet.
Where to stay // Hotels around Font St or Munson Ave are a shuttle ride/warm-up jog from the start line.
Where to eat // Try Traverse City breweries (Jolly Pumpkin or North Peak) or the Chateau Grand Traverse Winery.
Things to know // Registration opens in December, and often sells out, so register early.
More info // bayshoremarathon.org; traversecity.com

Opposite: Brandywine Falls in Cuyahoga Valley National Park; see monarch butterflies in Minnesota

MORE LIKE THIS
BEAUTIFUL MIDWESTERN ROUTES

BUCKEYE TRAIL, OHIO

Any runner in Ohio can consider themselves lucky. They're never more than two hours away from this enormous loop, which encircles the state from Lake Erie in the northeast to the Ohio River in the southwest. Hop on at either spot, or anywhere in between, and follow the 'blue blazes' – two-by-six-inch markings on trees or poles – across bike paths, dirt roads, and paved trails. A highlight is Cuyahoga Valley National Park, between Akron and Cleveland, where you'll lope past waterfalls, caves, wetlands, and the Hale Farm & Village, a historic homestead with demonstrations of 19th-century glassblowing and candle-making.
Start // **Headlands Beach State Park, outside Cleveland**
Finish // **Eden Park, Cincinnati**
Distance // **1444 miles (2323.9km)**
More info // **buckeyetrail.org**

KNOBSTONE HIKING TRAIL, INDIANA

Millions of years ago, a giant ridge arose more than 300ft (91m) above the plains in what would eventually become Southeast Indiana. Today, those hills are known collectively as the Knobstone Escarpment and this path, sometimes referred to as 'Indiana's Appalachian Trail', traverses them. The steep hills and bluffs, the 'knobstones', fill the route with challenging climbs and descents; you'll gain upwards of 10,000ft (3000m) along the route. But if you have strong legs and trail shoes, the resulting views of the farmland and hardwood forests below are worth it (the most rugged and scenic portions are toward the south, in Clark State Forest). When you cross one of the route's several streams, be sure to look down – you might spot the crystalline centers of cracked-open geodes underfoot.
Start // **Deam Lake**
Finish // **Delaney Park**
Distance // **60 miles (96.5km)**
More info // **in.gov/dnr/forestry/ properties/knobstone-trail-conditions- reroutes-maps/knobstone-trail-about**

SUPERIOR HIKING TRAIL, MINNESOTA

Hop on at one of more than 50 trailheads on this single-track trail, which stretches from the Minnesota-Wisconsin border up to Canada, or scout out one of the 2- to 8-mile (3.2km to 12.8km) loops along the way. The SHT, as it's affectionately known, traces the sharp-edged ridges of the appropriately named Sawtooth Mountains, making for undulating terrain. You'll traverse forests of aspen, birch, cedar, fir, and pine trees; spot waterfalls that tumble down into Lake Superior; and may even encounter the occasional moose, deer, bear or butterfly. The stunning vista at the northern terminus, 270 Degree Overlook, offers an aerial view of the forest, bluffs, and winding Pigeon River, which marks the Canadian border. Feeling competitive? Every September, the Superior Fall Trail Races offers marathon, 50-mile, and 100-mile distances.
Start // **Southwest of Duluth, near the Minnesota/Wisconsin state line**
Finish // **270 Degree Overlook, in Cook County**
Distance // **310 miles (498.9km)**
More info // **superiorhiking.org**

THE PORCUPINE MOUNTAINS AND THE LAKE OF THE CLOUDS

Hidden in Michigan's Upper Peninsula sits a vast, untouched forest and pristine lake that altered Drew Dawson's perception of the Midwest's natural treasures.

There was no way this existed in the Midwest. A friend, Rob, from Colorado had scoured the internet for an epic run we could do as training for a late-year 50 miler. Out of nowhere, he suggested a 26-mile (42km) route in these 'mountains' of Michigan's Upper Peninsula. We wanted incline, views, and an experience neither of us would forget. I scoffed at the suggestion until he uttered the name – the Porcupine Mountains, home to the gloriously titled Lake of the Clouds.

Causing my imagination to explode with the possibilities for adventure, I began making preparations. The mountains were named by the region's Indigenous Ojibwa people because their silhouette was similar to the shape of a porcupine. For one of the lakes hidden in its valleys, they chose a name that reflected the sky, the Lake of the Clouds. It's no wonder someone thought to preserve this wilderness for generations to enjoy, and the area was declared a state park in 1945.

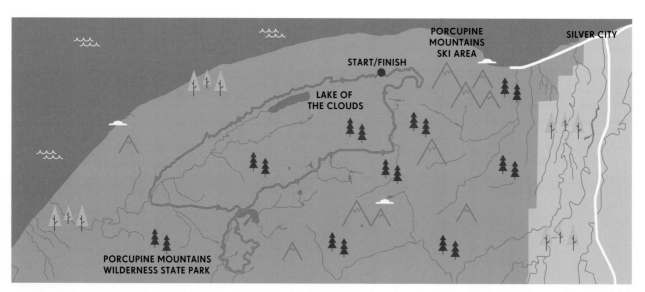

AROUND THE UP

The Porkies aren't the only reason to visit Michigan's Upper Peninsula. Touching three of the Great Lakes (Superior, Michigan, and Huron), there are thousands of miles of coastline to explore, plus waterfalls, springs, and other natural wonders. Essential stops are Kitch-iti-kipi (a uniquely colored freshwater spring), Tahquamenon and Bond falls, and Mackinac Island's suspension bridge.

"I will always recall the first time I looked out over the Lake of the Clouds, but I will also remember that there were almost no miles where I wasn't stopped in my tracks"

Unfortunately, airlines be airlining and, due to a system-wide network crash, my friend's flight and our adventure got canceled at the 11th hour. Facing a five-hour solo drive and already well behind schedule, I regretfully pulled the plug that summer.

Yet those names never left my mind. Every week, I googled them. Each time, images of an overlook appeared. In the valley lay an oval-shaped lake surrounded by a dense, untouched hardwood forest that seemed to go on for miles. And all this just along the border of Lake Superior, the greatest of the Great Lakes.

These images, this place, called to me. If only to disprove my initial assumption that this place couldn't exist in the Midwest, I felt compelled to go one October day. It was fall. The leaves were changing to the north. I called in sick to work. Five hours later, I arrived.

For the uninitiated, the Upper Peninsula, or UP, is the detached part of Michigan just north of the mitten and attached to Wisconsin. There are no major airports within hundreds of miles. The only way to reach it is by driving the single-lane highways that roll up and down through the mountains. If you drive as far north as you can, you'll eventually reach the mighty Lake Superior and the 'Yoopers' who call this home.

Don't let the freshwater fool you. If you arrive when the lake has been disturbed by a storm, you'll find icy, 10ft (3m) waves crashing into the shore. On the day I pitch up, that is precisely what welcomes me as I enter the park. An exposed view of the lake to my right looks out to a never-ending horizon.

Then, I disappear into the woods. At this time of year, you are surrounded by shades of yellow, orange, and red, lining both sides of the road. It's like driving through a box of colored pencils, and that multicolor show is what I experience all along the trail.

Starting from the Government Peak trailhead, I quickly learn that the elevation is not to be taken lightly. Slogging up the first hill, I huff and puff for 20 minutes until I see a clearing in the trees. I stop instantly. Below me and stretching for miles are the valleys of the Porcupine Mountains. Known colloquially as the 'Porkies', this landscape of rivers, streams, lakes and woodlands formed around volcanic and sedimentary rocks that were deposited in the area over a billion years ago, during a continental rift.

Running further along the escarpment, imagination once more becomes reality as I see the Lake of the Clouds in the distance. In all its majesty it sits there, calm and still, reflecting the blue sky above and the colorful leaves around it. The trail runs along the entire ridge above the lake for about 4 miles

(6.4km), and I can't help but stop every quarter-mile to steal a peek. This will definitely take longer than I anticipated.

But that's the beauty of an adventure. The unplanned moments and experiences are what we remember. I will always recall the first time I looked out over the Lake of the Clouds, but I will also remember that over the 26 miles (42km) around the park, there were almost no miles where I wasn't stopped in my tracks. I remember dipping my tired feet into Mirror Lake (another lake hidden in the park's valleys) while I ate my peanut-butter-and-jelly sandwich. Only for a second, for the water was very cold. Or struggling up the stairs of the lookout tower on Summit Peak, the highest point in the park, at 1958ft (597m). And slowing down every time I saw moose tracks, out of both fear and a lifelong goal to see the behemoth, preferably from a safe distance.

Self-supported, the run takes hours but they fly by. Before I know it I'm on hour seven and crossing Government Peak, on the southern side of the Lake of the Clouds. Looking across, I see Lake Superior in the distance, an indication that my car, and the end, are near. Now there's a decision to make. Legs fried, eyes heavy, I approach a fork in the trail. One way takes me up the final section of my planned route, with a final climb and descent to my car. The other fork will also take me to my car (I assume) but I'm not sure how.

Everything tells me to just be done. Call it a day, go get a milkshake and be on my way. Standing at the fork, however, my mindset flips. This entire trip was to discover something I didn't quite believe existed. I wonder what else might be revealed – there's only one way to find out. **DD**

Left to right: forest running; peaceful rivers in the Porcupine Mountains; a male elk in full bellow

Previous spread: Lake of the Clouds in Porcupine Mountains Wilderness State Park

Start/Finish // Government Trailhead
Distance // 26 miles (42km)
Getting there // That's the tough part. Michigan's Upper Peninsula isn't near any major airports. Ontonagon is a 6-hour drive from Milwaukee and 9 hours from Detroit. (Road trip!)
When to go // If you want a dazzling array of colors and comfortably cool temperatures, head there the last week of September or first two weeks of October, when the leaves peak.
Where to stay // Located about 30 minutes outside the park, Ontonagon has great Airbnbs, plus other rentals near a fun downtown. Check out Stubb's for a post-run drink, and great food at Syl's Cafe.
Things to know // This route is entirely on-trail with some decent inclines, so wear shoes with proper tread. Be sure to carry plenty of water and food.
More info // theporcupinemountains.com

 © Jo Crebbin / Shutterstock

Opposite: Split Rock Lighthouse State
Park near Duluth, Minnesota

MORE LIKE THIS
MIDWEST MARVELS

GITCHI-GAMI STATE TRAIL, MINNESOTA

The Gitchi-Gami trail runs parallel to part of the 300-mile (482km) Superior Hiking Trail, which in turn travels from Duluth, Minnesota, at Lake Superior's southwestern corner, to the Canadian border in the north. There are scenic treasures all along this popular backcountry camping route, one that gives you access to some of the best and most beautiful attractions without having to conquer too much technical terrain. This roughly 20-mile (32km) route connects three state parks: Tettegouche, Split Rock Lighthouse, and Gooseberry Falls. Running from one waterfall to another, the trail offers an experience to rival those of the California and Maine coastlines. Highlights include stunning stony shores and a lighthouse perched atop a 130ft (40m) cliff, which perhaps explains why its light can be seen for 22 miles (35km). If that weren't enough, a smooth, bike-friendly path will deliver you to these sites, most formed over 2 million years ago by glacial erosion.
More info // dnr.state.mn.us/state_ trails/gitchigami/index.html

MINES OF SPAIN, IOWA

Not the sort of name you might expect to see in Dubuque, Iowa. However, the Mines of Spain State Recreation Area boasts one of the coolest views in what is known as the Driftless Area of the Midwest, which comprises southwestern Wisconsin, northeast Iowa, and southwest Minnesota. The region is known for the bluffs that have formed over its river valleys, especially along the Mississippi River. One of the best is located here, albeit somewhat hidden away from the riverbank and railroad tracks. Indeed, if you only drive through the park or boat along the river, you will remain blissfully unaware of the spectacular natural features (there's also a canyon) just waiting to be explored. In October, there are 100-mile (161km) and 62-mile (100km) races held here, consisting of loops through the park with elevation gains of 14,000ft (4267m) in the longer event.
More info // minesofspain.org

DEVIL'S LAKE STATE PARK, WISCONSIN

Part of the 1200-mile (1930km) Ice Age National Scenic Trail, Devil's Lake, just outside Madison, Wisconsin, is the most visited site in the state annually. The centerpiece is the roughly 1-mile-long (1.6km) lake, but the adventure is the 5-mile (8km) route climbing the east and west bluffs overlooking the water feature. It is technical at points and includes steep climbs to the flat tops of the bluffs. In addition to a number of overlooks, the detours offer exceptional national wonders. Of note is a quarter-mile detour from the West Bluff Trail to the Devil's Doorway, a rock formation that's one of the most photographed spots in the state. It gets crowded in the warmer months. For a longer route, add on the 7 miles (11km) of connecting trails to Parfrey's Glen, a nearby gorge with walls of sandstone embedded with pebbles and boulders of quartzite, with a small stream running through it.
Start/Finish // South or North parking lots
More info // dnr.wisconsin.gov/topic/ parks/devilslake

LOOPING THE GENEVA LAKE SHORE PATH

While most people want you to keep off their property, a Wisconsin lakefront community will welcome you to see the lake – and their homes – from a different perspective.

When I first moved to Wisconsin, there was a lake – or was it a town – that kept coming up in conversation. It was called 'Lake Geneva' and turned out to be the name of both the town and the lake it sits on. Slightly confusingly, this body of water is actually called 'Geneva Lake' but, all the same, from what I gathered from lifelong Midwesterners, both Illinoisans and Wisconsinites considered the area a weekend-getaway paradise. Situated about an hour from Milwaukee, Madison, and Chicago, it drew many visitors seeking a break from city life.

Not one for tourist traps, I initially stayed away from Lake Geneva. Yet I never stopped hearing stories about it, two of which intrigued me. First was the mailboat that delivers the post to shoreline homes. Its primary appeal is that, each summer, teenage staff get the privilege of 'mailboat jumping'; that is, delivering and collecting mail by hopping on and off the moving boat as it arrives and departs without stopping. It is, by all accounts, a hoot, with more than the occasional jumper ending up in the water.

The second story was that of the Geneva Lake Shore Path. The name tells you most of what you need to know; that it's a

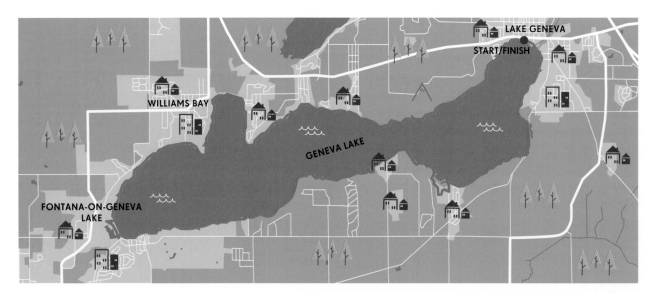

LAKESIDE LIVING

Of the 1000 homesteads on the lake, the most notable in size and architecture are Stone Manor, the largest estate on the lake and made of Bedford limestone; Driehaus Estate, a Georgian-style home built in 1906; and Alta Vista, a massive Italianate estate completed in 1920. The shore path takes you up close and personal with these properties and more, many of which have been maintained (or fully restored) for more than a century.

Left to right: life on the water at Lake Geneva; lakeside paths and secluded mansions tempt you further; urban distractions. Previous page: fall colors at Lake Geneva, Wisconsin

22-mile (35km) path circumnavigating the entire lake. But it doesn't tell the whole story. For that, you need to go back to 2500BC, when multiple Native peoples called the lake home. Spread across three principal settlements that existed in the area, their residents also traveled by boat, navigating their way along the shoreline.

Another key chapter in the path's history relates to the Great Chicago Fire of 1871, after which some of the city's very wealthiest residents sought land to build summer getaways. They chose Lake Geneva and, in a period Mark Twain dubbed the 'Gilded Age', by the turn of the 20th century the entirety of all lakefront property was owned by just 40 people. The kind of private ownership which, in America, is invariably signaled by 'Keep Out' signs, in these parts it came with an altruistic twist.

For instead of fencing off the lake and their homes, it was declared that a 20ft-wide (6m) strip of land extending from the shoreline be considered public domain. More than 150 years of development later, and now with more than a thousand homes on the lakefront, the decree still stands. This allows residents

and visitors alike to circumnavigate the lake, so long as they respect the properties they pass.

When I ran the trail the first time, I thought I was lost almost as soon as I started. Heading counter-clockwise out of Lake Geneva, when the public park ends confusion begins. With my mind trained to follow a sidewalk, it takes some adjustment to pass through a thin gap between bushes and a fence – and straight into someone's backyard.

On this run, fighting convention is the name of the game. Essentially, you run through countless backyards, one after the other. There are no fences to hop and homeowners are required to keep the 'path' clear. I use quote marks because this is a trail unlike any other. While some paved sections offer direction, other stretches are simply open areas of grass or dirt. Worn-down patches offer an indication of where to go but otherwise you just hug the lakefront.

None of which make it feel any less invasive or awkward, at least for the first few trips around the lake. After all, would you want someone wandering through your backyard? Probably not. Once free of such thoughts, however, you get to enjoy the run for what it is.

The fastest recorded times on this route are 2:21:43 for men and 2:36:32 for women. However, rather than beating the clock, this run is all about embracing a Midwest-vacation vibe. Above all, that means slowing down (occasionally chowing down) and taking in the sites.

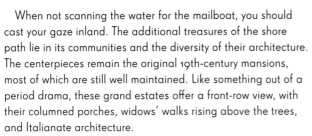

When not scanning the water for the mailboat, you should cast your gaze inland. The additional treasures of the shore path lie in its communities and the diversity of their architecture. The centerpieces remain the original 19th-century mansions, most of which are still well maintained. Like something out of a period drama, these grand estates offer a front-row view, with their columned porches, widows' walks rising above the trees, and Italianate architecture.

Between these historic landmarks you'll find an eclectic mix of architectural influences: Victorian, mid-century modern, Cape Cod. While some are set back hundreds of yards from the shore, others are so close to the lake's edge you'll run right past them.

Even with a comfortable pace, it's easy to work up an appetite over 22 miles (35km) with 300ft (91m) of elevation gain. When I'm not in a rush, I stop to enjoy a snack in the towns I pass through. There are three that line the water: Lake Geneva, Williams Bay, and Fontana-on-Lake Geneva. I typically start my runs in Lake Geneva, the largest of the three and the easiest to access. Along the way, it's hard not to stop for a bite in Fontana at Chuck's Lakeshore Inn or Gordy's; in Williams Bay, meanwhile, there's Harpoon Willie's and Steamers Coffee Shop. Finally, back in Lake Geneva, I recommend Oakfire's wood-fired pizza for a post-run treat. So many backyards later, it's the very least you deserve. **DD**

Start/Finish // Lake Geneva Riviera
Distance // 26 miles (42km)
Getting there // Lake Geneva has three major airports within driving distance: Milwaukee Mitchell International (50 minutes), Chicago O'Hare (70 minutes), and Chicago Midway (90 minutes).
When to go // Summers in Wisconsin are unbeatable, with lots of sunshine from late June through September.
Where to stay // The three main towns have rentals and hotels available in all. The most popular is Lake Geneva, whose bustling downtown has abundant shops and restaurants.
What to wear // Road or trail shoes work on this path and there is no technical terrain.
Things to know // Parking in the warmer months can be a nightmare. Best to park a couple blocks off the main roads or start at one of the many access points around the lake. It is also customary in Wisconsin to celebrate a run with beers, brats, and cheese.
More info // visitlakegeneva.com

Opposite: downtown Fish Creek and its marina in Door County; sunset over Lake Michigan in the Indiana Dunes National Park

MORE LIKE THIS
RUNS BESIDE MIDWEST LAKES

DOOR COUNTY

Another popular Wisconsin vacation spot. Located on a peninsula just above Green Bay, you'll find some of the clearest waters on Lake Michigan and even a designated Dark Sky reserve for stargazing. The Fall 50, an annual 50-mile (80.4km) road race, is held here in October but the area has plenty to offer in spring and summer, too, thanks to Peninsula State Park. One of Wisconsin's most popular parks, most runs here take you along the bay, through woodlands and also connect to the nearby town of Fish Creek and the village of Ephraim. Each has its own distinctive Midwestern charm and offers great places to stop for a bite to eat. Take Shore Rd through the park and the total route is about 10 miles (16km), point to point, between the two downtowns. There are various ways to shorten that distance using other paths in the park.

Start // Downtown Fish Creek
Finish // Downtown Ephraim
Distance // 10 miles (16km)

3 DUNE CHALLENGE, INDIANA DUNES

Located on the shores of Lake Michigan, Indiana Dunes National Park is home to long, sandy beaches whose towering dunes look out across the lake to the Chicago skyline. If you fancy a run on the sand, there are nine different beaches in the park. There's also the Calumet Trail, a flat point-to-point run of 10 miles (16km) with the added bonus, if you start early enough, of a beach day to follow. One of the area's most popular attractions is the 3 Dune Challenge. This 1.5-mile (2.4km) route takes you up – and down – the park's three tallest dunes, each higher than the previous: Mt Jackson, with an elevation of 176ft (54m); Mt Holden (184ft/56m); and finally Mt Tom (192ft/57m). If the increments don't sound too daunting, the loose sand and inclines of 40 degrees will certainly test your legs.

Start/Finish //Dune Acres, Indiana
Distance // 1.5 miles (2.4km) for the Challenge; 10 miles (16km) for the Calumet Trail

MACKINAC ISLAND, LAKE HURON

Where the upper and lower peninsulas of Michigan meet, there is an island on Lake Huron. Its original name is 'Mitchimakinak', in Ojibwemowin, meaning 'big turtle', due to the island's shape. It later became Michilimackinac, a name given by the French, before the English called it Mackinac. The island has had many lives: a sacred place for the Anishinaabe people who first inhabited the island; a trading post for French settlers; a site of battles during the War of 1812; and a cozy community on an island with zero cars. Taking a ferry across, you'll find a buzzing downtown in the warmer months with shops, restaurants, and lodging. You'll also find an 8-mile (13km) route around the entire island that never leaves the shoreline. The views, history, and parks are best experienced with an uninterrupted lake breeze. You'll see quickly why the entire island is on the National Historic Registry.

Start/Finish: In town on the south side of the island

WEST USA

SOUTH BOULDER CREEK TRAIL

Barbara Noe Kennedy celebrates the best of the West on this wildlife-rich trail in the shadow of Boulder's iconic Flatirons.

More than 20 years ago I moved east, from California to Washington, DC, for an internship that turned into my dream job at National Geographic. But I never shook the loss of being away from the West, its towering mountains, earthy pine forests, and emerald lakes. So, after I married David in 2014 (and whose brother, Mike, lives in Boulder, Colorado), I suddenly began visiting the West once more. And each time I went, I sucked in lungfuls of fresh air, lost myself in views of the expansive Flatirons, and felt wholly alive.

And nowhere did I feel that more than when running the South Boulder Creek Trail, which locals (Mike included) tend not to think of as that big a deal. But as someone not lucky enough to live near such an amazing place, I'll tell you why it is. The South Boulder Creek Trail is 3.6 miles (5.8km) of winding, fairly flat gravel and dirt. It traverses a stunning green space burgeoning with wetlands, meadows, and grasslands, including a remnant of the plains cottonwood riparian ecosystem, and all important wildlife habitats. You can do an out-and-back through this sublime natural realm, or else connect with other trails along the way, to go as short or as long as you wish.

On good days, there are always a lot of people out running or hiking, ready with a friendly nod. I've run the trail in all seasons – except for one winter visit when a surprise snowstorm covered the town in a white mantle, preventing me from heading out, and making me wish I had cross-country skis. In spring, bluebells, shooting stars, and especially wild iris decorate the grasslands, while in summer, sunflowers bloom in clouds of yellow. Raptors soar overhead, and some visitors report spotting deer and foxes. I've read that the bobolink is a common ground-nester and though I'm not sure I've ever seen one, they arrive at the meadows in summertime.

Most often I run the trail alone but, on this occasion, David and Mike have joined me.

I like to start at the gate along Marshall Rd, near Foothills Hwy, because it's near my brother-in-law's house, but there are various other access points. As soon as I enter the open space, the car traffic fades away and the wide dirt trail reveals fluttering grasslands, gnarled oaks, and multihued wildflowers. My stride picks up and the only sound I hear is the crunch of my feet on the dirt path. I run with a sense of anticipation because, within minutes, I've entered the world of the prairie dog. These poor little guys never fail to amuse

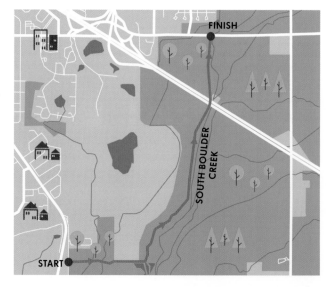

"As the car traffic fades away my stride picks up, and the only sound I hear is the crunch of my feet on the dirt path"

me; they should be used to runners and walkers given the numbers of us that pass through their homeland but, as you approach, they always become frenetically active.

Several stand sentinel with noses in the air, sniffing for danger and emitting their high-pitched warning cries. I try to reassure them as I stop and watch them, darting from hole to hole until, eventually, they get used to my presence and begin to relax. I pry myself away and, from here, the trail passes beneath a copse of oak trees – a welcome patch of shadowy coolness on hot summer days – and crosses over two waterways, Bear Creek Ditch and Dry Creek Ditch Number 2. The burbling waters run cool and fresh, their currents rippling in the sunlight, and eventually they will flow into South Boulder Creek.

We veer north, with South Boulder Creek to our right and flower-dotted meadows all around. The spectacular Flatirons rise in the distance, a view that truly takes my breath away (or maybe it's the 5000ft/1524m elevation). These striking, red-brown sandstone formations are one of Boulder's most iconic landmarks, named for their resemblance to clothes irons standing on end. Side by side, the peaks top out at between 6900ft/2103m and 7630ft/2325m and from this vantage I can take in the massive wall in all its lofty grandeur. Part of their appeal is that they're ever-changing, a radiant red in summer or frosted with snow in winter. Toward the end of the day, they take on a shadowy glow as the sun creeps behind them, sending fingers of golden light between the ridges.

If the Flatirons weren't enough, in the distance I spy Longs Peak, one of Colorado's majestic 'fourteeners', those mountains higher than 14,000ft (4267m). Specifically, a renowned 14,259ft (4346m) peak that has attracted climbers since the late 1800s. I, however, am happy to view it from afar. The trail continues, past a dilapidated barn and cornflower-rich grasslands, South Boulder Creek a constant companion and all painting a stunning Western scene. On hot days, I've seen young families picnicking along the creek's shores as kids wade into the stream. In colder months it becomes icy, carrying on its way regardless of whether humans are there or not.

Eventually, the trail passes beneath US Hwy 36 and South Boulder Rd before continuing on. Depending on how I feel, I turn around after 1.5 miles (2.4km) or 3.5 miles (5.6km). Whatever the case, the trail offers the gift of sublime nature in the heart of the urban landscape, precisely the reason it's an epic run. And it's not just me who thinks this an extraordinary place; by way of endorsement, in October 2023, this space was designated the official South Boulder Creek Natural Area, in recognition of its rich biodiversity. **BNK**

THE PRAIRIE DOG DILEMMA

Prairie dogs divide opinion. Besides being cute, they're a food source for coyotes and raptors, and their tunnels provide homes for snakes and burrowing owls. Detractors argue they threaten agriculture and open city spaces. Boulder's efforts to control prairie dogs began in 2022; they've since repopulated 6% of the land they were removed from, and occupy 8 sq miles (20 sq km) of the city's urban spaces.

Clockwise from top: looking south from Boulder toward the Flatirons; running the South Boulder Creek Trail; Colorado wildflowers in spring; an alert prairie dog. Previous page: the Flatirons around South Boulder

Start/Finish // Marshall Rd, off Foothills Hwy (and other points of entry)
Distance // 3 miles (5km), more if you wish
Getting there // Denver International Airport is an hour's drive to the trailhead.
When to go // The trail is runnable year-round but best done May through October.
What to wear // Dress for the weather, which is highly changeable between seasons.
Where to stay // St Julien Hotel & Spa and Hotel, Boulder.
Where to eat // South Side Walnut Café has homestyle American breakfasts and specialty coffees.
More info // Boulder Tourism Office: bouldercoloradousa.com

Opposite: the Mississippi River from Barn Bluff Trail; running the Chesapeake & Ohio Canal Trail

MORE LIKE THIS
WILDLIFE-RICH ROUTES

BARN BLUFF TRAIL, RED WING, MINNESOTA

Incorporating several trails (Midland, South, Prairie, Quarry, and North), this popular double loop kicks off with a steady, quad-burning climb as you make your way up 340ft (104m) Barn Bluff – including several sets of steps. As you get higher and higher, the views get better and better: breathtaking glimpses of the town of Red Wing; barges chugging up the Mississippi River; with luck, bald eagles and hawks soaring overhead; and migrating birds. Indeed, this portion of the Mississippi Flyway is one of the country's best places for viewing fall and spring bird migrations. Autumn has the additional advantage of fiery foliage colors. The Dakota people, who called the bluff He Nmi Can, considered the place sacred thanks to the presence of ancient burial mounds. The area is often windy, and the North Trail can become icy in winter.

Start/Finish // Small parking lot off E 5th St, Red Wing
Distance // 2.9 miles (4.7km)

CHESAPEAKE & OHIO CANAL TRAIL, WASHINGTON, DC

This historic canal towpath along the Potomac River, once the domain of mule-pulled canal boats, runs for 184.5 miles (297km) from Georgetown in Washington, DC, to Cumberland, Maryland. Today, the crushed, flat, gravel pathway provides the perfect place for a short – or long – run. You'll spy lock ruins, historic toll houses (several of which can be rented overnight), and picturesque river towns. Though most of the time, you're submerged in a woodsy, riverine realm alive with songbirds, deer, and red fox; spring wildflowers are sublime. You can choose any distance you like, but for a good run from DC, head up to 15 miles (24km) to Great Falls Tavern Visitor Center, where you can take historic tours and hop aboard a restored canal boat for a ride through a lock. For a shorter run, turn around at Fletcher's Boathouse (mile 3.1) or the Capital Beltway (mile 9.3).

Start // Off Water St, Georgetown
Finish // Great Falls Tavern Visitor Center
Distance // 15 miles (24km)

TONY KNOWLES COASTAL TRAIL, ANCHORAGE, ALASKA

Extraordinary views of downtown Anchorage, the Chugach Mountains, and, on clear days, snow-capped Denali, are the rewards of this paved, multiuse trail. But even more thrilling is the potential sighting of moose, beluga whales, bald eagles, and other wildlife. Starting in the heart of downtown Anchorage, the mostly flat trail scampers along the city's jagged coastline overlooking Cook Inlet and through pine-scented forests. You can go as far as Kincaid Park at Anchorage's western tip (though, of course, it's perfectly acceptable to turn around sooner; there are plenty of entry and exit points). Along the way, Earthquake Park showcases exhibits about the devastating earthquake that struck Anchorage in 1964; and Westchester Lagoon is a favorite spot to spy red-necked grebes and Canada geese. Note: don't jump off the trail and comb the beaches; the quicksand-like mudflats can be deadly.

Start // 2nd Ave at Cook Inlet
Finish // Kincaid Park
Distance // 11 miles (18km)

THE BIG SUR MARATHON

California's ruggedly stunning Highway 1 is a race venue that's perfect for deep thinking and self-reflection – if you can forget about the quad pain, that is.

© Courtesy of Big Sur Marathon Foundation / Ian Higuera

I t was mile 22 (35.4km) when I hit the wall. I remember it pretty clearly. My calves pulled up into a sinewy ball, muscles went into spasm, and I felt like I could no longer breathe. I had survived the brutal 2-mile (3.2km) ascent to Hurricane Point, and sailed across Bixby Bridge, spurred on by vast ocean views and the sound of crashing waves. Yet, here I was, with one last steep climb and just 4 miles (6.4km) to go, and finishing no longer seemed possible. Making matters worse, in that moment, it felt like if I didn't finish I'd probably end up in a life of ruins.

You see, the reason I was running the Big Sur Marathon along California's central coast in the first place was because life wasn't going quite as planned. I was in what you might call a rut. Heck, some might even say my life was a shambles. I was overweight, single, and inspired by nothing. My assets in life amounted to the computer I used for a job I didn't love and some debt. I was a beat-down 30-something writer and emergent alcoholic. Worst of all, I was starting to feel numb to it all.

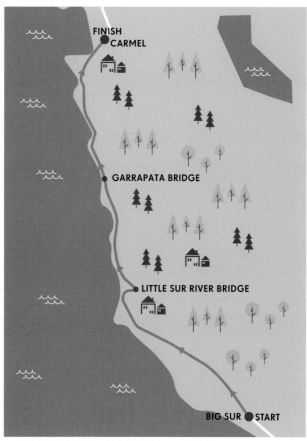

Perhaps more out of survival instinct than intention, I turned to the one thing in my life that had always remained a constant companion: running. My friend Brian had always had this beautiful poster of the Big Sur Marathon hung on his office wall. One day, I asked him if I could have it; the very next day I showed up to my own office with the poster in hand, and promptly hung it right beside that damn computer. And it stayed there for three full months as I trained for the 26.2-mile race that allows VIP access to one of the most beautiful stretches of highway on Earth, completely devoid of cars between the villages of Big Sur and Carmel, a stretch that is normally swarmed with road-trippers.

The Big Sur International Marathon hosts roughly 4500 runners, mostly from other states and countries. No one comes here to set any records or qualify for anything. Runners come to simply soak in the ocean views, rolling hills and rugged coastal wilderness.

The race's motto is 'running on the ragged edge of the western world'. Ragged is another way of saying it's really hilly. It has 2182ft (665m) of elevation gain and 2528ft (770m) of loss – it's not the race to try for that personal record. It's a run where you tune into the sounds of huge waves crashing against tall rock cliffs of tungsten and orange, where you can stare out across coastal mountains that ripple with verdant green ferns and redwoods so tall they seem to touch the sky. Even my training regimen began to lift me out of my malaise.

I was able to prep for all those hills with a few of my old familiar routes around my house, in the funky college enclave of Berkeley, a few hour's drive north from the race's start. I also made regular training trips up around the gorgeous stone buildings and quads of the University of California campus, as well along the paved trails of Inspiration Point in Tilden Park. Eventually, my body began to feel tighter, stronger. More importantly, my mind was clearer. Despite the fact that I had never run a marathon, and that my longest training run had only topped out at 18 miles (29km), I even felt ready.

On race day, I mingled among the other runners, including a handful of elites up front, a few diehards who use the Big Sur Marathon as a way of training for another upcoming race, and then, of course, a bunch of middle-of-the-packers, like me. Shivering with excitement and slightly chilly from California's icy coastal mist, we huddled together, talking about race strategies. My stated goal was simple: to finish. However, secretly, I wanted to do it under 4:10 so I could beat my friend Brian's time.

The race began slightly inland, but when California's glorious coastline finally revealed itself, the runners let out a collective gasp. The pace even picked up, and there were a few whoops and cheers.

At the midway point is Bixby Bridge, perhaps one of the most famous landmarks along the way. Race organizers had tuxedoed musicians playing on grand pianos here to energize us for the

back nine. The curving bridge provides what are perhaps the best panoramic views of the coast along the course.

Right about the time the views start to get monotonous in their beauty, there is more live music and some costumed race fans cheering us on from the sidelines. But there are also a few runners lying splayed out in front of the first-aid tents. That's exactly when I began to think about my own precarious state.

I stopped momentarily to take a deep breath, stretch my calves and scarf down a banana. Then I began moving again. Not fast, just forward. One step after another. I looked up at the clouds in the sky, then down to the crashing waves. I looked back at vaulting mountains behind us. That's when the proverbial lightbulb appeared. I actually began gaining speed. Working through it. Finding what I guess you could call 'the now'.

My mile 22 catharsis came and went in the blink of an eye. As I moved through the final miles I realized that, while I was here with 4500 other people, I was actually running this race alone. Likewise, my dissatisfaction with the world around me – my job, my computer – was about me. And if I could only focus on the me in every moment of every day, just as I was here in every step of this race, I knew I'd be OK. Some might call this runner's high.

Whatever it is, it freed my mind to take in the powerful beauty of the coast all the way to the finish. More importantly, it allowed me to finish that race in a Brian-beating 4:02:00. **GB**

Clockwise from left: runners on high; clifftop views keep things exciting; some hills help, most hurt; the coastal road is rarely closed to cars. Previous page: Bixby Bridge marks halfway

RACE WITH A VIEW

Big Sur Marathon founder Bill Burleigh was a Superior Court judge who commuted between Big Sur and Monterey every day. On his way home, Burleigh always passed a sign that indicated Big Sur was 26 miles away. Then lightning struck. The recreational runner who had never finished a marathon himself decided to test the waters. The first run took place in 1986.

"No one comes here to set any records or qualify for anything. Runners come to soak in the ocean views and rugged coastal wilderness"

Start // Big Sur, California
Finish // Carmel, California
Distance // 26.2 miles (42km)
Getting there // Monterey has an airport, but flights are cheaper to San Jose or San Francisco (100 miles/160km and 130 miles/210km north, respectively). There are shuttles to the start, from Carmel and Monterey.
When to go // Last Sunday of April.
Where to stay // Big Sur has some of the most beautiful campgrounds in the world, as well as some of the most honeymoon-worthy – and expensive – hotels in the world. More modest B&Bs can be found in Carmel or Monterey.
Things to know // Leave a few days to explore the coastal redwoods, killer restaurants, and Monterey Aquarium.
More info // bigsurmarathon.org

Opposite: cliffs and ocean views of
Acadia National Park, Maine

MORE LIKE THIS
RUGGED US COASTAL RUNS

OUTER BANKS MARATHON, NORTH CAROLINA

The Outer Banks is a string of barrier islands off North Carolina offering spectacular coastal views and amazing sand dunes. The Outer Banks Marathon starts in Kitty Hawk – where the Wright Brothers flew their way into the history books with the first powered flights – then cuts through the Nags Head Woods Ecological Preserve on a hard-packed dirt road, before heading out for several miles below the East Coast's largest sand dunes. The final miles take you rocketing past the arching Washington Baum Bridge and Roanoke Island.

Start // Kitty Hawk
Finish // Manteo
Distance // 26.2 miles (42km)
More info // outerbanks.com

MT DESERT ISLAND MARATHON, MAINE

With over 1500ft (450m) of ascents, this hilly marathon passes through six gorgeously preserved New England villages surrounding Maine's Acadia National Park. Runners will see the East Coast's only fjord, Somes Sound, and quintessentially New England scenes of golden trees, misty coasts and centuries-old maritime villages. It all starts in downtown Bar Harbor, heads over the ridges of the Champlain and Dorr Mountains, past the rugged cliffs and headlands of the island's southeast tip. It all ends with a fast mile-long descent to the charming village of Southwest Harbor, and a cup of piping-hot clam chowder.

Start // Bar Harbor
Finish // Southwest Harbor
Distance // 26.2 miles (42km)
More info // runmdi.org

CAPE LOOKOUT, OREGON

This rugged 4.7-mile (7.5km) out-and-back takes you through mossy fern forests and cedar groves, to a lookout over the Pacific Ocean. Fallen logs and slippery roots add some fun technicality and gentle switchbacks ease the climbing. Expect rain and mud – it is the Pacific Northwest, after all – and embrace it as you continue on for spectacular views of the cape, 400ft (122m) drops down to the sea, wildflowers, and the final vista, which feels like the edge of the world. The trail is easily accessed from Tillamook, Oregon, where you'll find world-famous cheese factories and access to excellent hiking, kayaking, and other adventuring along this less crowded portion of Oregon's coast.

Start/Finish // Cape Lookout Trailhead
Distance // 4.7 miles (7.5km)
More info // oregonstateparks.org

GRANDJEAN & SAWTOOTH LAKE LOOP

Traverse this wilderness loop in Idaho's Sawtooth Mountains and discover why a whiskey milkshake is the recovery drink of choice.

Nerves flutter as we lie in our tent on the eve of our run. The South Fork of the Payette River gently murmurs outside as moonlight cascades through the trees, here on the 44th parallel north; it's no wonder the Sawtooth Wilderness is an internationally designated Dark Sky Reserve. We buried the crackling warmth of our fire hours ago and wiggle deeper into our bags in the hope of succumbing to sleep.

Specifically, we're in Grandjean, located a couple of hours northeast of Boise and 30 minutes south of Stanley. A seasonally populated canyon, life revolves around the modest Sawtooth Lodge. Outfitted with an equally modest restaurant, dry cabins, and campgrounds (including a geothermal pool), the wilderness access is unparalleled. Tonight, we are staying at the campground at the terminus of Forest Rd 524, about a half mile (0.8km) away from the main lodge.

Though Grandjean is our favorite family camp spot, we've left the kids at home this weekend. Our goal (the 'our' being myself, my spouse, and our ever-eager border collie) is to run a clockwise loop through the Sawtooth Wilderness, covering 20.4 miles (32.8km) with 4022ft (1219m) of elevation gain. We are equipped with the following:

CamelBaks of water, margarita-flavored energy chews, peanut-butter squeezes, sunscreen, extra layers, GPS, a suspicious mid-life determination, and, most importantly, dog treats.

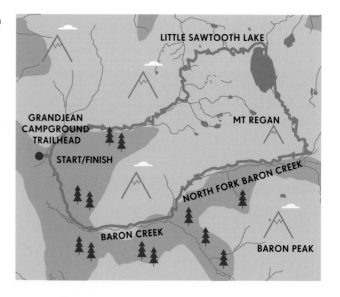

© Spring Images / Alamy Stock Photo

"Fallen trees force numerous detours and our quads burn with every squat under a tree limb, or a scramble over a trunk"

The morning of our run begins with steaming mugs of cheese grits and a trip to the pit toilets before we fill water bladders at the trailhead pump. A few cars line the parking area – likely overnight backpackers – but we suspect the lot will be overflowing by afternoon, when we return. The sound of a horse whinnying pierces the quiet, and my inner horse-girl smiles in delight.

A wide, sandy trail veers southeast along Baron Creek Trail but we are headed northeast, up reasonably graded switchbacks. This trail winds through knee-high meadows of delicate yellow columbine, fire-red Indian paintbrush, and waving purple lupine. On this section, runners can boast they've traveled part of the Idaho Centennial Trail, a once celebrated thru-hike that stretched from the state's southern to northern borders; the route is now all but disappeared due to a lack of maintenance and wildfires.

About a mile or two in, we break at a rock outcrop to squeeze in some peanut butter and prepare for a creek crossing. Safely on the other side, we encounter a fire-clearing crew. They step aside and we nod in gratitude, perhaps not realizing just how much gratitude their work truly warrants. The scent of fresh-cut wood permeates each deep breath, and my spouse and I become a little dizzy with the altitude and exertion. We're plodding along at over 7000ft (2133m) when we stop in unison, pointing ahead with the same question: 'Why are those deer wearing backpacks?' Upon closer inspection, the 'deer' are, in fact, pack-llamas accompanied by a fisherman, not an uncommon sight in this alpine lake region but a first for us.

We opt for another water break and study the map. In the upcoming sections, wildfire detritus makes navigation increasingly difficult. Fallen trees force numerous detours and our quads burn with every squat under a tree limb, or a scramble over a trunk. We aren't running anymore, simply trying to find our course. We use Observation Peak as a landmark and it eventually guides us back to our path. We continue climbing in relentlessly crappy conditions, with a full sun above and burnt forest as far as the eye can see.

On the final ascent, nothing positive happens except for this: in a moment of low morale, I tweak my ankle. Rather than check the injury, I attempt to unearth the guilty rock and throw it off the side of the mountain with a primal scream. Except this little ankle-twister is wedged in tight, impervious to my grunting efforts. The scene ends with cathartic laughter, a moment of comic relief.

SAWTOOTH LODGE

Sawtooth was built as a ranger station by Danish-born Emile Grandjean, Boise National Forest Supervisor from 1883 to 1922. After he negotiated with legislators to preserve the area, Grandjean's renown led to visits from a fellow outdoorsman, one Ernest Hemingway. During WWII, Sawtooth was occupied by the Civilian Conservation Corps, established as part of Franklin D Roosevelt's 1930s New Deal.

Clockwise from top: Sawtooth Lake; the trail gains altitude; alpine daisies and paintbrush wildflowers. Previous page: the North Fork Baron Creek Trail, south of Sawtooth Lake

© Nichimar / Shutterstock; J K Floyd / Shutterstock

© CSNafrger / Shutterstock

More assuredly, we crest 8800ft (2682m). With Sawtooth Lake finally in view, any ill will (even toward rocks) floats away on the breeze. I feel small but significant, tired but alive. I drop a pebble into Sawtooth Lake and concentric circles break the glass-like reflection of its surface: mountain peaks white with snow, a deep-blue sky free of clouds. The next few miles will be our favorite, filled with lush greenery and studded with one glacial lake after another.

We start the descent alongside North Fork Baron Creek and the overgrowth thickens. A splendid array of wildflowers and butterflies abound but our progress slows to bushwhacking. On our final creek crossing we head northwest, on Baron Creek Trail, back toward the campground. When we pass two riders trailing a third horse, I'm ready to throw myself across that Pinto rump, like a sack of potatoes. Instead, I grudgingly walk the last couple of sandy miles on my own two feet. Even pooch drags.

At Sawtooth Lodge, I use the changing-room shower to scrub away the trail dust and sweaty salt deposits. Then I step into the geothermal pool for the best soak ten dollars can buy. I sidle up to where the hot water is pumped in and rest my head against the pool's edge. The iconic, pointed crags of the Sawtooths are silhouetted against the fading light. My spouse pulls a flask from his towel and adds a healthy splash of whiskey to our huckleberry milkshakes. They are a hearty size and we scrape them dry, even after wolfing down loaded burgers from the lodge restaurant. I suspect we will sleep well in our tent tonight, the usual post-run balance of pain and pleasure tipped toward the latter by this moment of serenity. **KS**

Start/Finish // Grandjean Campground trailhead
Distance // 20.4 miles (32.8km)
Getting there // Both Boise (BOI) and Friedman Memorial (FMA) airports are a 2.5-hour drive to Grandjean Campground.
When to go // June through September, when temperatures are between 70-80°F (21-27°C); be prepared for snowy patches and tricky river crossings at any time of year.
Where to stay // Sawtooth Lodge (reservations required) or Grandjean Campground (first-come, first-served): sawtoothlodge.com/accommodations. Alternatively, Stanley, Ketchum, and Boise could also serve as your base camp and have the advantage of better amenities (read: showers, electricity, flush toilets).
What to pack // Water and/or water-pump (multiple creek and lake access points), trusted runner-friendly portable snacks, layers, sun protection, compass, and map/GPS; the area has no cell service.
Things to know // For full park regulations: sbbchidaho.org/pdf/sawtooth_reg.pdf

Opposite: the Stack Rock Trail near Boise

MORE LIKE THIS
OTHER IDAHO RUNS

RACE TO ROBIE CREEK
HALF MARATHON

With a placard marking the start line of 'the toughest race in the Northwest', this Idaho cult classic was first staged in 1978. Considered a rite of spring, local myths abound regarding this kick-off event to the area's racing season. Wild in more ways than one, yearly themes such as 'Staying Alive' and 'All Things Basque' crank up the fun. With volunteers providing 'whiskey courage' (and sometimes donuts) at the water stations, runners must first slog up the 2072ft (631m) climb to Aldape Summit, then suffer a pounding 1732ft (528m) descent to the finish. The race is held in April, with the start gun sounding at high noon. Registration is on President's Day in February, and spots fill within minutes.
Start // Fort Boise Park, Boise
Finish // Robie Creek Campground,
Boise
Distance // 13.1 miles (21km)

RIDGE TO RIVERS

Whether it's marathon training or a few undulating miles, the network of dirt paths linking public and private lands in the Boise Foothills provide solitude and time to appreciate nature. In fall, yellow blooms of rabbit brush and purple aster color the hills. In spring, pink mariposa lilies and arrowleaf balsamroot cheer an otherwise monochrome landscape; and very few fragrances beat the scent of sagebrush after rare desert rain. Start your run at one of several trailheads; locations include Camel's Back Park, Hulls Gulch, and the Military Reserve – each is popular for various distances and city views. Freddy's Stack Rock Trail (11.7 miles/18.8km) embarks from N Bogus Basin Rd and features a loop around Stack Rock, a prominent geological feature you can see from the Treasure Valley below. (Panoramic views of the valley are even better from Stack Rock.)
Start/Finish // N Bogus Basin Rd,
Boise
Distance // 11.7 miles (18.8km), out-
and-back
More info // ridgetorivers.org

TUBBS HILL

Never underestimate any nature trail accessible from a city center. Tubbs Hill Park and Nature Trail are located on a 165-acre (67-hectare) peninsula on the shores of Lake Coeur d'Alene. Pack a camera for this one because lake views are spectacular on this easy 2-mile (3.21km) loop. Begin at McEuen Park and follow the shoreline for a mile of mostly flat, lakefront trail; runners can even enjoy a quick beach break on the southwestern side of the loop. As the trail rounds the eastern edge of the peninsula, it begins to circle back through evergreen forest. Additional authorized trails and loops can be tacked on for more mileage but pay close attention to signage and stay on designated trails to help reduce damage and erosion to this popular nature reserve.
Start/Finish // Tubbs Hill Nature Park,
Coeur d'Alene
Distance // 2 miles (3.21km)

THE BADWATER 135

Due to its face-melting heat and altitude extremes, just reading about this iconic ultramarathon across the California desert will be harder than your morning run.

At mile 127 of the Badwater 135 ultramarathon, the pain I felt in my legs was no ordinary pain. It was an illuminating pain that, strangely, has lured me back to this race year after year. I'd say it's what lures a lot of us here. It's a pain that asks you who you are and who you want to be. No race on the planet cleanses mind and body quite like this one.

This was my sixth time running Badwater and yet I've never felt quite prepared for it. For some reason, knowing what's coming doesn't help. I'm always stunned when the car door opens at the start, exposing my prickly cool, climate-controlled skin to a veritable furnace blast. Fittingly, Badwater starts in Death Valley, California,

the massive desert region named by a group of pioneers who, in 1850, found themselves hopelessly lost here, with death being the almost certain outcome.

Badwater is designed to bring runners from the lowest point in the lower 48 to the highest point. Starting at Badwater Basin, racers plod along narrow desert highways all the way to Lone Pine on the east side of California's Sierra Nevada mountain range, before turning westward up to the top of Whitney Portal Rd at 8360ft (2548m), the base of the tallest peak in the lower 48 (the original course finished on the 14,505ft (4420m) summit of Mt Whitney until the park service shut it down due to safety concerns).

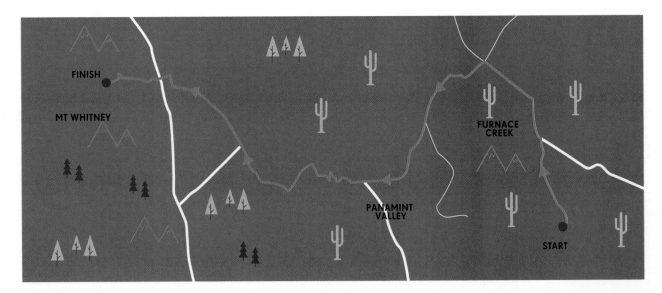

Even in the sport of ultrarunning, where the word 'extreme' is somewhat overused, the Badwater 135 stands out as a truly sadistic test of endurance. Considered by many to be the toughest footrace on the planet, its origin is firmly rooted in the age-old, ill-advised question: 'I wonder if I can do this?' Al Arnold, a fitness guru from Walnut Creek, CA, was the one asking and set off for an answer in the early 70s. Then, after two failed attempts, he successfully covered the distance in 1977, thus dooming hundreds of future adventure seekers to take on this same challenge. Despite running dozens of ultras through the years – even winning more than a few – I still consider the Badwater 135 to be the ultimate challenge.

As I arrived at the starting line of this latest edition my anxiety grew, and a familiar question arose: 'Do I really want to do this again?' It was mid-July, the hottest time of the year, because to race at some other time of the year would defeat the purpose. I guess you could say that purpose was to have such an intense clarifying experience that it would scrape out my insides and replace them with some deeper understanding of what I'm made of.

Every racer is required to bring their own support crew, as there are no aid stations along the course. Without a crew, racers might not survive the race, much less finish it. My crew were all rookies that year, but I was fairly confident they wouldn't let me die. Lined

> *"The pain in my legs was no ordinary pain – it was an illuminating pain that has brought me back, year after year"*

up at the start with my fellow adventurers, I glanced up to my right and saw the words 'sea level' scrawled on a rock face, 282ft (86m) above me. When the 10am start time arrived, we shuffled away from the line like a bale of turtles. I let the faster runners go ahead, reminding myself that Mt Whitney was a long 135 miles (217km) away and I should try to enjoy this early, relatively pain-free section. It wouldn't last for long. Not much later, my watch cruelly reminded me it was already 128°F (53°C). And that's the good news. The bad news was that the 200°F (93°C) surface temperature caused what I can only describe as a sort of open-space claustrophobia.

I moved through Furnace Creek and then past furrowed dunes on my way to Stovepipe Wells. It had taken 42 miles (67.5km) of slow gradual climbing just to reach sea level and this small town. Some racers were stripping down and jumping into a motel pool, but I just kept moving. I slogged my way through the 17-mile (27km) climb up to Towne Pass, 5000ft (1500m) above the desert floor. Then I scurried down the 10-mile descent to the Panamint Valley.

DOUBLE THE FUN

Distance is only half the challenge at Badwater, as the course crosses two mountain ranges for a cumulative elevation gain of more than 19,000ft (5790m). Nonetheless, there are a handful of men and women who have done what are known as the Death Valley 300 (a round trip), a Badwater Triple (three crossings) and even a Badwater Quad (two round trips).

From left: runners near the finish at Mt Whitney; dust devils; heat and dehydration are ever-present dangers. Previous page: temperatures in Badwater Basin can hit 130°F (54°C)

The setting sun meant mercifully cooler temperatures and the lavender sky was a beautiful reward for my hard work so far. As dusk turned to full dark, I was startled by a rattlesnake in the road. At mile 72, I passed the Panamint Springs Resort, then Father Crowley's Turnout, finally reaching mile 90 and the turnoff to Darwin, a small inhabited ghost town with a sign reading 'NO television, NO WIFI, NO cell signal, NO stores; visitors welcome.'

The pleasant 97°F (36°C) night-time temperature beckoned me to turn off my headlamp and take in the mind-blowing celestial show. A few hours later, dawn began to breach the horizon as I passed through the small mining town of Keeler, at mile 108. Up ahead was Mt Whitney and the stunning Sierra bathed in a dawn alpenglow.

I was fully energized as I finally reached Lone Pine at mile 122. The final, and arguably hardest, section of the race is this 13-mile (21km), 5000ft (1500m) climb up the foothills. As I made my way up, the temperature cooled and the wind picked up. Every S-curve through the towering pines brought a new view of the impossibly vast desert below. Then, the final turn revealed a small crowd near the finish line at 8300ft (2530m), causing me to unleash a hobbling sprint. It had taken me 26 hours and 15 minutes to get here. As I looked back one final time, I said to myself, 'Goodbye Death Valley – never again'. As I write this, I am currently signed up to run it at least once more. **CE**

Start // Badwater Basin
Finish // Top of Whitney Portal Rd, above Lone Pine, California
Distance // 135 miles (217km)
Getting there // Fly to Las Vegas, then drive 140 miles (225km) to Furnace Creek.
When to go // Third week in July.
Where to stay // The Furnace Creek Ranch (oasisatdeathvalley.com) is a good luxe option near the start. The Dow Villa Motel (dowvillamotel.com) has simple rooms near the finish in Lone Pine.
Things to know // Everyone focuses on the heat, but it's the dry air you have to worry about – start hydrating at least a week before your arrival.
More info // badwater.com

Opposite: welcoming the end of the Hardrock 100 Ultramarathon; training in Hawai'i

MORE LIKE THIS
GRUELING ULTRAMARATHONS

ARROWHEAD 135, MINNESOTA

The Arrowhead 135 takes place in the coldest part of winter in the coldest city in the lower 48 states, International Falls, Minnesota. The multipurpose Arrowhead State Trail is a mix of wide, flat trails and rugged, rolling hills with ice-cold lakes and streams. Expect to see moose and wolf tracks, as well as deer, lynx, foxes, and snowshoe hare. The southern section of the trail has vast areas of exposed rock and enormous boulders, detritus left behind from glacial erosion that ground down ancient mountain ranges. There are scenic vistas overlooking the lakes and old iron-ore mines, as well as massive stands of old-growth hardwoods. Pay attention and you might also spot osprey, snowy owl, and bald eagle nests along the way. The race ends near Lake Vermillion, but with a finishing rate below 50%, many racers find a warm place to bail out along the way.

Start // International Falls
Finish // Lake Vermillion
Distance // 135 miles (217km)
More info // arrowheadultra.com

HURT100, O'AHU, HAWAI'I

This trail race through the rainforests above Honolulu requires near-Biblical levels of endurance; not for nothing are the official race guidelines dubbed The Book of Hurt. Specifically, it's a course of 100 miles (160km), spread over five circuits that include 24,500ft (7468m) of elevation gain, along narrow forest trails choked with roots and rocks, while stretches offering respite from ground obstacles feature exposed ridges and near-vertical embankments. First staged in 2001 by the fledgling Hawaiian Ultra Running Team, the event went on to foster a tight-knit community of die-hards, not dissimilar to those found surfing on Honolulu's nearby beaches. With a 36-hour time limit, the field is restricted to 125 participants, with about 500 hopefuls vying for places. Entries are organized via a 'kukui nut' voucher system, earned via a range of criteria (including spending years on the waitlist without ever being selected). Should you make it to the start, you can rely on the services of the 'HURT Patrol' to steer you to the finish. This team of six HURT veterans is on hand to guide stragglers through tough periods, physical and mental.

Start/Finish // Honolulu, various
Distance // 100 miles (160km)

HARDROCK 100 ULTRAMARATHON, COLORADO

Founded in 1992 and one of the toughest ultramarathons in the world, the Hardrock may not boast the gonzo craziness of the Barkley but that's likely to be the last thing on the minds of competitors as they face the extreme elevation of the San Juan mountains, which has made the Hardrock 100 infamous. Starting (and finishing) in the town of Silverton, the Hardrock's 100-mile (160km) course travels through 13 mountain passes that stand between 12,000ft and 13,000ft (3658m and 3962m), and includes a high point, at Handies Peak, of 14,048ft (4281m). Along the way, runners must negotiate snowfields, scree slopes, and other technical terrain, and all within a 48-hour cut-off. The course record, set in 2022 by Spain's Kilian Jornet Burgada, is an impressive 21:36:24; the average finisher gets home in a little over 41 hours, invariably overnighting. Whether you're speedy or steady, all must kiss the 'hard rock' – a ram's head painted on a large boulder – which constitutes the race's finish line.

Start/Finish // Silverton
Distance // 100 miles (160km)

THE PIKES PEAK ASCENT

With more than 7800ft (2377m) of elevation gain in just 13.3 miles (21km),
the Pikes Peak Ascent is one of the most challenging half marathons in the world.

As a Coloradoan now located in the Pacific Northwest, completing the Pikes Peak Ascent had become a bucket-list running goal as soon as I started training more seriously a few years ago. I'd run several half-marathons in the past but the Ascent, held annually in September, famously offers what no other trail half-marathon does – namely, 7815ft (2382m) of altitude gain. Starting in Manitou Springs at an elevation of 6300ft (1920m), the race course is essentially one giant hill-climb to the finish line, on the summit of Pikes Peak at 14,115ft (4302m). Each year, 1800 people toe the start line for the race – most finish but not in typical half-marathon fashion; most finish in twice the time of their usual half, give or take 30 minutes.

As race days go, mine started out relatively inauspiciously. That is to say, I did what I always do, which is to doubt that all of my training and preparation have had any effect whatsoever, and to spend copious amounts of time panicking over useless minutiae. I had spent countless hours running hills in my neighborhood in Portland, but none compared to the sight of Pikes Peak above me. In awe of the mountain and the great challenge it presented, I began to overanalyze my outfit. Would I be warm enough, or would I be too hot? (What if the aid stations ran out of water?) At one point, with speakers blaring for runners to make their way to the start, I stared down at my shoes, wondering if my extra 2mm of lug height would be the difference between me finishing the race

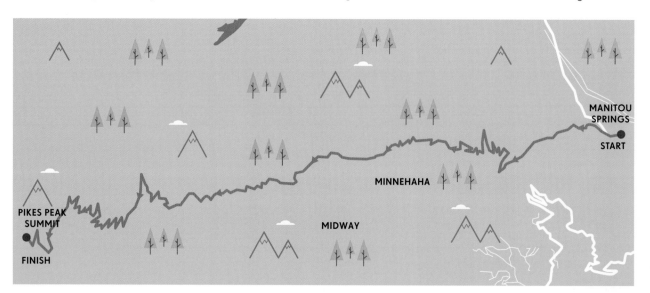

MANITOU
SPRINGS

START

MINNEHAHA

PIKES PEAK
SUMMIT

MIDWAY

FINISH

or getting stuck in the snow that was rumored to be blanketing the trail near the summit.

And yet, once the gun went off, the noise and anxiety became a low din as my body, followed by my brain, remembered exactly why running has become deeply important to me. And why the Pikes Peak Ascent had motivated me for the better part of a year.

Despite having lived in Colorado Springs (just north of Manitou) for almost 20 years, I had never summited the mountain of my childhood, nor had I taken part in the festivities of such an iconic event. The racers, the spectators, the energy of starting a new race in a familiar, meaningful place buoyed me with enthusiasm. As we ran through Manitou, past cheering fans and volunteers, my shoes gripped tight to the street, my hydration pack hardly wriggled, and I felt a surge of adrenaline-induced confidence. Plan A was a go; in my head, the Ascent was as good as finished. And then came the mountain.

Each year, rumors abound that the Ascent is a 'runnable' course because the altitude profile indicates only about 600ft (183m) of gain per mile. Challenging, to be sure, but doable. And each year, average runners like myself discover that those runnable portions of the course are few and far between, broken up by long stretches of hiking and, near the top, a zombie-walk to the finish line.

> *"Once the gun went off, my body, followed by my brain, remembered exactly why running has become deeply important to me"*

So there I was, approximately 3 miles (5km) in and already hiking, startled by the reality that moving mostly uphill for the better part of four hours at high altitude is, in fact, really hard. As I plodded through six, then eight, then 10 miles (16km), the group I was part of started to move with less energy; the enthusiasm with which I had run through the streets 6000ft (1829m) below had waned just like the oxygen in the mountain air.

A voice called from behind me: 'Anyone else starting to hallucinate a little bit?' I snapped my head up, awakened momentarily from my trance-like focus on the trail ahead. Due to a combination of the altitude, continuous climbing, and the confirmed presence of snow in late summer, things definitely felt a little hallucinatory. In spite of myself, or perhaps because of the ridiculousness of what I was doing – what we were doing – I laughed out loud. I couldn't help it, really, because at that moment I found it all hilarious. And strange. And beautiful. There we were, this worn-down group of professional sufferers,

PIKES PEAKS

In 1993, mountain-running legend Matt Carpenter famously set records for both the Pikes Peak Ascent and the Pikes Peak Marathon (see overleaf), on the same day. He ran the Ascent (as the first half of the Marathon) in a time of 2:01:06, then descended to notch a Marathon record of 3:16:39. Carpenter's Ascent was bested by pro trail runner Remi Bonnet's 2:00:20 in 2023; his Marathon record still stands.

Left to right: the Pikes Peak summit; you can get there by train, rally car or on foot; the Manitou Incline, a former cog railway; crossing the finish line in thin air. Previous page: scrambling to the boulder-strewn summit

shuffling up the side of a 14,000ft (4267m) mountain peak just for fun, a kind of silent camaraderie between us. This was not a new sensation, and yet it felt as fresh as the first time I'd experienced it – that peculiar joy at the convergence of suffering and beauty. At nearly 12,000ft (3658m) above sea level, reaching the point of exhaustion, enduring muscle fatigue and minor hallucinations, I took a moment to stop. Breathing deeply and taking in the ravishing beauty of an alpine landscape above the tree line, I noted a particular Colorado sensation, that of standing in snow while staring at a crystal-clear blue sky, sun bearing down on stark terrain.

Plan A was out the window. Plan B probably was, too. Moving as I was, the remaining 2 miles (3.2km) felt like 200 but that brief moment of pause on the trail, on the precipice of great personal accomplishment, gave me what I needed the rest of the way. Not a newfound sense of endurance or a latent talent for power-hiking but a simple appreciation of the privilege of treading where many others had before you. And the greater – yes, even epic – privilege of pushing yourself, totally spent, one foot in the front of the other, all the way to the summit. My new plan was Plan F – just finish, and on that day it was exactly enough. **TW**

Start // Manitou Springs
Finish // Pikes Peak summit
Distance // 13.3 miles (21.4km)
Getting there // Both Colorado Springs Airport (16 miles/28km) and Denver International (90 miles/145km) are within drivable distance of Manitou Springs, and offer shuttle/transit options.
Getting back // Ascent finishers are shuttled down from the summit to the starting area for post-race festivities.
What to wear // Given the altitude and exposed landscape, weatherproof gear is a must. Organizers update weather-related instructions close to race day.
Tours // Pikes Peak summit is accessible via car or train; the Pikes Peak Cog Railway operates daily to/from the summit.
More info // Registration: pikespeakmarathon.org. Given the Ascent's popularity, it's recommended signing up as soon as registration opens, usually March 1st.

*Opposite: the Garden of the Gods,
Colorado*

MORE LIKE THIS
THREE MORE ICONIC COLORADO RACES

THE PIKES PEAK MARATHON

The sister race to the Ascent, the Pikes Peak Marathon requires runners to turn around once they reach the summit and follow the same testing course back down to the start line. The Pikes Peak Marathon and Ascent are held over the same weekend but on different days; typically, the Ascent on Saturday and the Marathon on Sunday. Runners are permitted to compete in both races, otherwise known as 'the double', and both elite and recreational athletes are welcome to attempt this truly epic feat.
Start/Finish // Manitou Springs
Distance // 26.2 miles (42km)
More info // pikespeakmarathon.org

THE GARDEN TO PEAK CHALLENGE

A recent extension of the Pikes Peak events is the Garden to Peak Challenge. To complete it, participants must rack up two additional races, followed by either the Pikes Peak Ascent or Pikes Peak Marathon. The first supplementary event is the Garden of the Gods, a 10-mile (16km) race that takes place in the iconic Garden of the Gods Park, in Colorado Springs. The race is typically staged in June. The other event is the Barr Trail Mountain Race, a 12.6-mile (20.3km) out-and-back that takes place in July. The course runs from the Barr Trailhead up to Barr Camp and back, during which it offers a great insight into the challenges of running at high altitude, thanks to an overall gain of 7800ft (2400m). It's also worth mentioning that the Barr Trail, at its westernmost point, finishes on the Pikes Peak summit. Runners who complete the Garden of the Gods, Barr Trail Mountain Race, and a Pikes Peak event are eligible for exclusive awards – and serious bragging rights.
Start // Gateway Rd, Garden of the Gods Park (GotG); Barr Trailhead (BTMR)
Finish // Rock Ledge Ranch; Barr Trailhead
Distance // 10 miles (16km); 12.6 miles (20.3km)

KENNEBEC MOUNTAIN RUN

A lesser known yet similarly challenging race in southwest Colorado, the Kennebec Mountain Run is another gem in the Centennial State's trail-racing scene. Set in the rugged La Plata Mountains, Kennebec may be a smaller race but boasts a big-time course, weaving in a loop for 15 miles (24km) through the San Juan National Forest. Though longer than the Pikes Peak Ascent, the Kennebec Mountain Run is a little more forgiving on the altitude front, with just 3300ft (1006m) of elevation gain. That said, the course does top out at 12,200ft (3719m), at the top of Kennebec Pass, so a testing challenge followed by spectacular views of the surrounding landscape is pretty much guaranteed.
Start/Finish // La Plata Campground, Durango
Distance // 15 miles (24km)

MT ST HELENS 'BACKCOUNTRY RISE'

This trail-running course on Mt St Helens offers a unique opportunity to complete a race entirely within the renowned backcountry of the National Volcanic Monument, says Tyler Wildeck.

Of all the peaks in the Pacific Northwest, none stand out on the horizon quite like Mt St Helens. Looming above the Portland skyline, Mt St Helens profiles like a massive, snow-covered butte rather than a true volcanic peak. However, prior to 1980, Mt St Helens stood even taller – at 9677ft (2950m) and perpetually covered in ice and snow, it was one of the tallest peaks in the region. Until, that is, the May 18th eruption which led to a generational geological event and altered views of the Pacific Northwest forever.

When I first arrived at the start line of the 'Backcountry Rise', the area's 20-mile (32km) trail race, the first thing I noticed was the blast site. Located on Mt St Helens' northern flank, it looks as though a giant ice-cream scoop carved out half the peak. What happened, of course, is that when half the mountain collapsed during the 1980 eruption, it caused a landslide so explosive that 150 sq miles (388 sq km) of forest was either

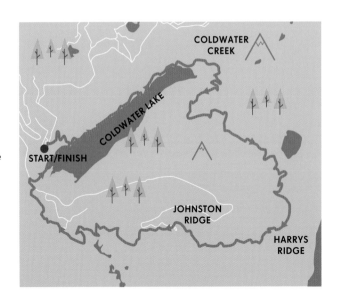

COLDWATER
CREEK

COLDWATER LAKE

START/FINISH

JOHNSTON
RIDGE

HARRYS
RIDGE

blown clean over or left standing and dead. Today, the slopes of Mt St Helens resemble a rocky graveyard more than flourishing mountain forests; the extreme conditions that so drastically reshaped the area resulted in the land being set apart for scientific research and, in 1982, designated a National Volcanic Monument. An acknowledgement of the formidable strength of the natural world, the monument was also designed to honor the memory of the 57 people who lost their lives in the eruption.

I learned all this while browsing in the Mt St Helens Science and Learning Center, the original volcano observatory for the region. It's also the unique (and highly informative) start line for a trail-running race, one that escorts runners to some of the remotest points in the Mt St Helens backcountry. First held in 2017, the race is an endurance challenge, to be sure, but also a real-time exploration of a natural landscape that has reinvented itself time and time again.

Those from the Pacific Northwest remember the day of the eruption with the kind of clarity reserved for extreme events. They recount how long the eruption seemed to last and how the ash created an eerie sensation of night during the middle of the day. And how, too, the lives of those lost in the largest volcanic eruption in North American history serve as a reminder that the power of the natural world often far supersedes our ability to conquer it.

I found 'Backcountry Rise' a profound experience, a way to explore this perilous connection by pushing my body to the limit in an environment that reminds me no matter how far I run,

"Some races are purely endurance challenges; some are so scenically beautiful it's hard to remember there's a race going on. This is both of these things and more"

how many early mornings I spend out on the trail keeping in shape, nature will always have the upper hand. I considered this as I made my way through the first few miles of the race, a mostly runnable section that skirted Coldwater Lake. Before the eruption, the lake had been named Coldwater Creek Canyon, but assumed its current form thanks to the landslide that more or less transformed the landscape instantaneously. Normally, I love connecting with nature when I run because of the comfort it can provide; the scenery, the wildlife, and the silence. But the further I ran into the Mt St Helens backcountry, the more I experienced a different kind of sensation. Not fear, exactly, but a kind of reverence for nature's resilience, the signs of which were all around me.

Never was this reverence more present than during my subsequent ascent of the most difficult climb on the course, a 4-mile (6.4km) section paired with a 2600ft (792m) increase in elevation. Predictably, any remaining warm sentiments regarding the landscape dissolved rather quickly, replaced only by heaving breaths, muttered curses, and sweat clouding

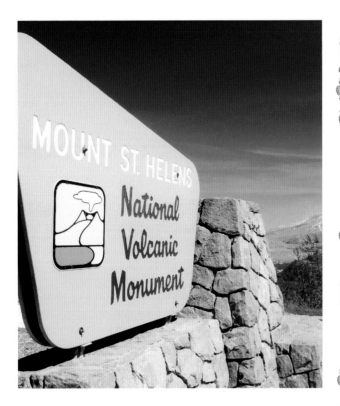

GIVING BACK

'Backcountry Rise' is not just a race but a chance to give back to the natural environment. A portion of race proceeds goes to the Mt St Helens Institute, which invests in critical wilderness research programs; while a partnership with the National Volcanic Monument allows for organized and sustainable trail maintenance here throughout the year.

Left to right: Coldwater Lake was created during the 1980 eruption; running Mt St Helens' Backcountry Rise; the National Volcanic Monument viewpoint. Previous page: wildflowers surround Mt St Helens

my vision. At one point, frustrated by the slowing pace but optimistic the summit would soon be reached, a runner next to me proclaimed optimistically: 'Only 13 miles left.'

So, my race of discovery became a race of endurance. And yet Mt St Helens rewarded my efforts with an unimaginably beautiful backcountry view: a glacially blue lake and a spectacular peak in the background. I couldn't help but pause, feeling as triumphant as I would at the finish line, still 10 miles (16km) away. For the rest of the race, in spite of the difficulty of the course, the stark beauty of the region was captivating, whether it was far-reaching vistas or the uninterrupted view of Mt St Helens itself, still towering over the surrounding landscape, continuing to morph and change even after nature's own cataclysmic intervention.

And even toward the end, after a long and testing downhill section, feeling spent as I stood at the bottom of the final, 500ft (152m) climb, craving a finish-line burrito, I couldn't help but imagine what the region must have looked like before. Different, surely, but beautiful all the same. And I imagined other runners, too, who ran through this backcountry long before me, and the versions of Mt St Helens they had seen, each as daunting and alluring as the view of it encountered.

Some races are purely endurance challenges; some are so scenically beautiful it's hard to remember there's a race going on. 'Backcountry Rise' is both of these things and more. It is a race unto itself – an epic adventure by definition and experience. **TW**

Start/Finish // Mt St Helens Institute Science and Learning Center, Toutle, WA
Distance // 20 miles (32km); race weekend also features a 50km (31-mile) race and a half-marathon
Getting there // The Center is accessible via paved road, though there's no public transport. It's about two hours from Portland, Oregon, or three hours from Seattle, Washington, both of which have international airports.
When to go // The race is typically staged in mid-August.
What to wear // Standard trail-running gear; many runners wear gaiters due to the loose, stony course.
What to pack // August is the hottest month of the year, with average temperatures in the low to mid 80s (26°C), so sunscreen is a must; a hat might also be a good idea.
Where to stay // Organizer Daybreak Racing (daybreakracing.com/backcountry-rise) procures special permits for registered racers to stay overnight in designated camping areas.
More info // Given the protected status of the surrounding landscape, racers must park and camp only at the MSH Science and Learning Center.

© neelsky / Shutterstock

*Clockwise from top: Crater Lake
viewed from Watchman's Peak; Mt
Hood and its Timberline Trail*

MORE LIKE THIS
VOLCANIC OREGON RUNS

DAYBREAK RACING'S 'WY'EAST TRAILFEST'

Staged on Oregon's most famous volcano, Mt Hood, the Wy'east Trailfest is a loop-style course that is suitable for anyone looking to explore the area's unique volcanic terrain. With three different distances available, this is a great event for runners of varying fitness levels, and while each course offers its own particular challenge, all share spectacular alpine views. An awesome venue for both fellow runners and supporters to hang out and cheer, the Mt Hood event is aimed at families with young runners; the 14k race is part of the USATF Mountain, Ultra, Trail Running Youth Initiative, a program run in co-operation with the American Trail Running Association (ATRA) and designed to increase participation in trail races among 14- to 18-year-olds, laying the foundations for excellence in future elite trail-running competitions.
Start/Finish // Mt Hood Meadows ski area
Distance // 14km (8.6 miles); 28km (17.3-mile) and 50km (31-mile) options available

TIMBERLINE TRAIL

For runners seeking a longer, less formal way to enjoy the Pacific Northwest's volcanic scenery, the Timberline Trail is one of Oregon's most famous backcountry expeditions. The 40-mile (64.3km) trail circumnavigates Mt Hood, offering picturesque views of the summit and the chance to encounter some of the region's most beautiful wildlife and seasonal flora and fauna. Some runners choose to break up the Trail into a couple of longer days, while others strive for the 'ultra' feat of completing the entire thing in a single day. The Trail can be entered and exited at multiple points, making it a great option for day trips as well.
Start/Finish // Various
Distance // Up to 40 miles (64.3km)

CRATER LAKE RIM RUN

The Crater Lake Rim Run has been held annually for 46 years (and counting) and continues to challenge racers from all over the world. Run on the scenic road circling the deepest lake in the United States, the event offers three race distances, all providing awe-inspiring views of Crater Lake National Park and the surrounding mountain peaks. Formed by the eruption of Mt Mazama nearly 7700 years ago, Crater Lake National Park is another example of the Pacific Northwest's unique natural history and provides the perfect backdrop for a challenging yet beautiful event. Due to Park permit requirements, participants are capped at 500 runners.
Start // Crater Lake Rim Rd (all races)
Finishes // The marathon finishes a few miles from Lost Creek Campground; the 6.7- and 13-mile races end on Crater Lake Rim Rd.
Distances // 6.7 miles (10.8km); 13 miles (20km); Marathon (42km)

Volcanic Oregon Runs

WHITE SANDS NATIONAL PARK

The bright, white gypsum dunes at this national park are like nowhere else on Earth, says Allison Burtka, and they make for an unforgettable run.

I've just walked up a steep, bright dune with my family, at White Sands National Park. At the top, it looks as if the rolling dunes go on forever. We're in New Mexico's Chihuahuan Desert, where the sand is so white it looks otherworldly, but inviting all the same.

We've got running shoes on, but we're not yet sure how runnable the surface is going to be. Loose sand can be frustrating and a park ranger we spoke to seemed to think that running on the dunes wouldn't exactly be fun. But my husband and I, along with our kids (a teen and a tween who run cross-country and track) like to run on trails. So, we decide to see how it goes.

We take off and the sand feels relatively solid under our feet. More compacted than it first appears, it doesn't feel at all like we're sinking, or churning up the terrain with every step. My kids increase to full speed, down the first hill and up another, until everybody's excited by just how unique this gorgeous landscape is. Traveling across dunes and ridges, sun shining all the while, it's exhilarating.

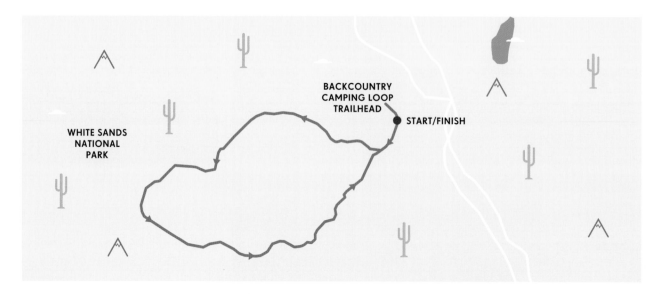

BACKCOUNTRY
CAMPING LOOP
TRAILHEAD

START/FINISH

WHITE SANDS
NATIONAL
PARK

© Courtesy of Allison Burtka

> *"We start running again and the sound of our feet striking the sand is satisfying. At the top of the dunes, all we can see in every direction are more crisp, white dunes"*

Unlike most sand, which is primarily quartz, the sand here is so much whiter because it's gypsum. White Sands is part of a 275 sq mile (712 sq km) gypsum dune field, the largest in the world. Which is, perhaps, why it feels like no place I've ever been.

Formerly a national monument, it became a national park in 2019. In the middle of our run, we stop for a water break and to admire the natural wonder around us. Beyond the dunes, the San Andres and the Sacramento Mountains look almost purple. We kneel down to touch the sand and notice it feels different from beach sand. It's cool, even though the sun is strong, and it doesn't stick to our skin and clothes like regular sand; I learn later that gypsum sand dissolves in water.

We start running again and the sound of our feet striking the sand is satisfying. At the top of the dunes, all we can see in every direction are more crisp, white dunes and, here and there, mountains in the distance. In some spots, the sand is dotted with short plants that must be especially hardy.

The route we're on is the Backcountry Camping Loop Trail although, technically, it's not so much a trail as a series of numbered posts to guide you around the dunes. Which seems kind of obvious, given the shifting sand prevents any trail from being maintained. We find that this is part of the adventure, trying to tell where the next post is and whether we're headed in the right direction.

Wherever we're on vacation, our family will usually find places to run. I feel like I experience a new place more fully when running through it, and breathing deeply, than I do any other way. The dunes do not appear to be a popular running spot – most people visit to hike, camp, and watch the sunsets. But for trail runners who don't mind uneven terrain and the challenge of hills, it's a special, if occasionally solitary, experience. Only after we finish the Backcountry loop do we see others out running, albeit on the main Loop Rd. It's flat and easier to run on, but the views are less exciting.

The Backcountry loop is 2.2 miles (3.5km), although we end up running 3 miles (4.8km), due to the back-and-forth nature of some stretches. At the park entrance, the main road is paved, with two lanes of traffic but not much of a shoulder; I wouldn't have felt comfortable running on that portion of it. Deeper into the park, however, the road widens and becomes hard-packed sand, with fewer cars. Later, driving on the sand feels strange, a little slippery, almost like driving on snow.

SECRETS OF THE SANDS

White Sands' gypsum comes from what was, millions of years ago, the Permian Sea. The shifting of tectonic plates caused mountain ranges to rise, including the gypsum-rich seabed. Water from melting glaciers then dissolved the gypsum and deposited it in Lake Otero. When most of that lake dried up, selenite crystals formed, which were in turn broken down into ever smaller grains before the wind shaped them into dunes.

Clockwise from top: the sand is 98% pure gypsum; the author making her mark; basic navigation aids; footwear for dunes. Previous page: the author setting off

We are at White Sands in early January, when the temperature is 55°F (12°C). It feels hotter than that but still comfortable – pretty much a perfect day. We bring plenty of water – and drink lots too – but clearly trying to run here in the summer would be treacherous, given highs can exceed 100°F (37.7°C).

Aside from its beauty, the park is historically and geologically significant. The gypsum is derived from an ancient seabed (see panel), subsequently carried upward by rising mountains, then washed down again in glacial run-off, into the Tularosa Basin. Humans arrived in the area about 11,000 years ago, hence the park also contains the world's largest collection of Ice Age fossilized footprints.

Once we've finished our run and caught our breath, we go to check out another trail up the road, Alkali Flat Trail. At 5 miles (8km), it's longer and flatter (the clue's in the name) than the Backcountry loop, and park rangers warn it's a trail on which it's easier to get lost. It's also worth remembering that twice a week, for an hour or two, the park and part of the nearby highway are closed for tests at the White Sands Missile Range, a US Army base (details are on the park website). As we leave the park in late afternoon, people are arriving to enjoy the sunset. That's something I'd love to do next time. On the plane ride home, I use the tracker to zoom in on the area where we'd been. The satellite image shows, amid the typical brown and green terrain, a huge white expanse. We won't forget the experience of running there. **AB**

Start/Finish // Backcountry Camping Loop
Distance // 3 miles (4.8km)
Getting there // El Paso International Airport (in Texas) is 98 miles (158km) away.
When to go // The colder months of the year, January through March.
What to wear // Light layers and sunglasses/hat. The sun is intense, reflected off the white sand, and it feels hotter on the dunes than it does in surrounding areas.
What to pack // A good hydration pack or water bottle, and sunscreen.
Where to stay // The small town of Alamogordo, 14 miles (22.5km) away, has a few hotels; Las Cruces, which is 52 miles (83.7km) away, has more hotel and dining options.
Things to know // The visitor center at the park's entrance is the only place to fill water bottles.
More info // nps.gov/whsa

*Opposite: Great Sand Dunes National
Park and the Sangre de Cristo mountains;
Michigan's Sleeping Bear Point*

MORE LIKE THIS
OTHER DUNE RUNS

SLEEPING BEAR DUNES, MICHIGAN

At Sleeping Bear Dunes National
Lakeshore in Empire, Michigan, the
Dune Climb is the main attraction, and
rightly so. The sand is loose, however,
and the climb is steep, so it's more
pleasant to hike than run. Several other
trails offer more runnable options and
the Sleeping Bear Point Trail is one of
them. With significantly less incline, only
part of the trail is on sand on this 2.8-
mile (4.5km) loop. Additionally, there's
a 0.5-mile (0.8km) spur that goes on to
Lake Michigan. The trail here passes
through a green forest and also a 'ghost'
forest (now-dead trees once covered by
shifting sands), and also offers great
views, both of the lake and Sleeping
Bear's other dunes.
**Start/Finish // Sleeping Bear Point
Trailhead
Distance // 3.3 miles (5.3km)
More info // nps.gov/slbe/
planyourvisit/trails.htm**

GREAT SAND DUNES NATIONAL PARK, COLORADO

At Great Sand Dunes National Park
and Preserve in Colorado, the dunes
are the tallest in North America. The
park encompasses many different hiking
options, with varied terrain over and
around the dunes. One of the forested
routes is Mosca Pass Trail, which is
3.5 miles (5.6km) one way. It begins
at Montville Nature Trail, which leads
0.5 mile (0.8km) through a wooded
area and the site, in the late 1800s, of
a former settlement. At its high point,
the trail has views of the dunes and the
wider San Luis Valley. A little further
on, the trail becomes Mosca Pass Trail,
running along a creek to a low pass in
the Sangre de Cristo mountains.
**Start/Finish // Montville Nature
Trailhead, Mosca
Distance // 3.5 miles (5.6km) each way
More info // nps.gov/places/mosca-
pass.htm**

OREGON DUNES NATIONAL RECREATION AREA, OREGON

Part of the Siuslaw National Forest,
the Oregon Dunes National Recreation
Area is notable for its widely varying
terrain; the landscape here includes
desert, forest, lakes, rivers, and ocean.
One option for runners is the Oregon
Dunes Loop Trail. Although parts of
the Oregon Dunes are open to off-
highway vehicles, this area is not. The
first 0.5-mile (0.8km) stretch is paved
and brings you to a viewing area. Next,
the trail passes into the dunes and out
to the beach, with post markers in the
sand. This part is fairly level and hard-
packed. At the ocean, turn south and run
along the beach for 1.5 miles (2.4km) to
an exit point that takes you back through
the dunes.
**Start/Finish // Oregon Dunes Day
Use Area, near Dunes City
Distance // About 4 miles (6.4km)
More info // fs.usda.gov/
recarea/siuslaw/recreation/
recarea/?recid=42465**

THE GRAND CANYON'S RIM TO RIM CHALLENGE

If you've ever had aspirations to hit off-road ultra-distances, few sights will inspire and ignite that extra gear quite like this one in Arizona.

S tanding on the edge of the Grand Canyon for the first time, I literally became weak at the knees. It was the night before I was going to attempt to tackle my bucket-list goal of running across the entire chasm and back with two friends – and yet my legs felt like noodles before I had taken a single stride.

This run is essentially an off-road ultramarathon with elevation gains and losses unlike any other in the world. Sure, some do this as an out-and-back – with a car waiting on the other side – but we were all in for the full 42-mile (67.5km) adventure.

After flying to Phoenix and picking up our rental car, we drove three and a half hours northwards with purpose, hoping to get our first glimpse of the 'Big Ditch' before the sun went down. We made it with 20 minutes to spare and scurried to an overlook at Mather Point. I actually felt my throat tighten and a lump start to form, as my legs started to ache. I couldn't even see the halfway point on the North Rim, but the view I did have was overwhelming enough.

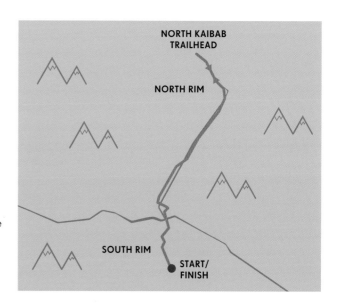

NORTH KAIBAB
TRAILHEAD

NORTH RIM

SOUTH RIM

START/
FINISH

Running across the Grand Canyon is known in running vernacular as Rim to Rim to Rim (or simply R2R2R) and it's one of the toughest trail runs in the world. I had previously run one 31-mile (50km) trail race, but it was mostly flat. I trained for months to prepare for nearly 21,000ft (6400m) of vertical gain and loss, including one workout that entailed running up and down a 2500ft (760m) mountain on a 6-mile (9.5km) loop – four times in a single day. And this still did nothing to prepare me for the debilitating heat. Temperatures here can soar to 120°F (49°C) in summer.

Anyone who has seen the Grand Canyon in person will agree that no photograph comes close to doing it justice. At 277 miles (446km) long, 20 miles (32km) wide and more than a mile (1.6km) deep, it's one of the most awe-inspiring views I have ever absorbed. Fortunately, when we started from the top of the South Kaibab Trail at 5.15am the next morning, it was pitch dark and all we could see was the light cast by our headlamps. That made this seem like an ordinary trail run with friends. What lay ahead, though, was actually a 4700ft (1430m) descent over 7 miles (11km) toward the Colorado River.

Running downhill on the smooth dirt was rather effortless, and it helped loosen up our legs in the surprisingly chilly weather. As soon as the sun began to rise, our focus shifted to the colorful sedimentary landscape that lit up as daylight broke. We were among blazing red and orange buttes, walls, and obscure rock formations created by ancient rivers and seas.

Just an hour in and we had already reached the bottom. We passed through a tunnel, roughly hewn through a massive granite outcropping, then rambled over a 440ft (134m) wooden-plank suspension bridge to reach the Phantom Ranch lodge, the only public accommodation at the bottom of the Grand Canyon. We pulled snacks from our backpacks and topped off our hydration packs at the first of five water pumps.

Once back on the North Kaibab Trail, my giddiness had burned off a bit as we jogged up mildly ascending gravel along Bright Angel Creek. We had now begun the daunting task of ascending 5700ft (1740m) over 14 miles (22km) to reach the halfway point at the North Rim. We passed the miles by soaking in the astounding red rock canyon scenery and spending long periods of time in solitary contemplation. We encountered a smattering of colorful wildflowers, massive yucca plants and cartoon-like agave stalks that towered 20ft (6m) into the air. By mid-morning, temperatures had reached almost 80°F (26°C), but constant cloud cover cast a merciful shadow.

We finally reached our turnaround point at about noon. It was so chilly and damp here we even put on our wind shells, knitted hats, and gloves for the descent. I hesitated for a moment, thinking that a one-way rim-to-rim run would have been sufficient to quell my adventurous quest. But all it took was a few strides back down North Kaibab Trail to know I'd be able to complete the journey.

ARE YOU R2R2R READY?

It takes most well-trained trail runners between 9 and 14 hours to complete the Rim to Rim to Rim run (R2R2R), across the Grand Canyon and back. But for perspective, Jim Walmsley, a professional runner from Arizona, did it in a record-shattering 5:55:20 in October 2016. The women's record of 7:52:20 was set by Colorado's Cat Bradley in early 2018.

From left: Kaibab National Forest near the South Rim; mule deer patrol the surrounding wilderness. Previous page: looking out over the Grand Canyon from the North Rim

That confidence carried me down the 14-mile (22.5km) segment back to Phantom Ranch with a bit of a spring in my step, even though by now temperatures had climbed back to about 90°F (32°C) and my legs were experiencing a new level of fatigue. We refilled our hydration packs and ate the last of our snacks. We had already covered about 35 miles (56km), but the vertical mile-high (1.6km) ascent over the final 7 miles (11km) of trail would prove to be the biggest challenge of the day.

As I pulled myself up South Kaibab, the first few miles jogging up the trail started out OK. But soon I was dragging and was reduced to a slow walking pace behind my faster friends. Every stair step on the trail seemed taller than the previous one and I began to wonder what would succumb first, my body or my mind.

Then, just as I was ready to sit down and give up, I suddenly remembered I had stashed a PayDay peanut caramel bar deep in a hidden pocket of my pack. I scarfed it down in three bites, took my last two gulps of water and within a few minutes I had renewed vitality and a fresh outlook. I suddenly felt like running.

Over the final mile or so, I ran with a consistent gait up the zig-zagging trail back towards the top of the South Rim, catching my flagging buddies along the way. Jogging side by side, we crested the final section of the South Kaibab Trail at 6.30pm. We high-fived and hugged. Of course, the day ended just as it had begun, as I stood on the edge of the Grand Canyon, weak at the knees. **BM**

Start/Finish // South Rim, Grand Canyon
Distance // About 42 miles (68km)
Getting there // Sky Harbor International Airport in Phoenix is 3½ hours from Grand Canyon Village; McCarran International in Las Vegas is 4½ hours away.
When to go // From March to April and mid-September to early November, all of the water spigots are turned on.
Where to stay // The Grand Hotel at The Grand Canyon, Tusayan, or Grand Canyon Lodge, North Rim.
Things to know // Carry at least $20 in cash just in case you need to buy additional food at the Phantom Ranch Canteen, at the bottom of the canyon.
More info // nps.gov/grca

From top: Acadia National Park; striding through the Observation Point Trail in Zion National Park

MORE LIKE THIS
US NATIONAL PARK EPICS

ACADIA NATIONAL PARK, MAINE

In 2017, trail runners Chris Bennet and Andrew Lombardi linked almost every high peak in this park on Mt Desert Island, including 1530ft (466m) Cadillac Mountain, and created the unofficial Acadia Mountain Marathon, a 26.2-mile trek with more than 7000ft (2100m) of vertical gain (not to be mistaken for the much mellower, and flatter, Mt Desert Island Marathon). That's a massive undertaking for most trail runners, but there are plenty of other trails ranging from 3 to 10 miles (4.8km to 16km) to explore. Just make sure you bring a rain shell as the Maine coast ranks second in annual precipitation to the Pacific Northwest.

Start // Lower Haddock Pond
Finish // Newport Cove
Distance // 26.2 miles (42km)
More info // acadiamountainmarathon. com

CUYAHOGA VALLEY NATIONAL PARK, OHIO

Boasting 125 miles (201km) of trails, this massive trail-runner's playground in northeastern Ohio is a stone's throw from several cities and towns in the Midwest. While numerous trails can be connected to run across the park, the Ohio & Erie Towpath Trail is an elegant 19.8-mile (31.8km) south-to-north route that was formerly used by mules from 1827 to 1912, as they pulled boats along the canal from Akron to Cleveland. Because it's an entirely flat route, it's as ideal for marathon training as it is a destination trail run.

Start // Botzum Trailhead, Bath Rd
Finish // Lock 39 Trailhead, Rockside Rd
Distance // 19.8 miles (31.8km)
More info // nps.gov/cuva

ZION NATIONAL PARK, UTAH

The most similar long-distance point-to-point run to running across the Grand Canyon can be found at nearby Zion National Park in southern Utah. While the arduous 48-mile (78km) northwest-to-southeast Zion Traverse is not for the weak of lungs, legs or heart, it's possible to run awesome out-and-back sections of that longer route, which includes the arduous run-hike up to Angel's Landing. Zion National Park boasts more than 130 miles (209km) of trails, and most of them offer distance glimpses or up-close viewing of the red rock geological features for which the park is known.

Start // Lee Pass, Kolob Canyons Rd
Finish // East Rim Trailhead, Hwy 9
Distance // 48.7 miles (78km)
More info // nps.gov/zion

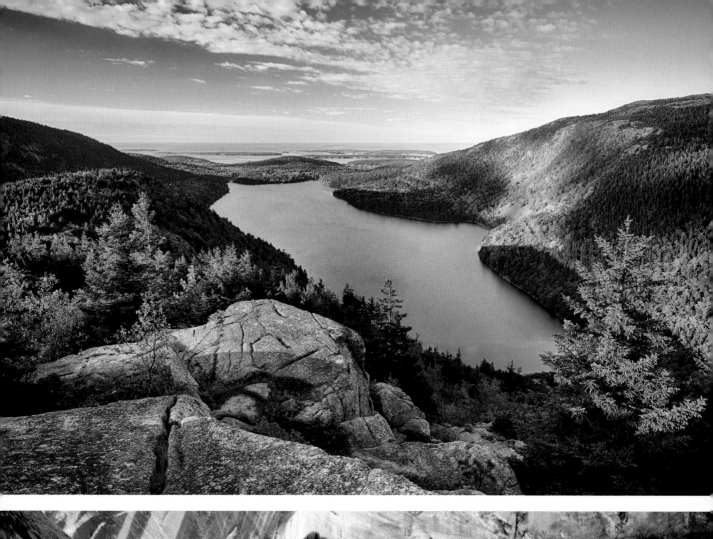

COMING TOGETHER FOR CHINATOWN'S FIRECRACKER RUN IN LOS ANGELES

Jinghuan Liu Tervalon enjoys traditional lion dancing, a fusillade of firecrackers, and sweet treats from local bakeries at this historic LA race with a modern social conscience.

I was introduced to this wonderful race through my first running club, Pasadena Pacers. In 2014, when I moved to that part of Southern California, I was a very green runner with limited understanding of the sport. I decided to join this particular club because there were various pace groups and the other runners seemed friendly. The official club race calendar included several local events, including the Chinatown Firecracker Run. I was daunted by the hilly nature of the course but, at 10k, figured I couldn't possibly fail. So I signed up.

Years passed. In that time I accomplished many of my running goals and traveled around the world for marathons. I also made a return to middle-distance races. My running journey took me a long way. Yet, looking back, the Chinatown Firecracker was, and still is, one of my favorites, thanks to the amazing race experience, the event's history and my own cultural connections.

'The history of Chinatown in Los Angeles is as vibrant as the city itself,' wrote the cultural historian Jenny Cho. Between 1850 and 1900, the Chinese population (around 3000) built its own enclave in the heart of LA. Known as Old Chinatown, it was demolished when the city authorities commenced the building of Union Station. Its replacement, New Chinatown, was built in 1938 and located around LA's Central Plaza.

Historically, New Chinatown has held an annual Golden Dragon Parade to mark the Lunar New Year. In 1978, local residents Edmund SooHoo and Helen Young decided to create a running race to add to the celebrations. SooHoo enlisted help from experts with relevant event experience. These included Fred Honda, head of municipal sports for Recreation and Parks, and

Andy Bakjian, the former Olympic wrestler and US Track and Field Hall of Famer. The narrow and hilly streets made creating a marathon challenging, so the organizers settled on a 10k. The first Firecracker took place in 1979 to great fanfare, drawing more than 1000 runners.

'Since day one, the Firecracker race has been a community event,' SooHoo explains. 'We wanted to create a race everyone could feel proud of. We had senior citizens volunteering to serve orange slices to the runners and they even brought their own knives and cutting boards. It was quite a sight, those tens of

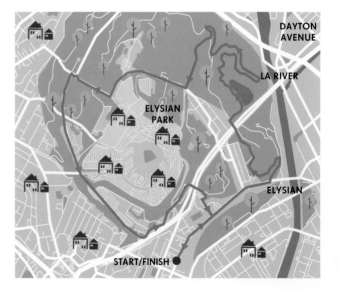

seniors all dressed in their knit caps, and our way of welcoming the runners to Chinatown.'

Today, the Firecracker's 10k is the oldest and largest running event in the United States to commemorate Lunar New Year. More recently, it has added a 5k option, a 1k kids run, plus a dog run/walk and 19- (or 50-) mile bike ride. Held every February, the event now attracts more than 8000 participants, cheered on by 30,000 spectators over the two-day celebration.

Entirely volunteer-run, the Firecracker's wider mission is to promote health and fitness in the greater Los Angeles area, as well as give something back to the Chinatown community that serve as hosts. 'All our proceeds are reinvested in support of elementary schools and non-profit organizations,' says Jennifer Gee, secretary of the LA Chinatown Firecracker Run Committee [LACFRC],

The Firecracker races draw a mixed crowd of both committed runners and casual joggers. What helps set them apart is the thoughtful integration of various aspects of Chinese culture. This begins the moment runners collect their race bibs at the race expo, where they are served a complimentary chow-mein as their pre-race, carb-loading meal. And whereas at other races you might hear the national anthem, or the crowd joining a countdown, the Firecracker achieves a special energy thanks to the 100,000 firecrackers popping in the air before runners get underway; adding to the theater are traditional

> *"The Firecracker is a unique experience, with an atmosphere unlike any other – where else would you see people drumming in the middle of the course?"*

Chinese lion dancers, performing elaborate routines. Such bursts of Chinese tradition extend well beyond the start line. In the kids' race, for example, held once the adults have completed their races, finishers are handed red envelopes containing chocolate coins. The exchange of red envelopes

© Tsuji / Getty Images; Kate33 / Shutterstock

between family and friends is a Lunar New Year tradition that symbolizes luck, prosperity, and happiness.

If that weren't enough, each year the design of both the official Firecracker race shirt and finisher medal incorporates the relevant sign from the Chinese zodiac. Plenty of runners complete 12 races in a row just to collect all 12 different medal and shirt designs: the year of the Rat, Ox, Tiger, Rabbit, Dragon, Snake, Horse, Sheep, Monkey, Rooster, Dog, and Pig. Many a diehard Firecracker fan will have all 12 medals framed and hung in their living rooms.

For runners who might not climb hills very often, the 10k course is a challenging one. Starting on North Broadway, in the heart of Chinatown, the route heads north. On the right-hand side is the recently built Los Angeles State Historic Park. The climb continues until runners reach Elysian Park and a small helipad. This is where runners get a beautiful view of Dodger Stadium, Downtown Los Angeles, Mt Wilson, and

Clockwise from left: lining up for the Firecracker race; Los Angeles' Chinatown developed in the 1930s; dim sum. Previous page: finishing the Firecracker

the Hollywood Sign. The course loops around the 110 freeway and, just when you might think the hills are over, they are most definitely not. Indeed, rolling hills continue on to Stadium Way, under the 110, and finally back to Broadway, where runners can sprint off a slight downhill to the finish line.

The 5k, in contrast, is an out-and-back course with the same start/finish line. Runners set off on Broadway but make a left turn on to Bishops Rd, then a right turn at Stadium Way. The climb continues, to Lilac Tce and Stadium Way. At the turn-around point, runners might very well feel like they've found another gear as, with the rest of the run downhill, a negative split is almost guaranteed.

LET'S DANCE

Firecracker Run organizers work with traditional Chinese troupes to produce both lion and, in relevant years, dragon dancing. Both are key celebrations for Lunar New Year, in China and around the world, intended to bring good luck and prosperity. A lion dance requires two performers, and a dragon dance typically nine, but both styles require years of intensive martial arts, dance, and acrobatics training, demanding strength, agility, and concentration.

Clockwise from left: lacing up; downtown's Chinatown; celebrating the Lunar New Year; traditional lion dancing in Los Angeles

The hilly course means that the 5k is more than just a soft option, as recent winner Angus Kwan-Yin Leung can attest. 'In 2020, right before the pandemic shut-down, I got second place,' says Leung. 'In 2023, aged 31, I was in the best shape of my life, so I signed up for the 5k as part of my training for the Los Angeles Marathon.' In the Year of the Rabbit, Leung went on to win (the 5k, not the marathon) in a time of 16:22. Leung describes the Firecracker as a 'unique experience', with an atmosphere unlike any other. 'Where else would you see people drumming in the middle of the course?' he says.

Modern Chinatown means different things to different runners. Second- or third-generation Chinese Americans, for example, might feel more nostalgic toward it than first-generation Chinese immigrants. Yet the aim of the Firecracker is to promote Chinatown's vibrant culture to as wide an audience as possible. 'In addition to promoting health and fitness,' says Jennifer Gee of the LACFRC, 'we want to attract those people who might not venture here very often. We want to educate people about Chinatown in Los Angeles because it has changed so much over the years.'

Illustrating those changes are the local businesses, whose involvement is another aspect of the race's appeal. By the finish line is one of the area's longest-standing firms, the Phoenix Bakery. Founded in 1938, the year of New Chinatown's opening, it is still operated by the same

family. The Phoenix Bakery is famous for its fresh-strawberry, whipped-cream birthday cake, handmade almond cookies and sticky sugar butterflies. During those years when my whole family took part in the race, we never missed a stop here for the guava Danish and boxes of almond cookies.

A more contemporary outfit, on the other hand, is the Homeboy Bakery. Located on Bruno St, near Chinatown Station on the city's A Line, it is part of the wider social enterprise, Homeboy Industries, the largest gang rehabilitation program in the world. The chocolate-dipped macaroons and the orange and cranberry granolas are my favorites to bring home after the Firecracker run.

Among the Chinese diaspora, food is, as you might expect, pretty important. Much like it is for runners, in fact, and each of us has our favorite. Michael Wong, a cybersecurity expert who has participated in the race for more than 10 years, swears by the Won Kok Restaurant, a dim-sum take-out whose value lies in the food if not the décor. 'The restaurant is a bit run-down,' Wong says, 'but you get amazing sweet-and-savory pork buns and egg tarts.'

And that's the beauty of it. For ordinary runners like me, with minimal chance of winning, what makes the Firecracker so special is the extent to which it captures the spirit of Chinatown. A fun day out for the whole family, it offers me the chance to test my fitness, celebrate Lunar New Year with my family, and reconnect with my own cultural heritage. **JLT**

Start/Finish // 943 N Broadway; Chinatown Central Plaza
Distances // 5k and 10k
Getting there // Take the A Line to Chinatown Station.
When to go // The race is held in February, close to Lunar New Year.
What to wear // February in LA is late-winter/early-spring season, with daytime highs of 70°F (21°C). Single, breathable layers are good (gloves optional).
What to pack // Not too much, to leave space in your suitcase for bakery treats.
Where to stay // Chinatown, Downtown Los Angeles, Little Tokyo, the Arts District are all close to the Firecracker start.
Where to eat // You're spoilt for choice, but Mama Lu's Dumpling House (700 N. Spring St) is ever reliable.
Things to know // For registration details along with a wealth of other information: firecracker10k.org

*Opposite: Griffith Park and the
Observatory are open to the public*

MORE LIKE THIS
CALIFORNIA CHALLENGES

ROSE BOWL HALF MARATHON (& 5K)

A beautiful and challenging tour of the
city of Pasadena, located in the northeast
part of Los Angeles. Starting at the Rose
Bowl stadium, a recognized National
Historic Landmark, runners pass along
South Arroyo Blvd, then across Old Town
Pasadena. You'll also spy one of the best
science and engineering schools in the
US, the California Institute of Technology
(Caltech), before looping back through
Old Town and climbing the hill by the
Norton Simon Museum. Having reached
the famous Colorado St Bridge, runners
eventually drop back down to the Rose
Bowl and finish there. The hills make the
event a tough one but the course is one
of the best ways to see major landmarks
of the city. A 5k option is also available.
Start/Finish // Rose Bowl, Pasadena
Distance //13.1 miles (21km)

GRIFFITH PARK TRAIL MARATHON
RELAY & 8K

Located in this iconic municipal green
space, the 8k course is a single loop,
starting and finishing on the fire road,
by the entrance to the Merry Go Round
parking lot at the bottom of Griffith
Park. The marathon relay comprises five
runners, each running 5.25 miles (8.4km)
with a combined distance of 26.25 miles
(42km). The relay has an elevation gain
of 799ft (243.5m) on each leg and the
course includes Upper and Lower Old
Zoo Loop and Beacon trail. Along the
way, runners have a breathtaking view of
downtown Los Angeles and the Griffith
Observatory. Whether you run the 8k as
a solo runner or join a relay team, you'll
encounter nearly all the running clubs in
and around the Los Angeles area.
**Start/Finish // Merry Go Round
parking lot**
Distance // 26.25 miles (42km)

CARLSBAD 5000

The City of Carlsbad lies on the north
coast of San Diego County. Known
as the world's fastest 5k, the race has
created 16 world records and eight
national records since it was first held, in
1986. Pick up your bib the day before the
race, and there's a reasonable chance
you'll get to meet Meb Keflezighi, the
former Olympic marathon silver medalist,
Boston Marathon winner and now
Carlsbad 5000 ambassador. In 2024,
the Carlsbad 5000 announced a new
course. Runners start at the intersection
of Grand Ave and Carlsbad Blvd, then
head southbound on Carlsbad Blvd. The
field turns round at the Tamarack Beach
Volleyball Courts, making its return
northbound on Carlsbad Blvd. The finish
is under the famous Carlsbad Sign, just
past the intersection of Carlsbad Village
Dr and Carlsbad Blvd.
**Start // Grand Ave and Carlsbad Blvd
Finish // Carlsbad Village Dr and
Carlsbad Blvd
Distance // 5k (3.1 miles)**

CONQUERING THE KALALAU TRAIL

The rugged, exposed, and hilly trail penetrates a nearly inaccessible wilderness, making it a memorable test of endurance for Alexander Deedy in one of Hawai'i's most beautiful places.

Even in a state as beautiful as Hawai'i, the Nā Pali Coast is notable for its stunning scenery. Nā Pali is Hawaiian for 'the cliffs', an apt name for a rugged and undeveloped stretch of Kaua'i's north coast, where verdant, razor-thin ridges plummet as much as 4000ft (1200m) to the Pacific Ocean. Near the middle of this untamed wilderness is Kalalau Beach, a sandy expanse that can only be reached by helicopter, boat, or the eponymous Kalalau Trail.

Kalalau is not a trail for the faint of heart. It wends for 11 miles (18km) along the base of Nā Pali's cliffs, at times becoming more akin to navigating a slackline than walking on a sidewalk. Its topographical profile could be the blueprint for a rollercoaster; the trail starts and ends at sea level, but trekkers will climb about 2500ft (762m) while navigating its ascents and descents. Most people who brave the trail do so on overnight backpacking trips, spending at least one night at the beach.

Kalalau's beauty, ruggedness, and the relative solitude it offers give it a special status in many hikers' hearts. It's certainly memorable for me, in part because Kalalau was my first long-distance trail run.

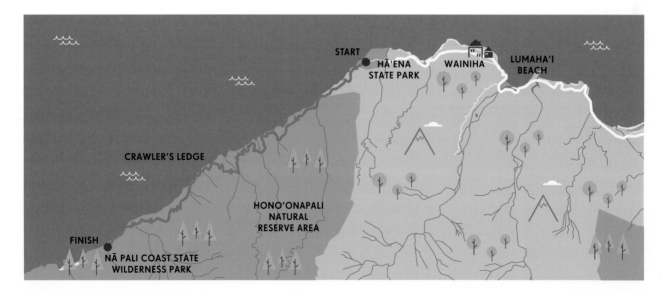

© Matt Munro / Lonely Planet

My Kalalau run was a result of youthful bravado. Shortly after my 27th birthday, a friend in his mid-50s was regaling me with stories of his annual run on the trail. I blurted something about breezing down the trail faster than him, and in that moment of unearned confidence I was committed.

Kalalau can be a soul-crusher from the very start. I had cobbled together sporadic training in the months leading up to the run, but I hadn't built a regimen that left me feeling prepared for the trail. I was all nerves when I started up the first mile, which is a steady climb to 600ft (183m). Within a few minutes, my chest was heaving and I was questioning whether I had the fortitude to continue for another 21 miles (34km). I got an energy boost near the apex, when the trail provides a stunning outlook of the Nā Pali Coast stretching ahead.

The second mile descends to Hanakāpī'ai Beach. It's a disheartening downhill because it's nothing but a bounce. The next section of trail is a steady climb to 800ft (244m), the tallest point along the route. Pacing the body and mind on such variable terrain can be a challenge for a new trail runner, and I was filled with doubt and trepidation during those first few miles. There's a good chance I would have pushed myself too hard, too early if I had been alone.

I ran Kalalau with two good friends. The guy who originally sparked my interest in running the trail backed out of the run after he injured a knee during training. I enlisted two co-workers who I knew were avid runners. We had agreed the day before to take the trail at our own pace and rendezvous at the beach

"My time didn't matter. What mattered is that I left Kalalau with an enormous confidence boost"

before the return leg. I figured both would quickly outpace me and I wouldn't see them until the end of the trail. We did spread out during the initial climb, but I caught up with one friend while he was filling his water from a stream at Hanakāpī'ai, and I caught up to my second companion shortly after. I realized maybe I wasn't as slow as I had thought.

After the first few drastic hills the topography smooths out a bit. The trail stays enshrouded in jungle for about the first 6 miles (9.6km), then the remaining stretch is more open. That drier section of trail affords some dramatic scenery. It's also home to a particularly precarious segment of trail that has been informally dubbed 'Crawler's Ledge' because the path becomes so skinny and the nearby drop into the ocean is so sheer most passers-by will slow to a crawl. I had heard of this infamous section prior to my run, but it turned out crossing that part without a top-heavy backpack that can compromise your balance isn't much of a problem, and I breezed past it.

My friends and I spread out a bit over the last few miles, staggering into the beach in our own time. We lingered there for about an hour and a half. We jumped in the ocean, explored a small cave on the far side of the beach, and refueled on PB&J

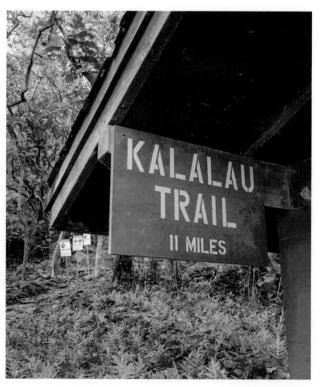

A DIFFERENT PERSPECTIVE

On the opposite side of Kaua'i from Hā'ena State Park and the Kalalau trailhead is a road that climbs from the sea up to Waimea Canyon and Koke'e State Parks, which preside over Kaua'i's uplands and offer lookouts from the top of Nā Pali's cliffs down onto Kalalau Beach. It's well worth taking a day to explore: Awa'awapuhi and Nu'alolo trails offer particularly dramatic overlooks.

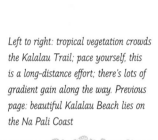

Left to right: tropical vegetation crowds the Kalalau Trail; pace yourself, this is a long-distance effort; there's lots of gradient gain along the way. Previous page: beautiful Kalalau Beach lies on the Na Pali Coast

sandwiches. Ninety minutes is hardly enough time to soak in the area's beauty, but we weren't there for leisure. So, we washed off the sand, slipped back into our shoes, and hit the trail.

We left Kalalau about 11.30am. The sun was high in the sky, and the climb out is a long, exposed section of trail over red soil. The relaxed paradise of the beach quickly felt a long way behind me as the sun's heat took its toll. Those 11 miles (18km) back to the trailhead were a slog for me. I alternated between stints of energized running and bouts of forceful walking. By the 800ft (244m) descent during mile 20, my legs were cramping. I submerged myself in the stream at Hanakāpī'ai to cool off before the final push. I finished the trail running, not walking, and I arrived back at the trailhead second of our little group of three. Later, when I texted my friend who made the annual Kalalau pilgrimage, I discovered I had bested his record time.

I didn't run Kalalau as part of a race. I didn't record a Strava time. I wasn't even competing against my trail-running companions. My time didn't matter. What mattered is that I left Kalalau with an enormous confidence boost. I had undertaken a personal challenge that seemed monumental just a few months prior, and I had done so on one of the most scenic trails in Hawai'i. I finished my first long-distance trail run healthy and happy, and a whole new world of backcountry adventures opened itself to me. **AD**

Start/Finish // Hā'ena State Park, Kaua'i
Distance // About 22 miles (35km)
Getting there // Lihue Airport is 37 miles (60km) south of Hā'ena. A shuttle provides transportation to the trailhead from several stops along Kaua'i's north shore.
When to go // Late spring through early fall. The rainy winter season can cause rivers along the trail to swell and create conditions that are unsafe for crossing.
What to pack // Sunscreen, food, and a water purification method because there is no potable water along the route.
Where to stay // Hotels and vacation rentals near Hanalei and Princeville are the best options.
Things to know // Everyone who goes past Hanakāpī'ai Beach at mile 2 (3km) of Kalalau Trail needs an overnight camping permit, even for day trips.
More info // dlnr.hawaii.gov/dsp/hiking/kauai/kalalau-trail/ kalalau-trail-routes/

*Clockwise from top: the Hoapili Trail
on Maui; the Aiea Loop on O'ahu;
volcanic action on Hualalai*

MORE LIKE THIS
HAWAI'I TRAIL RUNS

AIEA LOOP, AIEA, O'AHU

A 30-minute drive from Waikiki Beach, Aiea
Loop Trail provides a forest escape that
doesn't require fighting through a crowd or
ascending a mountain ridge. The trailhead
is at the top of a residential neighborhood,
in a park that surrounds a heiau – a
traditional place of worship for Hawaiians.
Mostly flat and well maintained, the loop
is a popular recreation spot for locals.
The first few miles of trail have a gradual
climb to an overlook with views of the
lush Halawa Valley and the H-3 highway,
one of the main arteries for crossing the
Ko'olau Mountains that run north to south
across O'ahu. Then the trail cuts back and
follows the ridge. It's a gradual downhill
to a stream crossing, and a final climb up
the steepest section of the loop just before
the finish. The trail can get muddy and slick
after rain, so be sure to wear shoes with
good traction.
**Start/Finish // Keaīwa Heiau State
Recreation Area**
Distance // 4.8 miles (7.7km)
**More info // dlnr.hawaii.gov/dsp/
hiking/oahu/aiea-loop-trail/**

HOAPILI TRAIL, MAUI

About 20 minutes from the resorts at
Wailea, Hoapili Trail provides an adventure
into an undeveloped stretch of Maui's
southern coast and a glimpse into ancient
Hawaiian history. The trailhead is at the
parking area for La Perouse Bay, a popular
surfing spot. From the parking area, the
trail bends along the coast and soon joins
a preserved section of the King's Hwy.
The King's Hwy was constructed about
500 years ago and originally stretched
for 138 miles (222km), circumnavigating
the entire island. The trail connected the
island's 12 subdivisions and was a crucial
route for transportation and commerce. It's
paved with loosely placed basalt rocks,
which makes for uneven footing. While
on the King's trail, stay on the path and
respect the nearby stone foundations of
old Hawaiian houses and other pieces of
cultural history. Hoapili crosses sections
of relatively recent lava flows, and
there is very little shade, so expect hot
temperatures on sunny days.
Start/Finish // La Perouse Bay
Distance // 5.5 miles (8.9km) round trip
**More info // dlnr.hawaii.gov/recreation/
files/2013/12/MauiNAHmap18.pdf**

MAKĀULA-'O'OMA TRAILS,
HAWAI'I ISLAND

Escape the Kona heat and venture into
the upland cloud forest on the slopes of
Hualālai Volcano on Hawai'i island. The
Makāula-'O'oma unit is a small segment
of the Honua'ula Forest Reserve, which
protects cultural and environmentally
important flora and fauna. Drive to the
end of Makahi St to reach the trailhead
and access a network of trails that forms
a rough figure-eight through the forest.
Going right from the trailhead will lead
runners up a series of switchbacks with
about 200ft (61m) of climbing. At the top
of the ascent, the trail travels along the
edge of the preserve, and runners can
choose to take the first junction for a
shorter loop or continue to the second
junction for a longer one. For anyone
hungry for extra steps, a couple of spurs
jet out from the figure-eight and end at
the reserve's formal boundary. The trail is
crossed with roots and can get muddy.
Start/Finish // Trailhead on Makahi St
**Distance // 4.5 miles (7.2km) of total
trails**
**More info // hawaiitrails.ehawaii.gov/
trails/#/trail/makula-ooma-trails/302**

THE MESA TRAIL

Easy-access wilderness on the outskirts of Boulder, Colorado holds a trail run so good it will turn burned-out pavement junkies into off-road addicts.

I probably would have quit running forever if it weren't for a run I did 25 years ago. Since then, I have probably run this trail more than a thousand times, as it sits just a stone's throw away from my adopted hometown of Boulder, Colorado. It has become much more than my favorite place to log miles over the years – it's my go-to destination for athletic fitness, deep thinking and self-calm, not to mention a special place to run with my dog or with friends, manage career stress, and even mourn the passing of my father.

Like a lot of runners, I was at a point of being burned out, broken down, and just plain bored of pavement, training for the same 10K runs and enduring the same kind of suffering through a big city marathon every year. Oddly, the same meditative – almost therapeutic – monotony that draws us to running often becomes the thing we despise most.

Then, by way of some unsolicited advice from a neighbor, I stumbled upon this utopian singletrack trail that helped change my life. Mesa Trail is a rolling, 6.7-mile (10.8km) dirt trail skirting beneath the iconic mountains that make up Boulder's western horizon line – most notably, Green Mountain, Bear Peak, and the Flatirons. Long one of the trail-running capitals of the US, Boulder has more than 40 unique routes and 300 miles (480km) of singletrack, dirt roads and craggy mountain ridgelines. And for many reasons, the utilitarian Mesa Trail is the best of the bunch.

I didn't know it at the time, but that first run on Mesa Trail stirred something in me. It's an idyllic route, one that spoils you with both mild and challenging sections, but nothing too steep that it cannot be run at a slow pace. Most importantly, it has a flow about it, a moderately undulating profile that continually rolls up and down without sending a runner's heart rate off the charts.

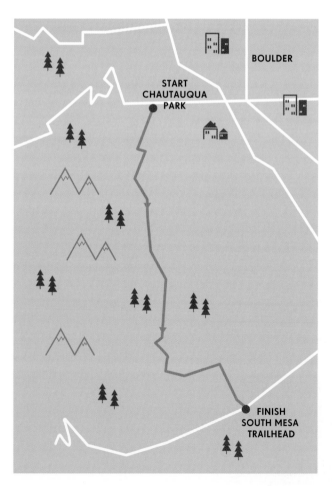

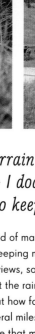

The day I finally decided to see what Mesa Trail was all about, I brought with me a bit of baggage. My angst and malaise toward running weren't the only things weighing me down – I was woefully out of shape. In fact, when I laced up my shoes and drove to the trailhead, I began to talk myself into just going for a short hike.

I started off from the stunningly expansive Chautauqua Park, immediately captivated by the impressive mountainscapes towering overhead. I was gasping for breath while adjusting to the thinner air of Boulder's 5430ft (1655m) elevation, so I began by walking the robust uphill section at the beginning. But the moment the route turned to a winding dirt track that disappeared into a thick forest, I was compelled to start running. Why? It's hard to explain, It was sort of a Forrest Gump moment. And like Gump, I haven't stopped.

When I started out, I had no idea where Mesa Trail went or wound up. There were plenty of signposts and maps, and no chance of getting lost, so I just followed the route as it twisted and turned, climbed and descended over the rolling foothills. Running over the dynamic terrain of Mesa Trail was a pathway into another world. Instead of the consistent gait I was accustomed to while running on the roads, I found myself running with a bit of a staccato pattern as I dodged rocks, roots and other obstacles, negotiated steep declines and sharp ascents, and used my arms

"The dynamic terrain was a pathway into another world – I dodged rocks and used my arms to keep my balance"

to keep my balance. Instead of maneuvering around pedestrians, obeying traffic lights and keeping my eyes peeled for cars, I found myself enjoying the views, soaking in the aroma of the pine trees and marveling at the rainbow of wildflowers along the trail. Without thinking about how far, how fast or how long I was running, I was already several miles along the trail and enjoying a mellow but enlightened vibe that must have been my first taste of trail-runner's high.

I finally turned around after running about 5 miles (8km) in 45 minutes – avoiding a long descent into a valley at the south terminus of the trail – and headed back whence I came. The way back was just as exhilarating, given that a trail looks and feels unique when heading in the other direction.

That afternoon, my Mesa Trail run was much less about running and all about the experiential moments I was having as I ran: the gusts of fresh air blowing in my face; my legs and feet meeting the unique challenges of the natural terrain; watching a deer prance

FLATIRON FUEL

After a morning run on Mesa Trail, locals refuel on the porch of the 120-year-old Chautauqua Dining Hall. The restaurant is known for its Colorado bistro cuisine, featuring favorites like the Cowboy Skillet (eggs, elk chorizo, baked beans, steak, jalapeno, and grilled sourdough toast) and the Denver Croissant Sandwich (eggs, ham, green peppers, onion, cheddar cheese, chimichurri aioli, and sliced melon).

From left: it's not only runners who love Chautauqua Park outside Boulder, Colorado; the iconic slanted shape of the Flatirons. Previous page: enjoying the flats near the Flatirons

through the grass in the distance; and the sound of bubbling Bear Creek as I hopped over rocks to the other side.

Though I didn't immediately become a regular trail runner after that, it certainly helped me rediscover my love for running. I returned again and again, often running all the way to the termination point at the South Mesa Trailhead and back, while also connecting adjacent trails to form unique loops on the fly, and eventually running to the high mountain peaks overhead. My staccato stride movements turned into a rhythmic dance, my long runs got longer, and in many ways Mesa Trail did eventually turn me into a trail runner. (And yes, my experiences running Mesa Trail even helped me become a better road marathoner.)

Now, 25 years on, I have run that trail, or some derivation of it, more times than I can count, in spring, summer, winter, and fall. It's the reason I never quit running and would never consider such a preposterous idea again. It has taught me such a lot about life, especially the notion that the journey is always the destination – not the time, distance, pace, and other stats your watch feeds you. I have now ventured far and wide around the US and the world to run inspiring trails and unfathomably long races. Ultimately, my sense of being as a runner, and perhaps my sense of being me in my adult life, will forever be firmly rooted on Mesa Trail. **BM**

Start // Chautauqua Park, Boulder
Finish // South Mesa Trailhead, Eldorado Springs
Distance // 6.8 miles (11km) (one way).
Getting there // Denver International Airport is an hour's drive to either trailhead.
When to go // Mesa Trail is runnable year-round, but the best months are from April to October.
Where to stay // St Julien Hotel, Boulder, and Chautauqua Cottages, Boulder.
What to wear // Trail running shoes with good traction and protection, appropriate running clothes for the season.
Things to know // There's wildlife aplenty on this trail throughout the year, including deer, foxes, black bears, coyotes, rattlesnakes, mountain lions, and a variety of birds.
More info // bouldercolorado.gov

Opposite: a dawn run on the Art Loeb
Trail over the Blue Ridge Mountains

MORE LIKE THIS
FAMOUS US TRAIL RUNS

OLD CROTON AQUEDUCT TRAIL, NEW YORK

An idyllic wooded run hidden within the urban gridlock of Westchester County, this flat, mostly dirt, trail follows the historic route of a 19th-century underground aquifer built to bring fresh water to New York City. With only a few mild rolling hills and entirely devoid of technical features, the 26.2-mile (42km) stretch is an ideal place for long runs, tempo runs, recovery runs, fartlek interval and other race-prep workouts. Shrouded by trees most of the way, the route occasionally offers picturesque views of the Hudson River and a variety of historic sites. Old Croton Aqueduct Trail offers numerous places to start out-and-back runs or long, one-way jaunts combined with a return trip on the Metro-North Railroad. Although it has numerous road crossings, it is a surprisingly continuous off-road running escape that's easily accessible via a short drive or train ride from Manhattan.
Start // Yonkers
Finish // Croton Dam Rd
Distance // 26.2 miles (42km)
More info // parks.ny.gov/parks/96/details.aspx

WATERFALL GLEN TRAIL, ILLINOIS

This wide crushed-gravel loop in suburban Chicago gradually rolls through classic Midwestern oak and maple woodlands, diverse native prairies and lush ravines as it encircles Argonne National Laboratory. That's the federal laboratory that once worked on nuclear reactors for the Manhattan Project in the 1940s but now primarily conducts clean energy and environmental research. One of the highlights of the trail is an overlook of a beautiful tiered waterfall on Sawmill Creek, built by the Civilian Conservation Corps in the 1930s. The preserve contains more than 400 native plants and more than 300 species of wildlife, including deer, foxes, coyotes, owls, and a variety of non-venomous snakes. This is a mild running loop with a few moderate climbs that have made it a popular place for local marathon training groups to do hill workouts and long runs.
Start/Finish // Waterfall Glen parking area, Darien
Distance // 9.5 miles (15km)
More info // dupageforest.org/places-to-go/forest-preserves/waterfall-glen

ART LOEB TRAIL, NORTH CAROLINA

This rolling 30.1-mile (48km) north-south trail has become one of the most famous in the eastern US, especially popular with long-distance runners. It meanders through the densely wooded Pisgah National Forest in western North Carolina, traversing several high peaks along the way, including Black Balsam Knob (6214ft; 1894m) and Tennent Mountain (6040ft; 1841m). Due to heavy logging in the 1920s and 1930s, many of the high points are treeless summits that reward you with expansive, 360-degree views. Named after a mid-20th-century naturalist from the Carolina Mountain Club, the trail can be conveniently parsed into four vehicle-accessible sections that range from 4 to 12 miles (6.4km to 19km) or run end-to-end for an epic ultra-distance journey.
Start // Davidson River Campground, Brevard
Finish // Daniel Boone Boy Scout Camp, Canton
Distance // 4 to 30.1 miles (6.4km to 48km)
More info // hikewnc.info

MORO CANYON, CRYSTAL COVE STATE PARK

Expansive views of the Pacific Ocean, steep hills, and coastal desert flora and fauna make this backcountry trail run both challenging and rewarding for Sharael Kolberg.

As I stood at the start line in my leggings and event T-shirt, bib number safety-pinned to it, I was antsy to hit the trails for the 6.2 mile (10km) run. As I lived nearby, the terrain was familiar but racing on it would be a new challenge. Specifically, the XTerra Laguna Beach, an off-road triathlon at Crystal Cove State Park in Newport Beach, California. Taking the running leg of a three-person relay team, my friend, Ian, would brave the cold Pacific for a 0.93-mile (1500m) swim, with another friend, Jan, tackling a hilly 15.5-mile (25km) mountain-bike ride.

Crystal Cove State Park, established in 1979, encompasses 3.2 miles (5km) of scenic beaches and stretches to inland canyons, with approximately 15 miles (24km) of trails spread across 2400 acres (971 hectares). This coastal chaparral landscape is home to a thriving ecosystem. During daylight hours, it's common to encounter cottontail rabbits on the trails, along with Western fence lizards, ground squirrels, California quail, and roadrunners, with red-tailed hawks soaring overhead. Occasionally, hikers, bikers or equestrians will come across a bobcat or rattlesnake.

With the swim and run completed, Jan tagged me in and I headed out to put my months of training to work. With good tread on my trail-running shoes, a waste belt stocked with water and Gatorade, as well as GU energy gels, I was prepared and confident as I started on the first 1-mile (1.6km) climb. Only a few moments into the race, my shoe had come untied. I bent down on the side of the trail to tie it, when a fellow competitor ran by and smirked; I'd failed to double-knot my laces, a rookie move.

Back in the action, I kept a pace I was comfortable with. Slow and steady. The good news was that, with the race literally at sea level, I didn't have to worry about altitude. The bad news was that the route had nearly 1000ft (304m) of elevation gain. After ascending almost 200ft (60m) at the start, on Moro Canyon Trail, I followed the trail signs and hung a left at West Cut Across – a trail that was little more than a half-mile (1km) long but which rose almost 400ft (121m). The route was so steep, I had to hike most of it.

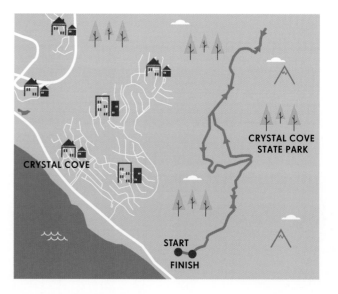

CRYSTAL COVE

CRYSTAL COVE STATE PARK

START
FINISH

© Anthony Fontanes / Shutterstock

Cranking up the tunes in my air pods, Gloria Gaynor's *I Will Survive* got me up the dusty slope. My selection also consisted of Kelly Clarkson's *Stronger (What Doesn't Kill You)* and *The Climb*, by Miley Cyrus. Only two years prior, I had created this playlist to lift my mood on my bad days, following intense chemotherapy to treat breast cancer. On those days, I couldn't even get out of bed. Now, those same songs were my anthem for undertaking something that, back then, I could not have fathomed doing. It felt good to be strong again, to be using my body and feeling my muscles, breathing deeply, dripping in sweat.

Ahead, there was a fork in the road and I followed the arrow signs to the left, passing a trail called Rattlesnake, until I got to No Name Ridge, where I turned right, still going up. This section was a mere 0.8 miles (1.3km) but included 200ft (60m) of steepness. As I trudged along, I ripped open an energy gel and washed it down with Gatorade in a flavor called Glacier Freeze, which seemed like a good idea since it was September and race-day temperatures were predicted to reach nearly 80°F (26.6°C).

Continuing on, I passed a sign that pointed to a single-track trail called Ticketron, which in turn led to the Deer Canyon Campground, a backcountry hike-in site with a picnic table and pit toilet. The park has three such campsites, while another, Moro Campground, was added in 2005. Located on a bluff overlooking the ocean, it has space for 27 RVs and 30 tents, and was created amid no small controversy. The campground replaced the long-standing El Morro Beach Trailer Park, a fixture in the area since the 1940s and home to among others, a community of artists and surfers.

CITIZEN SCIENCE

Between the Moro Canyon Trail and Crystal Cove State Park tunnel lies the Michael and Tricia Berns Environmental Study Loop. A joint venture between the state park and the Crystal Cove Alliance, its eight self-guided, interactive field stations give visiting citizen scientists a better understanding of the wide range of conservation work the Alliance oversees. The stations provide information on bugs, butterflies, and birds, as well as local hydrology, rock formations, and weather systems.

Clockwise from top: a snowy egret in the park; Crystal Cove landscape; running El Moro Canyon; run this way. Previous page: Crystal Cove State Park

On the final ascent I encountered day hikers, enjoying the trails from the Bommer Ridge access point off Hwy 73. They included some elderly walkers, passing me with their hiking poles as they huffed and puffed to the top. When I finally arrived at the turn-around point, a race volunteer high-fived me before I started back down toward the finish line. The pale-blue Pacific sprawled out in front of me, with sailboats dotting the horizon.

The fact I was now descending allowed me to appreciate the natural beauty of the area. The wide fire road was lined with fragrant coastal sage, prickly pear and cholla cacti, and an odd-looking lichen called Witch's Hair that draped from the vegetation. Nearing the end, I veered left at Poles trail, for a decline that dropped nearly 300ft (91m) in just under a half-mile. I chose my steps carefully on the uneven trail, so as not to twist an ankle. With a final right-turn, I was back on Moro Canyon Trail for the last mile or so. The crowd cheered as the announcer called out each participant's names as they crossed the finish line. Exhausted but elated, I was greeted with hugs from my husband, Jeff, and also from Jan. I wore my finisher's medal with a smile for a job well done.

On subsequent visits to Moro Canyon, when I'm out for a leisurely hike with friends on the trails, I remember back to race day and feel proud to have conquered such daunting hills. It's something hold as a metaphor for tackling life's challenges. **SK**

Start/Finish // Day-use parking lot, Moro Canyon Trailhead
Distance // 6.21 miles (10km)
Getting there // Located on Pacific Coast Hwy between Corona del Mar and Laguna Beach. Day-use parking is $15. The nearest airport is John Wayne, in Santa Ana.
When to go // Spring is the best time, for wildflower viewing.
What to wear // Sweat-wicking layers.
What to pack // Water with electrolytes, sunscreen, charged smartphone.
Where to stay // The Resort at Pelican Hill or the historic Crystal Cove Beach Cottages.
Where to eat // Crystal Cove Shake Shack or The Beachcomber at Crystal Cove.
Things to know // Phone service in the area is not always reliable.
More info // crystalcovestatepark.org/hiking-2

Opposite: Potato Harbor on Santa
Cruz Island; among giants in
Humboldt Redwoods State Park

MORE LIKE THIS
CALIFORNIA STATE PARK RUNS

ANZA-BORREGO DESERT STATE PARK, SAN DIEGO COUNTY

Anza-Borrego Desert State Park, near San Diego County, is California's largest, spanning more than 938 sq miles (2430 sq km). The landscape consists of a variety of cacti, spring wildflowers, agave, and groves of palms. The easy, 2-mile (3.2km) Pictograph Trail is situated in Blair Valley, off historic California Hwy S-2 (also known as the Great Southern Overland Stage Route). Along the path, runners will encounter ancient Native American petroglyphs and pictographs on the boulders and cliffs. To extend the run to 3 miles (4.8km), continue on to the Smuggler's Canyon overlook. The Pacific Crest Trail also passes through the park. Although this trailhead is easily accessible, with 500 miles (805km) of dirt roads, four-wheel-drive vehicles are recommended for most areas. Day-use fees are $10 per vehicle.

Start/Finish // Pictograph Trail trailhead
Distance // 2 miles (3.2km)
More info // parks.ca.gov/?page_id=638

SANTA CRUZ ISLAND, CHANNEL ISLANDS NATIONAL PARK, VENTURA COUNTY

Santa Cruz, at 96.5 sq miles (250 sq km), is the largest island off the coast of the United States. It is one of eight Channel Islands, each of which is surrounded by a Marine Protected Area that extends for 8 miles (13km) offshore. Located on the northeast end of the island is the hilly and moderately difficult Potato Harbor Overlook Trail that leads to stunning views of Potato Harbor. Keep your eyes open for sea lions frolicking in the kelp forest below. (There is no direct access to the beach.) While running on this narrow dirt trail, you'll pass through coastal sage scrub, grasslands, and chaparral. Native land mammals on the island include the rare island fox, the island deer mouse, harvest mouse, and the spotted skunk. It's also a great place for birdwatching.

Start/Finish // Trailhead begins at Scorpion Anchorage
Distance // 5 miles (8km)
More info // nps.gov/places/ooo/potato-harbor-overlook.htm

HUMBOLDT REDWOODS STATE PARK, HUMBOLDT COUNTY

For an inspiring and majestic run through the world's largest expanse of old-growth redwoods, head to Humboldt Redwoods State Park in Northern California. Situated on land originally belonging to the Sinkyone people, the park features 100 miles (160km) of trails spread across 83 sq miles (214 sq km). The area used to be logged but, thanks to the Save the Redwoods League, the enormous trees were spared when it became a state park in 1921. The cool, wooded coastal environment gets a high amount of rain, which keeps it lush and green. Along the wheelchair-accessible Drury-Chaney Loop trail, runners will meet giant redwoods that can grow to more than 350ft (107m) high, with a base diameter of up to 20ft (6m). It is also likely they'll see bright yellow banana slugs, a variety of ferns, mosses, squirrel, and deer.

Start/Finish // Avenue of the Giants, mile marker 43.9
Distance // 2.4 miles (3.8km)
More info // parks.ca.gov/?page_id=31000

BAY TO BREAKERS

*San Francisco's most famous running race is not about split times and speed records.
It's more like a fast-paced protest march through the streets, freak-flags flying high.*

Making my way up Howard St in the first miles of the Bay to Breakers race across San Francisco, I couldn't help but feel people were staring at me. I was an oddity that day – one of the few runners dressed up as, well, an actual runner.

On this cool Sunday morning in late May, I was surrounded by a woman wearing a panda costume; two men wearing black leotards, multicolored tutus and fluorescent yellow feather boas; and two more dressed up as the Blues Brothers. Nearby, a group of runners were dressed entirely in green, wearing cardboard signs decrying

oil drilling and deforestation and global warming. To my right were 'centipede' teams of identically outfitted runners, tethered together with a small cord. And then, of course, there were the naked people. Naked men, naked women, bandying about, wearing nothing but running shoes and lightweight backpacks.

When signing up for this event, I'm not sure I fully understood what the Bay to Breakers run was all about, or what it meant to so many people. Yes, it always attracts an odd collection of humanity, but perhaps even stranger was the notion that we were all there – 50,000 of us – to run 7 miles (11km) across San Francisco, from the

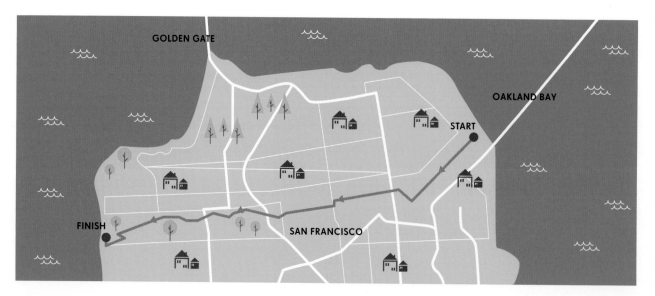

bay shore at its eastern edge to the Pacific ocean in the west.

For me, the Bay to Breakers was actually supposed to be a simple tune-up for an upcoming marathon. But it became pretty clear even before the race start that I was an outsider looking in. As my race wave approached the start line, a group of runners wearing inflatable rubber-ducky pool toys did some sort of choreographed warm-up dance. An Elvis impersonator belted out a few bars of *Love Me Tender*. In my wicking T-shirt, nylon running shorts, and a beat-up pair of Nike Pegasus, I actually felt a bit foolish, perhaps even some shame, that I had seemingly missed the entire point of what I now know is the most peculiar race in running, as well as one of the most significant events in San Francisco.

In fact, I cruised through the entire financial district, shortly after the start, contemplating what kind of costume I would wear if I came back to run it again in the future. Maybe a superhero? A bunny rabbit with big floppy ears? Maybe I'd just wear a brightly colored pair of Speedos.

It's the sort of event that makes you second guess things like personal time goals, which somehow feel a little inconsequential. Bay to Breakers has long been one of the world's most iconic running races, both because it's one of the oldest – it originated in 1912 – and because it so distinctively oozes the passionate energy of the city that spawned it. It was started as a way of lifting the city's spirits after the devastating 1906 earthquake. But decades later it transformed into the massive public party it is today. It's more than just a race. Much like San Francisco itself, it stands for self-expression, personal fitness, political activism, and counterculture.

'Yes, it is a big party, but it's certainly much more than just that. It's a San Francisco institution,' says one runner who has run on a fast centipede team almost every year for more than a decade. 'It's an excuse to dress up for fun, but also for whatever social cause you believe in.'

A few miles in, the two women beside me wearing pink sports bras, pink Spandex shorts, pink running shoes, and bright pink wigs seemed perfectly normal. The course zigzagged from Howard to 9th St to Hayes Valley, where I began the trudge up the notoriously steep Hayes St Hill – an ascent that climbs as sharply as 11% for 2000ft (600m). When I finally reached the summit, people were out in force, partying on porches, dancing to a street-side band playing – what else – Grateful Dead covers.

When the first wave of the American running boom swept the US in the early 1970s, Bay to Breakers grew from hundreds of participants to thousands. Shortly after, it ballooned into the world's largest running event. It has actually shrunk a bit since then – thanks to rising entry fees and buzz-kill citizens fed up with the debauchery – yet still attracts thousands of unregistered 'bandit' runners, as well as more than 100,000 enthusiastic spectators.

The Panhandle near Golden Gate Park and the Haight Ashbury neighborhood marks the halfway point. Here, I was passed by the first of many centipede teams. No other race in the world allows runners to compete while linked together as a team. Nowadays

RECORD SETTER

Held every year since 1912, Bay to Breakers has been run for more consecutive years over a given course and length than any other footrace in the world. During WWII, participation sometimes slipped below 50 registrants, but the race carried on without interruption. Meanwhile, it also became the world's largest running event; the 1986 race set a world record thanks to 110,000 runners.

Clockwise from top: essential race kit; the Golden Gate Bridge; 50,000-strong. Previous page: runner-revelers hit Alamo Sq

"I cruised through the financial district contemplating what sort of costume I might wear next time. A superhero? A bunny rabbit? Or maybe I'd just wear a pair of Speedos"

winning centipede teams run faster than a 5:30-mile pace, a true sight to behold as runners stride in unison just 5ft (1.5m) apart for the entire length of the course.

Running through Golden Gate Park, I passed the domed greenhouse of the Conservatory of Flowers and the manicured gardens fronting the Japanese Tea Garden. This is also the high point of the course, and running downhill along John F Kennedy Dr, the final miles went by in something of a blur. I realized I had abandoned my target long ago in favor of people-watching, so it felt good to finally pick up some speed. After a slight zigzag to Martin Luther King Jr Dr, I ran past the famous Dutch-style Murphy Windmill in the southwest corner of the park.

Turning onto the Great Hwy, I got my first glance of the ocean, its powerful waves breaking to my right the entire final hundred yards to the finish line. When it was over, I immediately felt an uncanny sense of remorse. Not because I didn't run as fast as I'd initially hoped, but because I had been paying attention to my time after all. I immediately headed to the beach to watch others cross the finish line and inhale whatever second-hand freakiness I could before the crazies started heading home.

I've run races all over the world and the truly great ones are a reflection of their physical and cultural landscape. In much the same way that your experience of the New York marathon is defined by the fact you get to run through all five boroughs, Bay to Breakers bares the soul of San Francisco. It's definitely not about running fast, nor even about running at all. It's about expression. **BM**

Start // Near Howard and Stuart streets
Finish // Great Hwy, Ocean Beach
Distance // 7.46 miles (12km)
Getting there // San Francisco International Airport is about 35 miles (56km) south of the start line.
When to go // The third Sunday in May.
Where to stay // Hotel Griffon (hotelgriffon.com) or Hyatt Regency San Francisco (hyatt.com) are good options near the start line.
What to wear // If you want to truly enjoy your experience to the fullest – and really fit in – wear a costume or run for a cause. That said, don't forget a good pair of running shoes – 7.5 miles is a long way to go wearing fake duck feet.
Things to know // This is one race where you should not forget your phone to take pictures.
More info // baytobreakers.com

RIght: dressed to impress for the
Las Vegas Half Marathon

MORE LIKE THIS
GREAT US FUN RUNS

ROCK 'N' ROLL LAS VEGAS HALF MARATHON, NEVADA

One of the biggest spectacles in running, this early November race sends runners up and down the Las Vegas Strip on one of the two nights of the year it's closed to car traffic. Beginning with a headliner music act and a pyrotechnic starting line, runners dash through the heart of Sin City, passing the famous 'Welcome to Las Vegas' sign, renowned casinos such as Mandalay Bay, Luxor, Excalibur, MGM Grand, Caesar's Palace, and The Bellagio, plus numerous wedding chapels, pawn shops, and the amazing light show of The Fremont Street Experience. There are also full marathon, 10km and 5km events, but the half-marathon distance is the sweet spot as far as seeing it all, with enough left in the tank to experience Vegas afterwards.

Start // MGM Grand Hotel Casino
Finish // Mirage Hotel Casino
Distance // 13 miles (21km)
More info // runrocknroll.com

GARMIN OLATHE MARATHON, IN THE LAND OF OZ, KANSAS

Shamelessly milking its close proximity to Kansas City, this fun, family-oriented event is perhaps the most specifically themed marathon in the US. With runners invited to dress as characters from *The Wizard of Oz*, there can't be many events inspired by a century-old children's story that became a wartime cinema smash and, today, a blockbuster Broadway musical. As the event's slick marketing proclaims: 'There's no place like [insert sponsor's name here].' In addition to the main event (26.2 miles; 42km), the family focus includes a 1.2-mile (1.9km) Munchkin Marathon, as well as a half-marathon (21km), and a 10k (6.2 miles). Whether you're a brainless scarecrow, cowardly lion or heartless tin man, all runners are invited to the Emerald City Festival that concludes proceedings. More serious athletes should note that the Garmin Olathe Marathon is USATF certified and therefore a qualifying event for the Boston Marathon, giving runners the chance to bag that much-prized 'BQ'.

Start // Garmin World Headquarters, 1200 E 151st St, Olathe
Finish // 151st St, Olathe South High School
Distances // 26.2 miles (42km), 13.1 miles (21km), 10k (6.2) miles, 1.2 miles (1.9km)

HATFIELD-MCCOY MARATHON, KENTUCKY & WEST VIRGINIA

Inspired by the Hatfields and McCoys, two feuding families who inhabited these parts in the 19th century, organizers claim this race captures the untamed spirit of the American frontier. Which may or may not occur to you as you push yourself over challenging terrain – a mix of trails and tar – and through the stifling humidity of the southern summer. Held in June, in the shadow of the Appalachian Mountains, the race is also notable for the fact it starts in Kentucky and finishes in West Virginia. There's no official time limit, and organizers are rightly proud of the dedication of their water-stop volunteers, who keep a watchful eye on the hydration levels of the entire field; some stops are themed, others provide iced water, and there's even a prize for the best stop. Spawning a movie and a mini-series, the original feud began with petty grievances and became murderous and dynastic. Today, the marathon named in its dishonor is started with a shotgun.

Start // Williamson, Kentucky
Finish // Williamson, West Virginia
Distance // 26.2 miles (42km)

PORTLAND'S EPIC PARK RUN

Forest Park is one of America's greatest urban wildernesses, a vast untamed oasis in Oregon where the trail running is so good you'll forget you're in a city.

Portland, Oregon has two tourist destinations that truly and reliably live up to the hype. One is Powell's City of Books, the independent bookstore that occupies a full city block on West Burnside. The other is Forest Park. (Sorry, Voodoo Doughnut.) Interestingly, they have a lot in common. Both are huge, exerting a gravitational pull that attracts visitors from near and far, and both are supremely satisfying places to lose yourself for an hour or two. Both are cathedrals – Powell's, to books; Forest Park, to nature.

But Forest Park is truly special in what it has to offer an especially picky outdoorsy and fit population. The bar is set quite high for greenspace in a city that is a short drive from both the ocean and the mountains. Sitting just across the Willamette River from downtown, it occupies a huge expanse just above the entire western shore. During my four years here, I've seen everyone on Forest Park's trails, from elite runners (Portland is home to quite a few) to families

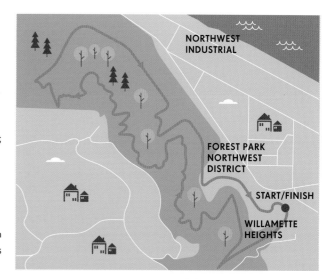

with dozing newborns. It's also a magnet for anyone craving a bit of tranquility and perspective within city limits. It's true, Portland is not exactly a high-stress city, but even we sometimes need a local escape, and that's exactly what I've come to rely on it for.

On a recent summer Sunday, I was in need of both tranquility and perspective. Between the usual work-life tension and a string of unusually awful news cycles, it had been a brutal week. I decided to tackle something a little more challenging than normal, a 12-mile (19km) combo of two of my favorite runs. But I was also in need of a bit of solitude, so I planned on spending some time on the less-traveled Wildwood Trail. I call my route the Chestnut Loop.

As I dipped onto I-84 from our neighborhood in the northeast, the lush green of Forest Park's southern tip peeked over the horizon. I knew I'd be there in 10 minutes, give or take, and already I felt better. Stretching more than 7 miles (11km) along Northwest Portland's western edge, Forest Park is immense. It's one of the largest urban forests in the country – a densely wooded 8 sq miles (20 sq km) or so, thick with Douglas fir, western hemlock, western red cedar and big leaf maple. Under this canopy is a network of trails, fire lanes, and paved sections – nearly 80 miles' (128km) worth, including the 30.2-mile (48.6km) Wildwood Trail (narrow, tortuous, and technical) and the 11.2-mile (18km) Leif Erikson Dr (wider and smoother).

My Chestnut Loop begins and ends at Lower Macleay Park, at the southern end of Forest Park. The fact that it's just a short hop away from excellent bagels and coffee means parking spots can be scarce up here, but that day I lucked out. I locked the car and was on my way.

The Lower Macleay Trail starts out paved but within moments I was on dirt, following Balch Creek into the woods. Less than a mile in, Lower Macleay meets the Wildwood Trail at a structure called the Stone House, also known as the Witch's Castle. The Stone House, or what's left of it, dates to 1929 and once served as a rest station with bathrooms and running water. Damaged badly in a 1962 storm, the building was stripped and abandoned. Today it's a graffiti-covered oddity and a common backdrop for selfies. Had I continued straight on Wildwood, I'd eventually end up at Pittock Mansion and the Oregon Zoo. I took a hard right – deeper into Forest Park.

Wildwood is a fun topographical scribble. Immediately I was climbing and clambering – rocks and roots are near-constant obstacles. I settled in and tried to find some sort of rhythm. The next 5 miles (8km) were nearly all uphill, some of it gentle, some not. Much of it is the sort of terrain you fast-hike rather than run. And I was OK with this, because I don't come to Forest Park to run fast. I come to Forest Park – with apologies to Thoreau – to run deliberately.

On Wildwood – and in Forest Park in general – it's easy to 'run deliberately', to focus not on things like pace but on things like, well, anything else. Apart from birdsong, the occasional plane humming high above, and, of course, my own footfalls, Forest Park was a

SECRET SQUATTERS

In 2004, it was discovered that a man and his 12-year-old daughter had been living in Forest Park, secretly, for four years. They had dug their camp into a hillside and built a small vegetable garden nearby. The father, a Vietnam vet, had been homeschooling his daughter using old encyclopedias. The story even inspired a book, and later a film called *Leave No Trace*, which starred Ben Foster as the father and premiered at the Sundance Film Festival in 2018.

Clockwise from above: fall envelops the Portland skyline; another ascent in Forest Park; there are many obstacles down in the woods. Previous page: the park offers a mixture of paths and lesser-trodden trails

"After miles of climbing and juking over technical terrain, I was grateful for the break"

© Danielle D. Hughson / Getty Images

deep-green sea of calm. I exchanged nods with other runners but, for me, this is always a solo run.

At around 6 miles (9.5km), where Wildwood intersects with Firelane 1 in a large clearing, I slowed to catch my breath. Once ready for more, I plunged downward, dropping an exhilarating 270ft (82m) over the next half-mile. In fact, it's literally all downhill from here. But the terrain remains tricky, so it's impossible to zone out. Instead I focused on the trail 5, 10, 20ft ahead, anticipating minor turns and obstacles and adjusting my form, almost unconsciously, step-by-step. Paradoxically, I find, this sort of hyper-focus frees up other parts of my brain to sort themselves out – like a hard drive defragging itself in the background. Herein lies the magic of all great trail runs.

Once I reached Chestnut Trail, I was on narrow singletrack, hemmed in by weeds, as it snaked lazily downhill before dumping me on the much wider Leif Erikson. After nearly 8 miles (5km) of climbing and juking over technical terrain, I was grateful for the break. I shook out my arms and opened up my stride for the final few miles.

Closer to the end, distraction was easy to come by: walkers and runners appeared more frequently – this is the part where you tend to see families with small children, and other casual strollers – and cyclists come and go. It's also where I began to catch occasional glimpses, through the trees to my left, of the Willamette River and Northwest Portland's industrial district down below. It is a gradual re-introduction to civilization, but by now, I was ready for it. **MR**

Start/Finish // Lower Macleay Park Trailhead, off Northwest Upshur St

Distance // 12.1 miles (19.5km)

Getting there // The Lower Macleay trailhead is about 30 minutes from Portland International Airport (PDX). Head west on NW Upshur St, which dead-ends at the trailhead. There is a Nike 'Biketown' bike-share hub about half a mile from the Lower Macleay Trailhead.

When to go // Late spring to fall is generally the safest bet, as winter's heavier rain can trash dirt trails.

Where to stay // All downtown hotels are a short ride from Lower Macleay Park, via bike, public transit or car.

Things to know // Beyond the trailheads, drinking water is non-existent. Tuck a map of the trail system into a pocket. Don't expect to rely on GPS; mobile reception in Forest Park is very spotty.

More info // forestparkconservancy.org/forest-park

From top: jogging in Central Park and
in Wissahickon Valley Park

MORE LIKE THIS
WILD US CITY PARK CIRCUITS

CENTRAL PARK, NEW YORK CITY

This 843-acre (341 hectare) sanctuary, established in 1857, sits smack in the middle of Manhattan, running approximately 0.5 miles/0.8km wide and 2.5 miles/4km long. Everyone from runners, triathletes, and cyclists to harried residents and tourists flock here day and night to escape Manhattan's hustle and bustle. Runners will find a surprisingly complex web of paths and trails, but the most popular routes take advantage of the Park Drives. The 'full loop' (just over 6 miles/9.6km) takes you on a tour of the park that includes the Harlem Hills and Lasker Rink in the north, the Metropolitan Museum of Art on the east side, and the Sheep Meadow and Strawberry Fields on the west side. Bonus: you can breathe easy. After years of pressure from activists, the park officially went car-free in the summer of 2018.

Start/Finish // Engineers' Gate, 2 East 90th St
Distance // 6.1 miles (10km)
More info // centralparknyc.org

UNIVERSITY OF WISCONSIN-MADISON ARBORETUM, MADISON

'The Arb', as locals affectionately refer to it, is one of best runs in Madison, Wisconsin's state capital. This spectacular green space, established in 1932, extends over more than 1200 acres (486 hectares) and it's hard to overstate both the variety of flora and fauna and its importance. The miles of trails will take you into prairies (albeit small ones), wetlands and forests, where you'll encounter rare species such as the Franklin Tree and maple-leaf oak. Today, the Arb serves as a living laboratory and, depending on the season, you'll also see abundant wildflowers (up to 500 native Wisconsin species). A popular route is the 6.2-mile (10km) loop starting at the Visitor Center. From Longenecker Dr, take the junction with Arboretum Dr, then run northeast for 2 miles (3.2km). At N Wingra Dr, loop back west, along Vilas Park Beach, passing the zoo and on to Edgewood College. From Nakoma, take Manitou Wy to Seminole Hwy, McCaffrey Dr, and back to where you began.

Start/Finish // UW Arboretum Visitor Center, Longenecker Dr
Distance // 6.2 miles (10km)

WISSAHICKON VALLEY PARK, PHILADELPHIA

Inside this 1800-acre (728 hectare) gorge lie 57 miles (92km) of trails, including Forbidden Drive (aka Wissahickon Valley Park Trail), a gravel road that follows Wissahickon Creek for 5 miles (8km). The park's upper trails are narrower, steeper and more rugged. Heavily wooded, the park includes several landmarks, including the historic Valley Green Inn roadhouse and Philadelphia's last remaining covered bridge. For a quick 4.25-mile (7km) loop, park at the Kitchens La lot and take the Orange Trail (near the Monastery Stables) along the creek's eastern edge. Follow the Orange Trail north past Fingerspan Bridge and Devil's Pool, then cross at Valley Green Rd to return south on Forbidden Dr to the Kitchens Lane Bridge, and back to the parking lot.

Start/Finish // Monastery Stables, 1000 Kitchens La
Distance // 4.25 miles (7km)
More info // fow.org

CARIBBEAN &
CENTRAL AMERICA

SEEING SAN JUAN, PUERTO RICO

Old San Juan is a colorful mosaic of Old World architecture, cobbled streets, glittering Caribbean views, and reminders of an uneasy past.

Sweat flows from my pores in the early-morning humidity but I barely notice. My attention instead is drawn into the sensory panorama unfolding before me as I make my way through Old San Juan's cobbled streets, a riot of color provided by brightly painted buildings, magenta bougainvillea, and a red-and-black caterpillar plodding across the sidewalk. I taste salt on the breezy Caribbean air as the aromas of tropical hibiscus and freshly cut grass enter my nostrils.

Over the past few years, I have found myself in San Juan on several occasions, for work but also for play. And each time, regardless of where I'm staying – whether within the old town itself or in Condado, a resort-filled neighborhood about 2.5 miles (4km) away – I have done this loop-run around San Juan's perimeter. It never fails to entrance me, as the city reveals herself, bits and pieces of present and past.

A gleaming white monument to Christopher Columbus rises at the old city's entrance, towering above the Plaza Colón. And, depending on where I'm coming from, I generally consider this my starting point. When Spanish conquistadors led by Christopher Columbus landed on what is now Puerto Rico, in 1493, the Taíno Indians were living

here, though they called it Borikén (Great Land of the Valiant and Noble Lord).

The Taíno were known for many things, including the development of a universal language and creating a complex

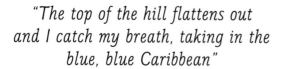

> *"The top of the hill flattens out and I catch my breath, taking in the blue, blue Caribbean"*

religious cosmology; and they thought Columbus was a god. 'They became his slaves,' Jonathan Caraballo, a guide at Discover Puerto Rico, told me. 'Then, one white man was killed and there was blood. They realized that white men weren't gods, so the Taíno rebelled and were killed with guns.'

By 1515, the Taíno population had fallen from more than 20,000 to 4,000 and the Spanish had colonized the island. In 1521, they moved the capital originally established at nearby Caparra to its current location, building Spanish-style houses with iron balconies, baroque churches, and palm-shaded squares inside a stone fortification wall.

Puerto Ricans hold varying views of Columbus. 'He was a tyrant,' Caraballo told me. '[For Puerto Ricans], it's a love/hate relationship. We mention him in our anthem but we don't like him.' Pablo Garcia Smith, a guide with Spoon, which offers food tours, had a different view. 'By virtue of our colonial heritage, we just say that's the way it was,' he says. 'Columbus was brutal and bloodthirsty but he was a

man of his age. We're in a different time... those events don't impact us directly.'

I mull over this as I make my way north up Calle Norzagaray, following the shadows of Castillo San Cristóbal, built by the Spanish to protect the city against land-based attacks. The top of the hill flattens out, with views of the fortress off to the right, and I catch my breath inside one of the sentry boxes, taking in the blue, blue Caribbean.

As I continue along Norzagaray, passing the colorful La Perla barrio, another fortress rises in the distance. This is Castillo San Felipe del Morro, built between the 16th and 18th centuries to guard the entrance to San Juan Bay. Its foreboding front gate, accessed via a long, straight pathway, speaks of that dominant power from another time.

Onward, I follow an unnamed road (a continuation of Norzagaray), past the Escuela de Bellas Artes de San Juan. The road makes a sharp left and, down the hill, an impressive red-doored gate tucks into the old stone wall, framing the turquoise-blue sea beyond. San Juan once had five main gates, each with a different function. This one, La Puerta de San Juan, was the city's formal entrance, where dignitaries would disembark from their galleons and walk up the hill to Catedral Basilica Menor San Juan Bautista, to thank God for a safe voyage.

SAVE-A-GATO CAT SANCTUARY

Feral cats have lived in Old San Juan since the Spaniards arrived; some even call them national treasures. When numbers boomed in the early 2000s, Save-a-Gato began trapping, neutering and returning cats to the streets, as well as leaving daily food and water. However, the NPS has recently begun plans to relocate hundreds of cats from the Paseo del Morro. Rats, anyone?

Left to right: the leafy lanes of San Juan; filling up with mofongo; explore San Juan by the shore; run along the Paseo del Morro. Previous page: the view from Castillo San Cristóbal

This is my favorite part of the run. I enter the gate and turn right, winding along the waterside Paseo del Morro, with the fortress's steep walls soaring above. It's beautiful and seemingly a world away from the city; it's also where I find myself in a feline wonderland, a veritable sanctuary where stray cats are fed and looked after by the Save-a-Gato nonprofit. The cats sit on the rocks, loll on the pathway and plead to be petted. The pathway wraps around the fortress's base, ending after just under a mile (1.2km), and rarely do I see people here, in this secretive corner of San Juan.

Backtracking to the red gate, I continue straight along the Paseo de la Princesa, back to Plaza Colón. Along the way, the Fuente Raíces makes me pause; the fountain, with its depictions of the island's Taíno, Spanish, and African peoples, was built in 1992 to commemorate the 500th anniversary of Spain's 'discovery' of the New World. While it seems potentially offensive, many Puerto Ricans have shared their pride in this mix of cultures, beautifully seen in their unique cuisine and music. *Mofongo*, for example, is an African-rooted dish of green plantains, garlic, and pork that is purely Puerto Rican; and Spanish-inspired *lechon* is roasted suckling pig cooked over an open fire. I'm only beginning to understand these complexities and each time I visit this multifaceted, mystical, sweet-scented city, I learn a little more. **BNK**

Start/Finish // Plaza Colón, San Juan
Distance // 3.2 miles (5.1km)
Getting there // Luis Muñoz Marín International Airport, then take an Uber.
When to go // It's best to run in the early morning to beat the heat and the crowds.
Where to stay // Hotel El Convento.
Where to eat // Santaella.
Tours // Every good run should end with food, and one of the best ways to get to know Puerto Rico's cuisine is with Spoon tours (thespoonexperience.com).
Things to know // If you are staying in Condado, you can run up the wide promenade along Av Luis Muñoz Rivera leading into the old town, with informative placards about history, flora, and fauna along the way.
More info // discoverpuertorico.com

Opposite: the views from the Presidio, San Francisco; Jacksonville's lions

MORE LIKE THIS
RUNS THROUGH HISTORIC DISTRICTS

THE PRESIDIO, SAN FRANCISCO, CALIFORNIA

Wooded trails wind throughout this old Spanish-style military base. And if that's all there was, we'd be happy. But it's the scenic vistas out to the San Francisco Bay, Golden Gate Bridge, and Alcatraz that make a trot through this 1500-acre (607-hectare) national recreation area particularly stunning. There are many hidden trails and roads to run, but a good loop follows the Presidio Promenade Trail to the Golden Gate Bridge, then circles back on one of the numerous roads and paths (there are signs) along the water by Crissy Field, a reclaimed wetland ecosystem. Along the way, you'll spy remnants of the old military outpost, including Battery Bluff, the Main Parade Lawn, and red-tile-roofed buildings now containing restaurants and offices. Pockets of forestland make you forget you're in a city at all. Among many options for add-ons, head out and back across the Golden Gate Bridge.
Start/Finish // Lombard Gate
Distance // 4 miles (6.4km)

CORPUS CHRISTI TRAIL, TEXAS

This region of Texas was once inhabited by the Indigenous Karankawa people, and Corpus Christi Bay was identified by Europeans as a strategic vantage point as far back as the 16th century. The Corpus Christi Trail runs for 9 miles (14.4km), from the barge docks to Cayo del Oso. The northernmost point is on North Shoreline Blvd and the route heads south, mostly on sidewalks, with the ocean your constant companion as you look out across Corpus Christi Bay to the Gulf of Mexico. You might also spot the occasional aircraft carrier, courtesy of the US Navy, which has a base in the bay. In addition to martial attractions, there's also the Art Museum of South Texas, as well as Texas A&M University, which marks the southern terminus of the trail. When you're in need of refreshment, there are numerous coffee stops, although the most popular are a few blocks inland, on S Alameda St and adjoining roads.
Start // N Shoreline Blvd
Finish // Texas A&M University
Distance // 9 miles (14.4km)
More info // visitcorpuschristi.com

ST JOHNS RIVER, JACKSONVILLE, FLORIDA

A great urban run through some of Florida's more historic neighborhoods. Start at the statue of the three lions, in San Marco, and make your way along San Marco Blvd, heading north. The architecture is distinctive, thanks to the ambitions of the city elders who, in the 1920s, redeveloped much of the area in an Italian Renaissance style (the lion statue was inspired by the Lion of Venice, in the Piazza San Marco). In a relaxed residential area, the sidewalk eventually brings you to the banks of the St Johns River but you'll need to negotiate various junctions as you pass beneath the Acosta expressway and Hwy 9. We recommend you persevere because once you reach the Friendship Fountain (1.3 miles/2km), head across the iconic Blue Bridge – worth a run of its own. Once over, pick up the Northbank Riverwalk and head toward Riverside, turning round at the arts market (1.8 miles/2.9km), at I-95, and heading back toward the lion statue.
Start/Finish // San Marco lion statue
Distance // 6.2 miles (10km)
More info // visitjacksonville.com/directory/northbank-riverwalk

AROUND THE MOGOTES

*Immerse yourself in rural Cuban life among tobacco fields, thatched drying houses,
and wooden farmsteads set against a backdrop of gnarly limestone cliffs.*

t's 7 o'clock-ish on a warm winter morning in Cuba and I'm gently massaging my hamstrings in a sun-dappled square in the center of Viñales, overlooked by a diminutive church and a ring of slender palm trees. Chickens cluck, a dog barks, and a septuagenarian Chevy rattles past, its driver exhaling cigar smoke through the open window.

Suitably warmed up, I start running tentatively down the main street, its sidewalk lined with young pines, before turning right on Calle Adela Azcuy and jogging past the village's deserted baseball diamond. Within what seems like minutes, I'm in open countryside trotting along a rust-red track that cuts through a patchwork of well-tilled agricultural fields backed by an imposing cluster of dome-like *mogotes*, the precipitous limestone cliffs for which western Cuba is famous.

Dotted with tropical vegetation and indented with numerous caves, Viñales' *mogotes* are revered by rock-climbers who come here in ever increasing numbers to tackle the walls of Cuba's

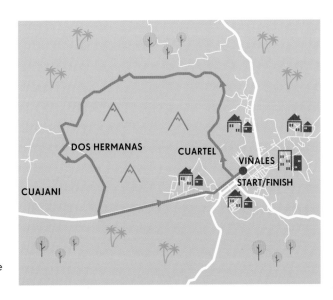

proverbial Yosemite. Bathed in an ethereal sunlight, all is quiet this morning, save for the faint rustling of leaves and the black outline of a turkey vulture circling overhead.

My aim is to jog anticlockwise in a rough circuit around the base of the shadowy *mogotes*, the highest of which reaches nearly 1000ft (304m), exiting on the other side, where a quiet country lane leads back to the village. It's a run I've done several times in the past, although, with paths branching off in multiple directions and a noticeable dearth of signage, it's hard to remember my exact route. I'm not unduly worried. In rural Cuba you're never far from a congenial *guajiro* (farmer), happy to put you back on track if you get lost.

Viñales is the nation's tobacco capital. The deep-green plants, which are at their lushest in February, dominate every rural vista, framed by small pastel farm buildings and elegant royal palms. Tobacco farming in Cuba remains an old-fashioned labor-intensive business, and the signs of human endeavor are all around. More than once on my running circuit, I am forced to veer to the side of the track to make way for a machete-wielding farmer on horseback or a rickety wooden cart pulled by oxen.

Despite the absence of clear signage, route navigation is surprisingly easy. The *mogotes* provide an omnipresent reference point, while the well-trodden tracks I'm running along are flat and wide, if sometimes a little muddy. I quickly find myself in a broad valley on the far side of the main *mogotes* known colloquially as the Valle del Palmarito, where a light mist

"Within what seems like minutes, I'm in open countryside trotting along a rust-red track"

still hangs over the tobacco plantations like a thin bridal veil.

With the village behind me, the landscape has become increasingly agricultural. I observe several contented-looking cows, a stout ceiba tree, a field replete with pineapple, and an A-frame tobacco house covered in palm fronds where the wrinkled leaves are hung up to dry.

Running confidently on the north side of the *mogotes*, I am forced to stop where the route has been temporarily flooded and blocked by a shallow river. Deciding to wade through rather than turn around, I bend down to take off my shoes and socks, just as a sombrero-wearing *guajiro* on horseback rears up in a cloud of dust. Barely breaking stride, he motions for me to climb up behind him, lending me his outstretched palm as he steadies his trusty steed. Gratefully, I scramble up and enjoy a brief ride across the muddy water before sliding clumsily to the ground on the other side. No words are exchanged. The farmer merely raises a hand in farewell as he trots away. It's one of those unique only-in-Cuba moments that, over the years, I've learned to expect and cherish.

The track ultimately meets a dirt road where, after checking my bearings, I jog left and glide past a secluded ecological farm embellished with fruit trees. I soon arrive beside the Mural

VALLE DEL PALMARITO

Just northwest of Viñales, Palmarito is easily accessible on foot from town. Since catastrophic 1980s floods, no one has lived in the valley permanently. Instead, farmers commute in daily, primarily on horseback, and most farm work is still done by plow and oxen. Palmarito is also home to several caves (one is swimmable), and is infamous for hosting cockfights.

Left to right: a farmer in Pinar del Río; a church in Viñales; the Mural de la Prehistoria in the Viñales valley. Previous spread: the mogotes near Viñales; drying tobacco in a hut

de la Prehistoria, a bizarre open-air fresco – one of the largest in the world – that adorns a giant cliff-face on one of the more prominent *mogotes*. Etched in bright primary colors, the mural was painted in the early 1960s by Cuban artist Leovigildo González Morillo, with the help of some local farmers, and depicts a handful of prehistoric animals set alongside some sketchy images of Indigenous people. I run swiftly past the adjoining tourist complex, over a well-tended lawn that fronts an open-sided restaurant, and join a quiet tarmacked road on the other side. Here, I am able to open my stride for the first time since leaving Viñales. I breeze confidently along the smooth asphalt, which cuts through a narrow cleft between two limestone *mogotes* and deposits me on the main drag between Viñales and Moncada.

The road isn't busy and this is no American-style highway. Bereft of white lane-markings, the slender thoroughfare is about as traffic-heavy as a bucolic backroad in 1930s Britain. Passing 'vehicles' include bicycles, a train of horses, several antediluvian American cars, and an obligatory oxen cart with a couple of farmers swaying around in the back. It's 1.2 miles (2km) back to Viñales, which gives me plenty of time to absorb the details of the surrounding countryside. Gnarly trees and abundant greenery soon give way to the first houses of the village: low one-story buildings with covered porches held up by simple columns. A little over an hour after setting out, I'm back beneath the church bell tower, re-massaging my legs and wondering what I'm going to have for breakfast. **BS**

Start/Finish // Main square in Viñales
Distance // 7.5 miles (12km)
Getting there // The nearest airport is José Martí International, in Havana. From the Cuban capital, you can catch a daily Viazul bus (viazul.wetransp.com) to Viñales (3½ hours).
When to go // Between November and March when it's dryer and cooler.
What to wear // Waterproof shoes are useful on this run.
What to pack // You may want to bring a small towel to wipe your feet after the river.
Where to stay // There are hundreds of casas particulares (private homestays) in Viñales.
Where to eat // Tres Jotas (facebook.com/BarTapas3J) is Viñales' favorite tapas bar. Aside from offering great small plates, it serves formidable mains, including lamb cooked in a red wine sauce.
More info // lonelyplanet.com/cuba/pinar-del-rio-province/vinales

*Opposite: a statue of Ernest
Hemingway between Cayo Coco
and Cayo Guillermo*

MORE LIKE THIS
RUNS AROUND CUBA

CAYO GUILLERMO

Pint-sized Guillermo is a 5 sq mile (13 sq km) coral island off the northwest coast of Cayo Coco that's joined to its larger neighbor by a bridge. It's known for its flocks of flamingos, white-sand beaches, and erstwhile Ernest Hemingway connections. This was one of the American author's favorite fishing grounds and there are numerous sites named after him. Start this run on the Hemingway Bridge, home to three statues of the great scribe, before setting off along the cayo's only road, past briny salt lagoons and low tropical foliage toward Playa Pilar at the island's northwestern tip. After a few laps of the beach (deemed by many as Cuba's finest), head back the way you came but cut left this time at the Hotel Gran Muthu and divert along a chain of wide sandy beaches that front several low-rise resorts back to the bridge.
Start/Finish // Hemingway Bridge
Distance // 10 miles (16km)
More info // cayoguillermocuba.net/index.html

MATANZAS

Initiate this fleet-footed tour of Matanzas on the waterfront next to a sturdy Spanish fort known as the Castillo de San Severino. From here, run east, beside the sparkling bay to the city center crossing the Rio Yumurí on the handsome stone Concordia bridge and proceeding along Calle 272 to Plaza de la Vigía, where the city was founded in the late 17th century. Jog along waterside Calle Narváez, an avant-garde art street, and then cut back along Calle 290 to equally artsy Parque de la Libertad. This is where you start your assault on the Ermita de Monserrate, puffing up Calle 306 to a renovated church on the summit dating from 1875. The lofty bastion perched high above the city was built by colonists from Catalonia in Spain as a symbol of their regional power. The views over the city and the adjacent Yumurí valley are stunning.
Start // Castillo de San Severino
Finish // Ermita de Monserrate
Distance // 3.1 miles (5km)
More info // lonelyplanet.com/cuba/matanzas

CIENFUEGOS

Cienfuegos, the so-called 'pearl' of Cuba's south coast, is an attractive neoclassical city with an enthusiastic sporting culture. Start this run with a lap or two of Parque José Martí, the handsome main square, before running east along the pedestrianized 'Bulevar' to El Prado, the Parisian-style boulevard that bisects the city north to south. Head south past elegant colonnaded buildings and, within just under a mile (1km), you'll be jogging along the Malecón, the palm-lined sea drive that borders one of the Caribbean's finest natural bays. When the Malecón runs out, you'll be deposited in the hallowed domain of Punta Gorda, Cienfuegos' erstwhile upper-class neighborhood that advertises its riches with colorful clapboard houses and grand eclectic palaces. Punta Gorda ultimately narrows into a single-lane street before terminating in a romantic park with a gazebo and shady trees. Turn around here and retrace your steps.
Start/Finish // Parque José Martí
Distance // 5 miles (8km)
More info // lonelyplanet.com/cuba/cienfuegos

RUN
8 TUFF MILES
ON ST JOHN

Beginning at sea level and reaching 999ft (304m) in elevation, this hilly, hot, and gorgeous annual run on the Caribbean island of St John more than lives up to its name.

The race was meant to start at 7am, well before the sun reached its hottest. I had jogged a craggy path over to Cruz Bay, the larger of St John's two island towns, from my resort just a half hour earlier. From Honeymoon Beach, a knotty trail hitched with roots led straight into town, if you could bear the knotty obstacles. I'm not much of a trail runner myself, but it beat paying $20 for a ride in an open-air taxi first thing in the morning. So off I

went, one foot in front of the other, mindful of the potential for a twisted ankle.

8 Tuff Miles draws runners from all around the US Virgin Islands. By the time I made it to the race's start, a large crowd had formed. The ferry connecting the much larger island of St Thomas with petite St John had unloaded tons of hopeful runners. It wasn't the eight miles I was worried about; that part I could do in my sleep. It wasn't even the unforgiving heat and

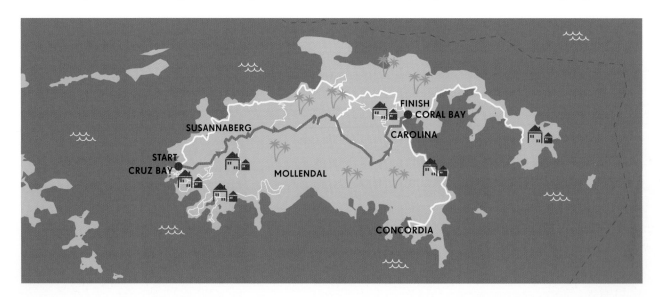

"Was it possible to keep running uphill forever? This race would probe our innermost demons, find out whether or not we could pull ourselves up and out"

humidity, though I typically ran at home, in New York; back there, on this February morning, it was likely a lung-bruising 20°F (-7°C).

You see, 8 Tuff Miles is called tuff because of its terrain. Almost entirely vertical, the race runs serpentine up the volcanic island's Mt Bordeaux, from sea level to a stunning 999ft (304m) above the water, and then back down again into the town of Coral Bay on the other side. By 7am, it was already 80°F (27°C). Pretty soon it was 8am, and the temperature was steadily climbing.

The fireball sun had made an appearance. Runners were pacing back and forth in the typical, itchy way that runners do before a race. We dripped sweat. We drank water. We talked about water. We went to the bathroom. We talked about having to go to the bathroom. We made friends in the crowd. I found a fellow tourist who had come to the island and who was running here for the first time, like me. Then, finally, two hours after the race was slated to begin – this was Caribbean time, after all – the race got underway and a flood of writhing, wet, slippery bodies headed toward the first hill.

There is, in most road races, a certain feeling of relief when you crest a major hill. You know that the worst is behind you, that what comes around a corner next will be less terrible than what lies behind you. Not so with 8 Tuff Miles. Every switchback that disappeared up into the mountains only turned into another switchback, more elevation, the terror of the realization that we were nowhere near the top. Was it possible to keep running uphill forever, without respite? This race would probe our innermost demons, find out whether or not we could pull ourselves up and out.

Normally, I had cheering squads on race courses, people I knew, places where I could expect to see familiar faces. But my family had decided to stay back at the resort for our last full day of Caribbean sun. I couldn't blame them, of course. It was their vacation, too, and I had chosen to do this wild thing all on my own. But it meant that I was out here on the road alone, my only companions the heat and the hills and, yes, the occasional peek-a-boo blue from the cliffs, as a switchback turned into a view of the stunning undulating cerulean seas hundreds of feet below.

For a while, I kept pace with the girl I had met in line. We couldn't talk much. It wasn't the kind of race that lent itself to conversation. When you're running uphill, it's best to lean into

ON THE UP

Running up the spine of a volcanic island is an incredible feeling. The best vantage point of the race is from mile 5.5 (8.8km) to the end, where the road permits a view of the island's southeast. Every year, runners gather in February to best one another at this truly grueling – and spectacular – race. Those looking for a scenic, challenging and, yes, hot race should consider this largely uphill pavement run, a unique island event that draws many returning racers.

Clockwise from top: snorkeling off the coast of St John; running 8 Tuff Miles; reaching the finish line is a big achievement

the road and look straight down. It helps with the vertigo, and with the feeling that the climb will never end. Still, we stayed side-by-side for a clip, her feet swishing, my feet swishing, the sticky tar gripping both of us, until she pulled ahead, or maybe I did. Long gone were the pace leaders; that race was won, somehow, at a sub-6:00 pace and by the same guy who ran it year after year, a lithe man named Jeremy, who practically popped over the hill and landed clear on the other side.

I struggled, however, to put one foot after another. The road turned. I turned. I resisted the urge to walk, even though my pace had slowed to a crawl. And then, suddenly, I could see a sign heralding the end to at least some of my pain. At a lookout at the top, where volunteers at a water station held a sign. It read '999', and it signified the highest elevation we would reach on the course. Along with my cup of water, I was handed a string of race-souvenir beads. I had made it. I had survived the worst of it. It was all downhill from here.

On the backside of the mountain I enjoyed a stunning view, a slow and steady 3-mile (4.8km) jog of the coastline, its features becoming clearer by the minute. Soon I was at the bottom, with the wind at my back, running across the finish line and right over to Skinny Legs Bar and Grill, where all participants joined in an impromptu celebration, knocking back beers and wiping off the day's workout. It was over. We were tuff enough. What a thrill it was to be alive in the Caribbean sunshine, down from the mountains, hot sun blazing. What a thrill. **HS**

Previous page: Cruz Bay, where the race starts

Start // Cruz Bay, St John, USVI
Finish // Coral Bay, St John, USVI
Getting there // Fly into St Thomas' Cyril E King Airport, and take a taxi to one of the hourly ferries to St John; allow an hour to get from the airport to St John.
When to go // The race is on the last Saturday in February.
Where to stay // Try St John Villa Rentals (stjohn-villarentals.com) for St John options.
Where to eat // At the Longboard St John, order the signature 'frozen painkillers'.
What to wear // Conventional running sneakers, hot-weather running gear, a water belt.
What to pack // With some of the most beautiful beaches in the Caribbean, you'll want to make sure you pack plenty of bathing suits and sunscreen.
Things to know // The race often begins late, so don't forget water (and more sunscreen).
More info // 8tuffmiles.com

*Opposite: beaches are great for
running with some resistance;
Trinidad & Tobago's marathon*

MORE LIKE THIS
CARIBBEAN MARATHONS

MARATHON BAHAMAS

Elevation-wise, the Marathon Bahamas
is almost the polar opposite of 8 Tuff
Miles, but this hot-weather, winter
Caribbean race has a lot in common
with its island cousin. Looping through
Paradise Island, Cruise Port and some of
the area's historic districts, this is still a
challenging race that defines Caribbean
running. Guests on the island will find
no shortage of places to stay and no
shortage of places to eat, especially
at the Baha Mar complex, which has
an abundance of dining concepts for
those looking to extend their vacation.
The Bahamas is further north than many
other Caribbean islands, offering more
favorable running conditions for those
who prefer a warm-weather race but
a more manageable climate. The 6am
start accounts for the hot weather and
the mostly flat, out-and-back marathon
takes place on firm pavement – a good
opportunity to run a personal best.
Start // Western Esplanade, Nassau
Finish // Montague Beach, Nassau
More info // marathonbahamas.com

TRINIDAD & TOBAGO INTERNATIONAL MARATHON

A colorful expression of both athletic
prowess and local culture, this four-
decade-old race has long drawn elite
competitors from around the world to
the islands. You'll need to fly into Piarco
International Airport, on Trinidad, which
is about an hour's drive from the start of
the race. The Hyatt Regency, in Port of
Spain, is one of the best accommodation
options for runners who plan to stay on
the island; it's 30 minutes from where
the race begins and very near where it
concludes. Runners should be aware
that, in recent years, the race has been
prone to postponement or rescheduling,
so build some flexibility into your
planning. While on the island, check
out The Meena House, an avant-garde
Indian dining experience, where chef
Umesh Meena offers degustation and
vegetarian menus.
Start // St Mary's Junction, Freeport
Finish // Queen Park Savannah, Port
of Spain, Trinidad
More info // ttmarathon.com

RUN BARBADOS MARATHON

The 40-year-old Barbados Marathon is
an undulating race with comprehensive
views of the island: that means ocean
views, local communities and green
countryside. Leading right into the
holiday season – the race takes place
in early December – means that runners
can enjoy the warmth of Barbados
during one of the most festive times of
year. Guests on the island can check
into the Crane Resort, an affordable
accommodation 35 minutes from the
race's start, or the Fairmont Royal
Pavilion on the west side of the island,
a more upscale property 25 minutes
from the start and finish. The marathon's
double-loop of a half-marathon course
may be a mental challenge for some
runners, so it's wise to come prepared.
When the race is over, celebrate
success in this invariably hard-fought
event with dinner at Cocktail Kitchen in
St Lawrence Gap.
Start/Finish // Barclay's Park,
St Andrew
More info // visitbarbados.org/
runbarbados-marathon-weekend

RUNNING JAMAICA'S REGGAE MARATHON

Natalie Preddie reconnects with her family in Jamaica at this December event, which features a half marathon as well as 10k and 5k road races, plus a great post-race party.

Rows of tiki torches light a path into the darkness and I can feel the pre-race energy buzzing in the crowd around me. The air is warm, and I can smell the ocean, even though the low early-morning light means I can't see it yet. I am in Jamaica, my paternal family's home, the place where my father was born and raised before emigrating to Canada almost 50 years ago. It's the first time I've been back since my grandpa passed away, and I am here for the Reggae Marathon, my first 10k (6.2-mile) event.

Prior to this moment, I hadn't been a runner – I'd barely even run for the bus. Eight weeks ahead of the race, however, I sat by my grandfather's hospital bed, telling him about the 10k I'd been invited to but wasn't sure I could complete. He nodded his head, ruminative at first, then with slow conviction.

He furrowed his brow and, after a thoughtful pause, spoke with characteristic authority. 'If you fail to qualify yourself,' he announced, 'you qualify yourself to fail'. A line he had repeated for as long as I could remember and a testament to the power of education, preparedness, and tenacity. In this instance, however, it meant I needed to start training.

My grandpa was almost 97 when he passed away and was active until the end. He lived alone in Scarborough, Toronto, and went for a walk every day, come snow, rain or shine. At 90, he hiked Mt Sinai – and helped the younger hikers who were struggling. He would often visit friends, some 20 years his junior, in old-age homes. He never stopped moving forward and, as his granddaughter, it was expected that I wouldn't either.

I downloaded an app that would guide my training and started jogging around the block daily. Every day I ran a little further and was excited to tell my grandpa when I visited him in hospital. I was invited to capture my progress on video for a Canadian women's lifestyle channel, giving me a wider audience but also greater accountability.

'Yeah?' my grandpa exclaimed when I told him I had finally gotten up to 10k.

My grandpa had always feigned astonishment when I presented him with a recent accolade or triumph, whether it

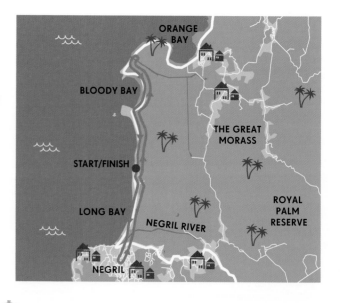

"I ran, breath heavy, face red, sweat dripping into my eyes, until I leapt over the finish line and onto the soft, white sand"

was learning to skate or singing in church, or from landing an audition to making an honor roll. But despite his gasps, he was never surprised. 'Of course you did,' he would say, 'you're a Preddie.'

It was those words that I heard as the starting-gun fired and the runners began down the dark road. Despite the early hour, supporters cheered from the sidelines and I suddenly felt self-conscious. I took a deep breath. 'Don't make a fool of yourself,' I imagined my grandpa warning me. I shook the doubt from my head and tried to find a rhythm to my pace.

Grandpa was one of my strongest connections to Jamaica. His accent was strong, too, and his stories would carry me to the warmth of the Caribbean sun, birdsong surrounding me while I ate fresh mangoes under a shady tree. He would tell me stories of growing up in the Jamaican countryside, his move to Kingston, his world travels, and his true opinion of Jamaican politicians. He would sing a combination of folk songs and hymns, and when he did, I felt compelled to join him.

In his final weeks, grandpa began slipping between the present and his teenage years, in 1930s Jamaica. He was no longer my grandpa, then, but a young man with the whole world in front of him. I sat at his bedside while he told me about climbing trees and eating fresh fruit with his friends, flirting with girls and his hopes for when he grew up. When we talked about my impending race in Jamaica, any recognition was a distant flicker behind his eyes. 'We're in Jamaica,' he smiled. 'We try and go down Kingston, yuh?'

'Yes,' I replied.

As the sun rose on race day, so did the temperature. I quickened my pace and lengthened my stride. I pictured my grandpa solemnly nodding as I ran, encouraging me along the route. As the light filled the now bright-blue sky, I saw him

PARTY TIME

The Reggae Marathon is a weekend-long event. Runners are welcomed on Saturday with the 'world's best pasta party', letting you load up on carbs at Jamwest Beach Park. Race day dawns early, with a 5.15am start to avoid the heat of the day. Finishers are rewarded with a post-race party: live reggae ensures it's the coolest fete you're likely to attend, especially if you scoop a share of the US$10,000 prize pot.

Left to right: refueling on local food; Negril's Seven Mile Beach; marathon camaraderie; post-run partying. Previous spread: team spirit on the Reggae Marathon

and his friends climbing those palm trees, eating star fruit and bananas, hollering at me from the branches. I was his granddaughter, I was a Preddie, and I was making him proud.

My grandpa passed away a couple weeks before the run. I lost a symbol of resilience, solemnity, and the strength of his unwavering conviction in my abilities. I lost a connection to Jamaica, my family, my past, and consequently, my future. I felt like there was more to say and to understand.

As race day approached, I considered canceling, staying home to grieve my loss. But as the fog of grief took on a new shape, I decided that the ultimate tribute would be to run this race. I needed to feel that connection again – I needed to go 'home'.

And so here I was.

The sun beamed high in the clear sky and I could see the finish line in the distance. People were cheering, banging pots, high-fiving and encouraging runners to the end. Faster and faster, I ran, breath heavy, face red, sweat dripping into my eyes, until I leapt over the finish line and onto the soft, white sand of Seven Mile Beach. Immediately, I was overwhelmed with emotion, and doubled over to both catch my breath and hide my sobs. I watched the tears fall to the sand as celebratory reggae played in the background and friends congratulated one another.

Standing there, on the land of my ancestors, I felt pride and strength. I felt the power of accomplishment and my connection was no longer lost. It was here and stronger than ever. When my grandpa smiled, it was big and it was infectious. His eyes would disappear into his cheeks as he showed all his teeth, an attribute passed on to my siblings and me. It was this smile, this emblem of joy, that filled my face as I celebrated my accomplishment with a refreshing jump into the Caribbean Sea. **NP**

Start/Finish // Seven Mile Beach, Negril, Jamaica
Distance // 3.1 miles (5km), 6.2 miles (10km), 13 miles (21km)
Getting there // Shuttles from surrounding hotels will take runners to the starting line and back again afterwards.
When to go // Arrive two to three days before the run to take part in the vibrant pre-race parties.
What to wear // Once the sun rises, it is very hot, with an average temperature of 89°F (32°C). It can also be very humid, so opt for your lightest run gear.
What to pack // Island wear: Swimsuits, shorts, and sandals.
Where to stay // Rockhouse Hotel (rockhouse.com).
Where to eat // Enjoy a fresh, delicious farm-to-table mean at Zimbali's Mountain Cooking Studio (facebook.com/zimbaliretreatsjamaica).
Things to know // Staying a few days after the race to enjoy the island is a must, and sunsets on the west coast are particularly awe-inspiring.
More info // reggaemarathon.com; visitjamaica.com

© Courtesy of Reggae Marathon

Opposite: the tasty finishing venue for the Big Easy Half Marathon; San Diego's Silver Strand beach

MORE LIKE THIS
MUSIC-THEMED RUNS

BIG EASY HALF MARATHON, NEW ORLEANS, LOUISIANA

Held over Halloween weekend, the Big Easy half aims to take advantage of the numerous other events being held in the city. For music lovers that means jazz, and there are countless venues to visit, from Preservation Hall to the Maple Leaf Bar. Starting and finishing at the Blue Crab Restaurant and Oyster Bar on Lakeshore Dr, the 13.1-mile (21km) route travels east, through the neighborhoods of Lake Shore-Lake Vista, and Lake Terrace-Lake Oaks. Passing the top end of Franklin Ave, the course then loops back just north of the Southern University at New Orleans. While the half-marathon has a four-hour time limit – this being the Big Easy there's a certain amount of flexibility – the event also offers both a 10k (6.2-mile) and 5k (3.1-mile) run. Whichever you choose, finishers can look forward to an authentic New Orleans feast at the Blue Crab's post-race party. Enjoy live music (jazz, obviously) and great seafood, before venturing on to the French Quarter.
Start/Finish // 7900 Lakeshore Dr
Distances // 13.1 miles (21km), 10k (6.2 miles), 5k (3.1 miles)

THE MUSIC & MILES HALF MARATHON, ELIZABETHTON, TENNESSEE

With just 367ft (112m) of elevation gain over 13.1 miles (21km), the course is the only part of this popular event that will leave you flat. That's thanks to the numerous live-music performances staged along the route. Drawing on the musical heritage of the state that nurtured legends such as Johnny Cash and Dolly Parton, this intriguing half showcases contemporary country talent. Against a backdrop of the Appalachians, the race is held in Carter County (not named, sadly, after June Carter Cash) and boasts a festive atmosphere designed to motivate and energize. The course starts on Main St, follows sections of the Tweetsie Trail to the Happy Valley Baptist Church, before heading back. Along the way you'll cross Elizabethton's historic covered bridge, built in 1882. The 134ft-long (41m) structure spans the Doe River, a tributary of the mighty Watauga, which runners will glimpse at various points. Finisher's medals come in the shape of a guitar.
Start/Finish // Main St
Distance // 13.1 miles (21km)

SILVER STRAND HALF MARATHON, SAN DIEGO, CALIFORNIA

This event blends inclusivity with one of the best beachside runs in the US, not to mention great tunes spun by local DJs. The course follows historic Hwy 79, specifically along Silver Strand, the 4.5-mile (7.2km) State Beach that runs from Coronado to Imperial Beach and separates San Diego Bay from the Pacific Ocean. Held over Veterans Day Weekend, usually the second in November, the Silver Strand Half also offers a 10-mile (16km) run, along with a 12k (7.4 miles) and Veterans Day 5k (3.1 miles). The last named is intended to honor service personnel, particularly those who have suffered injury or disability as a result. Organizers of the event are keen to welcome challenged runners from across the country. Along the various routes, athletes may well spot whales or dolphins, who migrate from summer through fall, before the event closes with a California beach party, soundtracked once again by local DJs.
Start // Coronado
Finish // Imperial Beach
Distances // Half-marathon (13.1 miles/21km), 10 miles (16km), 12k (7.4 miles), and 5k (3.1 miles)

SUNRISE OVER THE RIVIERA MAYA

White-sand beaches, street art, and a hidden Maya temple form the backdrop to this morning run in Playa del Carmen, a former fishing village turned Caribbean playground.

The palm trees are dark silhouettes as light breaks on the eastern horizon. Out on the beach, two workers are raking up small piles of sargassum. An older couple stroll along the shoreline and a few seagulls glide past in the cool tropical breeze. The sea beyond is as flat as pond water and shimmers with golden light under the early morning rays.

It's dawn on the coast of Playa del Carmen, a vibrant city perched on the so-called Riviera Maya. This corner of the Yucatán Peninsula is the stuff of photoshopped postcards, with miles of powdery white-sand beaches lapped by cerulean Caribbean waters and vibrant coral reefs hidden just offshore.

My wife and daughters are still slumbering away at a guesthouse a few blocks inland. I had tiptoed out of the room, shoes in hand, feeling slightly guilty at the thought of experiencing the sunrise without them. But it is our last day in Mexico and for months I had been daydreaming about making an early-morning run on this stretch of coastline. I was eager to traverse the beaches within easy reach of town, while also taking in a mix of iconic and little-known sights.

I take one last look at the ever-changing colors of sea and sky, then set off at a slow run up the beach. I veer closer to the waves, searching for hard-packed sand while dodging patches of sargassum washed up on the shore. The developments thin into coastal scrub and denser patches of palm trees as I make my way north, and soon the steadfast rhythm of the waves is all that I can hear. After a mile, the sands widen near the lovely shoreline crescent of Punta Esmeralda. Just in from the

crashing waves, a tiny lagoon makes for an enticing natural wading pool. But this early in the day, only chattering grackles are taking advantage of this waterway.

Turning inland I run along Quinta Avenida (Fifth Ave), a treelined thoroughfare paralleling the coast for more than 2.5 miles (4km). After the uneven beachfront, the smooth paving stones allow me to shift into a higher gear as I glide along the road. The low-slung buildings to my right seem almost prosaic, were it not for the colorful murals periodically bursting into view.

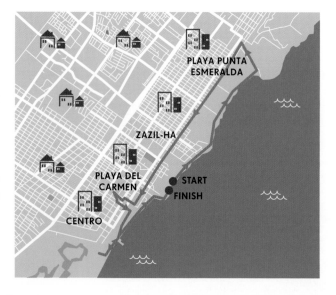

PLAYA PUNTA ESMERALDA

ZAZIL-HA

PLAYA DEL CARMEN

CENTRO

START
FINISH

A mile further, cars disappear as the avenue transforms into a pedestrian-only district. Still early in the day, the boulevard is mostly empty, apart from shopkeepers sweeping their storefronts, pulling merchandise out to the sidewalk and chatting with neighbors. It's a dramatic contrast from the carnivalesque atmosphere of the previous evening, when throngs of visitors mingled in the cool night air, packing the restaurants and bars, while roaming mariachi bands and costumed dance groups held mini-performances in the street.

For most visitors, the beach and Quinta Avenida are the only parts of Playa del Carmen they'll see, but I am eager to have a look at a little-known square a few blocks inland. The Plaza 28 de Julio is an open expanse named not for a military victory in the distant past, but for a steamy July day in 1993 when the then tiny city of Playa del Carmen (population 15,000) officially separated from Cozumel and became the capital of a new municipality. Since then, Playa has become one of the fastest growing cities in Latin America, reaching a population of 100,000 by 2005, then tripling to 300,000 today.

Anchoring one end of the plaza is the Palacio Municipal (City Hall). I slow my pace to a walk as I enter the courtyard. Covering the wall are dreamlike murals depicting elements of the Maya cosmovision – a towering pyramid, an open-handed deity, and a stalk of corn from which humans were created. Hidden in the corner of the painting are several key buildings in Playa that connect strands of the past: a small temple, a colonial church, and the very building that surrounds me.

SUPER CENOTES

Just inland from the Punta Esmeralda is the Cenote Punta Esmeralda, a small crystal-clear natural pool hidden in lush forest. The Yucatán is home to thousands of cenotes: sinkholes formed by the collapse of limestone that gradually fills with water. Most are startlingly clear with turquoise water that gives an otherworldly aspect. To the Maya, they were gateways to Xibalba, the underworld, revered as sacred sites.

Clockwise from top: there are Mayan ruins throughout the Yucatán; scarlet macaws; downtown Playa del Carmen. Previous page: dip your toes in Playa del Carmen's sand

I unpause my running watch as I continue west to a much better-known plaza. The temperature is rising as I reach the edge of Parque los Fundadores, Playa's liveliest gathering place. In the afternoons and early evenings, crowds gather to watch elaborate performances – including the *voladores de papantla*, a group of four 'fliers' who ascend a 98ft (30m) pole and secure themselves with ropes. They then launch themselves into the air and make a slowly spinning descent to the accompaniment of flute and drum beats. Nearby, the massive arch of the Portal Maya frames the seascape. I jog out onto the beach and skirt through the ferry terminal as a bright-orange vessel bound for the nearby Cozumel pulls from the dock.

Soon, I'm back on the sands following the waterline south along Playacar Beach. Backed by seafront condos and sprawling resorts, this strand feels exclusive but it's open to all as long as you arrive along the shoreline. I've come to seek out a hidden Maya site that a friend had told me about. After about a quarter mile I head up an unmarked path and soon catch sight of the Xaman-Há ruins. Nearly swallowed by the forest, the low-rise structures were once a key departure point for Maya pilgrims to Cozumel, home to a temple dedicated to the goddess of fertility and the moon.

I stick to the beach on the final mile back to my starting point. Although the sands are no longer empty, I enjoy seeing families setting up near the waterfront and fellow runners jogging past. I push the pace for the last half mile, relishing the tropical sun now blazing intensely. A few minutes later I'm kicking off my shoes and dashing into the water. There's simply no better way to finish a run than by diving into the Caribbean Sea. **RSL**

> *"I take one last look at the ever-changing colors of sea and sky, then set off at a slow run up the beach"*

Start/Finish // Playa Mamitas
Distance // 6 miles (9.7km)
Getting there // Located an hour's drive north of Playa del Carmen, Cancun International Airport has direct flights to the US and Europe. Frequent ADO buses travel directly from the airport to the city center.
When to go // PDC is a year-round destination, though if you come from December through April you'll find cooler temperatures and you won't have to worry about hurricanes.
Where to eat // On weekend nights, Plaza 28 de Julio fills with food vendors hawking tacos stuffed with *cochinita pibil* (spiced slow-roasted pork), *marquesitas* (crunchy sweet-filled crepes), and other delicacies.
Tours // Free walking tours operated by Estación Mexico give insight into key historical and cultural sites in Playa del Carmen.
More info // playadelcarmen.com

© Dmitry Eagle Orlov / Shutterstock

Opposite: Mérida's Catedral de San Ildefonso

MORE LIKE THIS
RUNS IN THE YUCATÁN

COZUMEL

An easy and scenic 11-mile (18km) ferry ride from Playa del Carmen, the island of Cozumel has glorious beaches, a handful of Maya temples, and some fine resorts to unwind in after a day of adventures. It's also a famous spot for divers and snorkelers, with biologically diverse coral reefs just offshore. You can get in some serious road mileage on the east side of the island, where a separate dedicated biking-walking path runs for some 12 miles (19.3km) past wild, untouched beaches. For something a little less remote, the town of San Miguel de Cozumel makes a fine setting for a run (best in the morning to beat the heat). You can take in the twin-towered Corpus Christi Church, and the fountains and sculptures of Parque Benito Juarez before heading up to Plaza de las dos Culturas, which commemorates the Maya before the Spanish onslaught. From here, follow the waterfront south, admiring the breezy views all the way to the International Cruise Terminal.
Start // Corpus Christi Church
Finish // International Cruise Terminal
Distance // 5.6 miles (9km)

MÉRIDA

One of Mexico's oldest cities, Mérida has a historic center lined with grand mansions and centuries-old churches, some of which were built atop former Maya temples. Rise early for a run along the cobblestones before the pedestrians and traffic hit the streets. A good starting point is the Plaza Grande, a photogenic square surrounded by architecturally striking buildings including the 16th-century Catedral de San Ildefonso. From here run north along Calle 60 passing a handful of other small leafy parks. At Parque de Santa Ana, jog over a couple of blocks to the Paseo de Montejo, Mérida's most impressive boulevard. It's lined with palatial 19th-century houses, some of which have been transformed into museums. If you're around on a Sunday, you can join local runners and cyclists, who flock to the Paseo from 8am to noon, when the street closes to vehicle traffic. A good turn-around point is the circular Monumento a la Patria, which celebrates Mexico's Indigenous heritage.
Start/Finish // Plaza Grande
Distance // 3.6 miles (5.8km)

PROGRESO

On the north coast of the Yucatán, Progreso is a major shipping hub but it feels far more laidback than most port cities. Day and night, the Malecón (seaside promenade) is the place to be, with open-sided restaurants, cafes, and even a small amusement park overlooking a wide sandy beach. And you'll never have to worry about running through traffic, as the city made the decision back in 2021 to close a long stretch of the waterfront to vehicles. Greet the morning out on Playa León, a wilder stretch of beach anchoring the west end of the Malecón. From there, you can head east for 1.5 miles (2.4km), enjoying views over the palms and inviting sands. Along the way, you'll pass the Puerto de Altura, a pier that stretches an astonishing 4 miles (6.4km) into the Gulf (alas it is not open to the public). Afterwards, cool off with a swim in the ocean.
Start/Finish // Playa León
Distance // 3.2 miles (5.1km)

© Witold Skrypczak / Getty Images

HAVANA'S EL MALECÓN

For a window into what makes Cuba's capital tick, hit the road along the city's seafront and be prepared for sensory overload.

As heavy drops of saltwater hit me in the face, the distinctive aroma of tobacco leaf mixed with diesel fumes drifts over from the houses opposite. A lone trumpeter sitting on the seawall, unperturbed by the crashing waves, diligently practices his arpeggios. I couldn't be running anywhere else in the world but Havana.

Buoyed by an unusual burst of early morning energy, I hasten steadily in the direction of the iconic Hotel Nacional, eyes fixed on the road ahead. In front of me, the Malecón, Havana's evocative 4.3-mile-long (7km) sea drive, curls its way around the city's northern shoreline in a protective embrace. Long a favored meeting place for courting couples, wandering musicians, amateur fishers, daring divers, day-dreaming Florida-gazers, and assorted tourists in Che Guevara T-shirts, this is the city's most expressive and typically Cuban thoroughfare. Local habaneros like to call it the world's longest sofa, a potent slice of open-air theater, where half the city shows up at sunset to meet, greet, date, and debate.

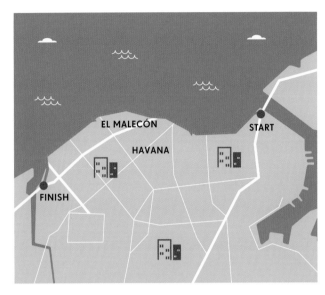

"Local habaneros call it the world's longest sofa — it's a potent slice of open-air theater, where half the city shows up to meet, greet, date, and debate"

For me, it will always be Cuba's most entertaining running route, the first place I visit when returning to Havana after a lengthy break. Here, amid the crashing waves and mildewed buildings, I feel I can reconnect with the city and quickly work out what has changed since I was last in town. In less than an hour, I've got a primer on the city's mood and a visceral reintroduction to its sights, smells and sounds.

Indeed, there have been plenty of changes over the years. Back in the 1990s, during Cuba's cash-strapped 'Special Period', I used to run along the Malecón in the pitch dark during the crippling *apagones* (power outages). It was rare to see a car here in those days, let alone a tourist bus. These days, the traffic is a little thicker, but the sights are no less unique.

The starting and finishing posts for my Malecón runs are two Spanish-built forts dating from the 16th century that stand like historical bookends 4.3 miles (7km) apart. The Castillo de San Salvador de la Punta guards the jaws of Havana harbor. The Torreón de la Chorrera overlooks the mouth of the Río Almendares to the west. In between are gallant equestrian statues depicting heroes of Cuba's independence wars.

Cruising westward, I get distracted by a dazzling new sculpture outside the Hotel Deauville. Unconsciously, I veer dangerously close to the curb to get a better view, but a honking motorbike-and-sidecar quickly snaps me to attention. Running the Malecón

isn't just a test of fitness, it's a full-on obstacle course. I continue through the tightly packed residential quarter of Centro Habana towards Vedado, battling loose paving stones, slippery seaweed, gusts of ocean spray, tangled fishing twine, and belching Buicks. By far the biggest obstacle is the sea itself. Even today's mild swell in the Straits of Florida is enough to send huge waves crashing over the Malecón's battered ocean defenses. On one occasion, I swear I was stung by a jellyfish.

The fabulously eclectic Hotel Nacional, visible along most of the route, is probably the Malecón's most famous landmark. Running beneath its manicured gardens is a wide section of sidewalk where, in the evenings, bottles of rum are passed around, puros (cigars) are lit, and asthmatic Chevys glide past. This morning, a few scattered survivors of the previous night's festivities are engaged in a half-hearted after-party.

I hear a guitar being quietly strummed, and a tentative roll on the bongos. The sounds serve to revive me as I forge on towards the concrete façade of the US embassy. Marking the halfway point, the building has always been the least gregarious part of the route. Due to security concerns, loitering is strictly prohibited. There have been times when I've merely bent down to retie my shoelace and an officious Cuban policeman has blown his whistle and ushered me on.

Today, the embassy is eerily quiet as I run past looking out for any new political billboards that might have sprung up since

THE MARABANA

The increasingly popular Havana marathon – aka Marabana – happens every November and draws more than 3000 competitors from around the globe. It's a two-lap standard 26 miles (there's also a one-lap half-marathon, plus events for 5km and 10km distances). The race makes the most of the city's iconic Malecón, running the entire length of the seductive sea-drive – twice!

From left: locals in the 'living room' of Havana; cruising the Malecón; all quiet in the afternoon; a historic lighthouse. Previous spread: a sunrise run on the seafront

my last visit. My favorite is the cartoonish depiction of a Cuban revolutionary facing off against a bearded Uncle Sam. 'Mr Imperialist, we have absolutely no fear of you!' it cockily proclaims.

The Malecón becomes more modernist beyond the embassy, the weathered house-fronts of Centro Habana giving way to the wider avenues of Vedado. I run past a line of plush-looking private restaurants that testify to Cuba's recent economic defrosting. A bevy of leather-faced fishermen stand on the seawall by the Torreón de la Chorrera, their rods aimed toward Florida.

Once, in tougher economic times, I stopped for a short rest here. Taking off my shoes to air my toes, I fell into a pleasant lunchtime siesta. When I awoke 20 minutes later, my shoes were gone. With a mixture of embarrassment and annoyance, I tiptoed in bare feet along the frying-pan hot sidewalk to Habana Vieja in search of a shoe shop – not an easy thing to find in Fidel Castro's Cuba. The memory of my comical robbery makes me smile as I turn around and head with fresh vigor back to my accommodation. Havana is a vibrant, complex, and endlessly riveting city, but it can be maddeningly frustrating at times. Yet, stoked with a runner's high on this ridiculously seductive sea-drive, I can't help but love it. The tempestuous waves, the tangerine sunsets, the sauntering lovers, the petulant billboards, and the weather-beaten buildings crying out for a face-lift. There really is nowhere else in the world I'd rather go running. **BS**

Start // Castillo de San Salvador de la Punta
Finish // Torreón de la Chorrera
Distance // 8.7 miles (14km)
Getting there // José Martí International Airport is Cuba's main entry point. To get to the eastern end of the Malecón (starting point for this run), get a taxi into the city center.
When to go // November to March.
Where to stay // In a privately run casa particular (Cuban home-stay). Hostal Peregrino (hostalperegrino.com) is conveniently located close to the Malecón.
What to wear // Light, breathable running gear – it's hot and humid even in the 'winter'.
Things to know // The Malecón is a long out-and-back run. If you're still acclimatising to the heat and humidity, take it easy on the first day and turn back near the US embassy.

From top: musicians in
Santiago de Cuba; the Plaza
Mayor of Trinidad

MORE LIKE THIS
CUBAN RUNS

SIERRA MAESTRA

The frighteningly steep road between the villages of Santo Domingo and Alto del Naranjo in Cuba's remote eastern mountains is generally considered to be the toughest climb in the country – for cars! Runners will need strong legs, lungs, and resolve. Lying deep inside Cuba's Sierra Maestra, close to Fidel Castro's secret ridgetop HQ during the revolutionary war, the road climbs 2300ft (700m) in a mere 2.5 miles (4km).The road is paved but unrelentingly steep with a killer 45-degree section near the top. Few cars attempt it, leaving it to the preserve of burly Russian trucks and the odd equally burly runner. If you're up for it, avoid the heat of the day and be prepared for high levels of humidity. There's a hotel and basic facilities at Santo Domingo, but nothing at Alto del Naranjo save for magnificent cloud-forest views.

Start // Santo Domingo
Finish // Alto del Naranjo
Distance // 3 miles (5km)

TRINIDAD TO LA BOCA

Trinidad is Cuba's showcase Unesco town with cobbled streets and historic architecture. La Boca is a scruffy little beach village, mostly snubbed by tourists, with potholed roads and a shabby authenticity. The short run between them, along a bucolic backroad amid tussocky fields with the Escambray mountains winking in the background, is a rural joy. Limber up in the attractive hub of Trinidad's Plaza Mayor before pitching south on Calle Desengaño (delusion street), which starts cobbled but quickly turns to asphalt before crossing a railway line and curving out of town. It's roughly 3.1 miles (5km) to La Boca from here, with little to bother you bar the odd bicycle and ancient spluttering car. You'll enter the village on a narrow street lined with pastel bungalows and hit the beach where the Guaurabo river empties into the Caribbean. Soak up the local ambience before retracing your steps.

Start // Plaza Mayor, Trinidad
Finish // Beachfront, La Boca
Distance // 3.5 miles (5.7km)
More info // lonelyplanet.com/cuba/central-cuba/trinidad

AROUND SANTIAGO DE CUBA

Cuba's second largest city can be a hot, frenetic place. Start this run early in the morning before the streets get overrun with motorbikes and doused in sticky tropical heat. Hit the asphalt in Plaza de Marte and jog down Calle Aguilera to diminutive Plaza de Dolores. Cut a block south into Calle Heredia and step through the remnants of last night's parties to the central hub of Parque Céspedes. From here, head west on Masó into the French-flavored Tivoli quarter, sprint up the terracotta Padre Pico steps, and then dash down to the harborfront and artsy Parque Alameda. Run north with the water on your left past the erstwhile Bacardí rum factory as far as the train station where a right turn will deposit you on a wide avenue known as Paseo de Martí, from where you can track back past the Art Deco turrets of Moncada barracks to where you started.

Start/Finish // Plaza de Marte
Distance 3.7 miles (6km)
More info // lonelyplanet.com/cuba/eastern-cuba/santiago-de-cuba

A RAINFOREST RUN IN COSTA RICA

*A fast, flat trail in Cahuita National Park mixes pristine
Caribbean beaches, tropical rainforest, and wildlife encounters.*

The Caribbean isn't made for running. Sunning, yes. Running, not so much. The vibe is baggy T-shirts and bare feet, not Lycra and technicolor shoes. Yet, here I am, pounding along a wonderfully forgiving sand-on-dirt trail in Cahuita National Park, the sound of the surf to my left, howler monkeys doing their thing somewhere behind me, and the jungle coming to life in the dawn.

On a family holiday to Costa Rica, this is my time – the sun pink on the horizon, the trail empty, and my kids still sleeping off their jet lag back at the guesthouse. Just after the park entrance I stop and scan the trees. Yes, it's still there – a day-glow yellow coil, high up on the side of a trunk. It's an eyelash pit viper, its banana-bright skin warning of its deadly venom. The reason I know this is that yesterday we made the best decision of our trip – on our first day in the country, we had spent six hours here with a wildlife guide. In Pierre's enthusiastic company we learned how to spot sloths, tarantulas, Jesus Christ lizards, and more.

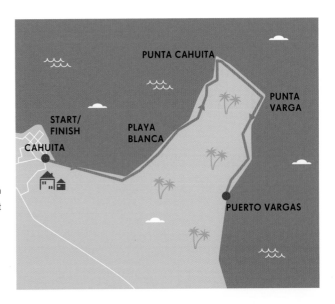

"The spider's web is the biggest I have ever seen and spans the entire width of the path – clearly not many people have made it this far recently"

For iguanas, we looked on sunny branches high up, where they bask in the sun undisturbed. If we crunched over freshly discarded almond shells, we were probably standing under a troop of capuchin monkeys. If we heard a strange coughing in the distance, it was a toucan and we should keep our eyes peeled for the source of the sound.

So this morning I am keen to put my new-found knowledge to the test. But first I have to put some distance between me and the park entrance, where a few other early birds are out, binoculars at the ready, walking at the snail's pace of the wildlife spotter.

I get into my stride, my breath coming easily, and realize what a great trail this is for running – I'm 8oft (25m) from the crashing surf, the promise of a beach on my left, but my trail is broad and shady, made of soft, rich earth covered with a thin layer of windblown sand. As running surfaces go, it's perfect – quiet, springy and wide enough that I can look around. I open my stride.

Soon it's just me and the trail and any dawn critters I come across. At my running pace, there are lots of animals I'm not going to spot – such as anything that relies on camouflage. But there's plenty that I stand a much better chance of seeing than I did yesterday, even without the eagle eyes of my guide. I'm running on my own, up before the crowds, fast and quiet. The

onshore breeze carries my scent away behind me. And the ever-present crashing of the waves masks the sound of my breathing and footfall. The element of surprise is on my side.

I come to an area where blue land crabs scuttle into their holes as I pass and I catch my first new spot – two crab-eating raccoons are out hunting. They look startled, but as I see them I stop dead and they run parallel to me into the jungle, giving me a wonderful view – fox-like faces made mischievous by bandito eye-stripes.

When I reach the Río Suárez, I look nervously at the mudbanks upstream. I've been running just 10 minutes, yet this is as far as we'd made it yesterday. Pierre had told us that caiman sometimes bask here. Of course they aren't out this early, and even if they were, I'm nowhere near them. But still, I take off my shoes and socks and tiptoe quietly across the cool creek.

From here on, it's virgin territory to me. I re-enter the jungle and as I round a corner I almost trip over a coati, the strange long-nosed cousin of the raccoon. He ignores me and carries on about his business, long tail pointing to the sky like a hushing finger as he sniffs out insects in the path. I carry on with a buzz in my belly from the feeling that somehow I'm a guest in his world.

Now the trail starts to change character as the forest to my right turns into swamp. The path moves further inland and there's a long section of boardwalk carrying me over the fragile, wet and crawling-with-god-knows-what shallows below. I realize

Usually, the three-toed sloth stays pretty high in the rainforest canopy, which makes it tricky to spot. But once every three weeks or so, it has to make a trip to the ground – to poop. So if you see a sloth slowly clambering down toward ground level, looking furtive and perhaps a little desperate, give it plenty of space as you observe – it will be feeling very vulnerable.

From left: a rainforest trail in Cahuita National Park; eyes peeled for the eyelash viper; three-toed sloths hang out high above. Previous spread: jungle meets surf at Punta Cahuita

how unfrequented this area is, just a mile or so further than most tourists come. I'm picking my way around the edge of a mangrove, planning my route over a fallen tree ahead when all of a sudden... Whoa! I stop dead in my tracks, the rim of my cap pressing against the biggest spider's web I've ever seen, my arms windmilling for balance.

A huge, beautiful golden orb weaver sits at its center, the yellow spots on her back matching the stripes on her long furry legs. She's mesmerizing. Her web spans the entire width of the path, so clearly not many people have made it this far recently. I clamber over a tree to avoid disturbing her and, after a few more minutes, I find myself at the end of this jungle peninsula. I stop and walk onto the beach. It's not sand here but coral and shells, white under the sun and scratchy underfoot. I stand and catch my breath. Like something out of a kid's cartoon, a couple of the shells start cautiously sneaking away from me. I pick one up, and am presented with the purple pincer of an annoyed hermit crab inside.

Out at sea, a line of white surf breaks over the reef. It's a sound that has been accompanying me, as regular as my breathing, for the past 10 minutes. It's 6.40am. The sky no longer holds any of the color of dawn. The air promises a hot day already. I look at the trail stretching round the headland in front of me, inviting me forward. Back in Cahuita, my children still sleep. This place was made for running. I run on. **PP**

Start/Finish // Cahuita, Costa Rica
Distance // 8 miles (13km)
Getting there // Cahuita is in southeast Costa Rica, a 4.5-hour drive from the international airport at San José. It makes an ideal first stop in the country.
When to go // You can visit year-round, but March/April and September/October are the driest months. In November and December the trail sometimes floods.
Where to stay // Playa Negra Guesthouse (playanegra. cr), where owner Pierre moonlights as a wildlife guide.
Things to know // Keep your eye out for three-toed sloth, yellow eyelash viper, coati, golden orb weaver spider, blue land crab, poison dart frog, Jesus Christ lizard, iguana, toucan, monkey, and caiman.

INDEX

Iowa, USA 180
Minnesota, USA 174, 180
New York, USA 256
North Carolina, USA 256
Nova Scotia, Canada 18, 14-17
Ohio, USA, 174
Oregon, USA 224, 270-3
Québec, Canada 54
Virginia, USA 132-5
Washington, USA 190-3

Trinidad & Tobago
Trinidad & Tobago International Marathon 294

U
USA
Acadia National Park, Maine 94-7, 236
Alaska 26-9, 56-9, 60, 66, 194
Anza-Borrego Desert State Park,
    California 262
Arrowhead 135, Minnesota 212
Art Loeb Trail, North Carolina 256
Assateague Island, Maryland 118
Atlantic City Boardwalk, New Jersey 86
Austin, Texas 136
Badwater 135 Ultramarathon, California 208-11
Barkley Fall Classic, Tennessee 148
Barkley Marathons, Tennessee 144-7
Baxter State Park, Maine 98
Bayshore Marathon, Michigan 170-3
Big Bend National Park, Texas 136
Big Dog Backyard Ultra, Tennessee 148
Big Sur, California 92
Big Sur Marathon, California 196-9
Boston, Massachusetts 100-3, 162
Boulder, Colorado 252-5
Brooklyn Bridge, New York City 168
Buckeye Trail, Ohio 174
Camden Hills State Park, Maine 98
Cape Lookout, Oregon 200
Cape May Loop, New Jersey 86
Caprock Canyons State Park, Texas 136
Carlsbad 5000, California 244
Central Philadelphia, Pennsylvania 124
Channel Islands National Park, California 262
Charleston, South Carolina 112
Chattanooga Riverwalk, Tennessee 162
Chesapeake & Ohio Canal, Washington, DC 194
Chicago, Illinois 164-7
Chicago Marathon, Illinois 104
Corpus Christi Trail, Texas 282
Crater Lake Rim Run, Oregon 224
Crystal Cove State Park, California 258-61
Cuyahoga Valley National Park, Ohio 236
Dartmouth College, New Hampshire 74
Daufuskie Island, South Carolina 114-17
Deception Pass State Park, Washington 66
Detroit Riverwalk, Michigan 158-61
Disney Marathon, Florida 104
Door County, Michigan 186
Downtown Philadelphia, Pennsylvania 130
Elizabethton, Tennessee 300
Embarcadero, San Francisco 168

Fire Island, New York 118
Fort Lauderdale A1A Marathon, Florida 80
Galveston Seawall, Texas 12
Garden to Peak Challenge, Colorado 218
Garmin Olathe Marathon, Kansas 268
Geneva Lake, Wisconsin 182-5
Gitchi-Gami State Trail, Minnesota 180
Grand Canyon, Arizona 232-5
Great Sand Dunes National Park, Colorado 230
Griffith Park Trail Marathon, California 244
Hardrock 100 Ultramarathon, Colorado 212
Hatfield-McCoy Marathon, Kentucky 268
Hawaii 212, 246-9, 250
Heather Meadows, Washington 66
Hope Point Trail, Alaska 62-5
Hudson River Waterfront Walkway,
    New Jersey 82-5
Humboldt Redwoods State Park, California 262
Huntington Beach, California 80
Indiana Dunes, Michigan 186
Jacksonville, Florida 282
Jekyll Island, Georgia 118
Kalalau Trail, Hawaii 246-9
Kennebec Mountain Run, Colorado 218
Key West, Florida 138-41
Knobstone Hiking Trail, Indiana 174
Lighthouse Trail, Texas 132-5
Little Rock, Arkansas 154
Lookout Trail Loop, New Jersey 86
Los Angeles, California 238-43
Madison, Wisconsin 274
Miami, Florida 126-9
Mines of Spain, Iowa 180
Mt Desert Island Marathon, Maine 200
Mt Marathon, Alaska 26-9
Mt St Helens, Washington 220-3
Myrtle Beach Marathon, South Carolina 80
Napa to Sonoma Half-Marathon, California 24
Narragansett Town Beach, Rhode Island 74
Nashville, Tennessee 112
National Mall, Washington, DC 92, 150-3
Newburyport, Massachusetts 70-3
New Orleans, Louisiana 12, 108-11, 130, 300
New York City Marathon, New York 104
New York City, New York 124, 274
Niagara Falls, New York 88-91
Ohio River, Kentucky 120-3
Old Croton Aqueduct Trail, New York 256
Oregon Dunes Recreation Area, Oregon 230
Outer Banks Marathon, North Carolina 200
Philadelphia, Pennsylvania 274
Pikes Peak Ascent, Colorado 214-17
Pikes Peak Marathon, Colorado 218
Pittsburgh, Pennsylvania 162
Portland, Oregon 270-3
Quoddy Head State Park, Maine 98
Race to Robie Creek Half-Marathon, Idaho 206
Red Wing, Minnesota 194
Ridge to Rivers, Idaho 206
Rockaway Beach Spring Half Marathon,
    New York 76-9
Rock'n'Roll Las Vegas Half Marathon,
    Nevada 268
Rose Bowl Half Marathon, California 244

Salt Lake City, Utah 154
San Antonio Mission Reach Trail, Texas 130
San Diego, California 300
San Francisco, California 264-7, 282
Savannah, Georgia 112
Sawtooth Mountains, Idaho 202-5
Self-Transcendence 3100-Mile Ultramarathon,
    New York 148
Sleeping Bear Dunes National Lakeshore,
    Michigan 230
South Boulder Creek Trail, Colorado 190-3
St Petersburg, Florida 142
Superior Hiking Trail, Minnesota 174
Tampa, Florida 142
Timberline Trail, Oregon 224
Tongass National Forest, Alaska 56-9
Tubbs Hill, Idaho 206
Upper Peninsula, Michigan 176-9
Utqiagvik, Alaska 60
Waterfall Glenn Trail, Illinois 256
West Hartford, Connecticut 74
West River Parkway, Minneapolis 168
White Sands National Park,
    New Mexico 226-9
Wissahickon Valley Park, Philadelphia 274
Wy'east Trailfest, Oregon 224
Yosemite National Park, California 92
Zion National Park, Utah 236
US Virgin Islands
St John 290-3

W
waterfront runs
Alaska, USA 56-9, 66, 194
Alberta, Canada 42
BC, Canada 8-11
California, USA 80, 168, 196-9
Cuba 308-11
Florida, USA 80, 126-9, 138-41, 282
Georgia, USA 118
Hawaii, USA 246-9
Illinois, USA 164-7
Jamaica 296-9
Kentucky, USA 120-3
Louisiana, USA 12
Maine, USA 94-7, 200
Massachusetts, USA 12, 162
Mexico 302-5
Michigan, USA 158-61, 170-3
New Jersey, USA 82-5, 86
New York, USA 76-9, 88-91, 118, 168
North Carolina, USA 200
Nova Scotia, Canada 14-17
Ontario, Canada 44-7
Oregon, USA 200
Pennsylvania, USA 162
Rhode Island, USA 74
South Carolina, USA 80, 114-17
Tennessee 162
Texas, USA 12, 282
Virginia, USA 118
Washington, DC, USA 194
Wisconsin, USA 182-5

Epic Runs of North America
September 2024
Published by Lonely Planet Global Limited
www.lonelyplanet.com
10 9 8 7 6 5 4 3 2 1

Printed in China
ISBN 978 1 83758 1948
Text & maps © Lonely Planet 2024
Photos © as indicated 2024

Publishing Director Piers Pickard
Illustrated & Gift Publisher Becca Hunt
Senior Editor Robin Barton
Editors Mark Mackenzie, Polly Thomas, Nick Mee
Senior Designer Emily Dubin
Designer Jo Dovey
Image Research Heike Bohnstengel
Index Vicky Smith
Print Production Nigel Longuet

Lonely Planet Global Limited
Digital Depot, Roe Lane (off Thomas St),
Digital Hub, Dublin 8,
D08 TCV4
Ireland
STAY IN TOUCH lonelyplanet.com/contact

Authors Alexander Deedy (AD); Alison Mariella Désir (AMD); Allison Burtka (AB), Barbara Noe Kennedy (BNK);
Brendan Sainsbury (BS); Brian Metzler (BM); Charlie Engle (CE); Christopher Beanland (CB); Fiona Tapp (FT); Gabi Mocatta (GM);
Greg Benchwick (GB); Hannah Selinger (HS); Isabella Noble (IN); Jinghuan Liu Tervalon (JLT); Joe Bindloss (JB); Kaidi Stroud (KS);
Karla Zimmerman (KZ); Mark Remy (MR); Matt Phillips (MP); Natalie Preddie (NP); Piers Pickard (PP); Regis St Louis (RSL);
Sharael Kolberg (SK); Stephanie Case (SC); Stephanie Vermillion (SV); Tamara Elliott (TE); Tyler Wildeck (TW)

Cover illustration by Ross Murray (www.rossmurray.com).